THE REVELATION:

Every Eye Will See Him

TABLE OF CONTENTS

Introduction

In recent years, in efforts to bring various evangelical segments together, popular Christian theologians have labeled the categories of *Theology Proper,* (regarding the attributes of the Godhead) and *Soteriology,* (regarding how a person is saved) as *"primary,"* while labeling most other elements of theology as being *"secondary"* in importance. In this effort, eschatology has been commonly reduced to being *secondary,* resulting in many churches either neglecting to teach on the subject, or simply offering a few vague propositions with little biblical explanation. These propositions are often partnered with caveats like "We shouldn't divide over this." or "This is not the focus of the gospel." The popular conclusion has become that any serious study on the *end-times* is at best fruitless, and more likely counterproductive.

As a result, many Christians have been deprived of the truth that eschatology is a primary focus of the gospel. The second coming of Christ, while not being the primary *application* of the Gospel, was always meant to be the effective *hope* of the Gospel. The purpose of the Great Commission, given at Christ's first coming, was to gather all people for salvation from the judgement that would occur at his second coming. Every New Testament exhortation was given to motivate the Church to persevere, through all trials and tribulations, in the hope that is fulfilled at the return of Christ. The many prophecies regarding Christ's return were meant to encourage the Church to watch for the signs of his coming, while standing guard against the deceptions that would obscure its nearness as the day draws near.

Downgrading the importance of eschatology has led the Church to look for hope in this world rather than in the return of Christ. As a result, much of the Church has assumed that its purpose is to *change* the world, rather than to call people *out of* the world. Because of this belief, many churches are turning to humanistic pragmatism, rather than the guidance of the Holy Spirit, as the means of fulfilling the Great Commission. In this motivation, the church is finding itself in the throes of a great apostasy, which is becoming so pervasive that it has become increasingly difficult to discern; a state which Peter expressly predicted.

> *... that there shall come in the last days scoffers, walking after their own lusts, and saying, "Where is the promise of his coming? for since the fathers fell asleep, all things continue as they were from the beginning of the creation." ~ 2nd Peter 3: 3-4*

Jesus and his Apostles warned repeatedly that this apostasy would precede the rise of *the Antichrist,* prior to Christ's second coming. *The Revelation* was given to express this teaching in a clear chronology, incorporating every remaining unfulfilled prophecy to close the Canon of Scripture. In the immediate generations after the Apostles died, writings were found that gave relatively consistent explanations of these teachings, with clear references to the original texts, leaving little room to misinterpret the ideas that these texts meant to communicate.

While current technological advancements have made it easier to observe the current trends in geopolitics and culture, and to demonstrate that the Scriptures exclusively predict these trends, the Church is turning away from these evangelistic tools altogether. Instead, many churches are gravitating towards an artificial unity, sensually entertaining experiences, and a degraded idea of love as the means of salvation for the world. This false love is reaching outside of the Church to unify with pagan religions, social movements, and political agendas toward a supposed "common good," that promises hope to the world, but will only serve to prepare them to receive *the Antichrist* in the coming years.

So why another book on The Revelation?

Several years ago, I was asked to lead a men's Bible study in a small church near Grand Rapids, MI. Based on some things I had witnessed in the church over the years, I felt a course on prophecy and eschatology was necessary. In this church, I found several people getting caught up in the latest pop theories about the *end-times,* having their origins further and further from the texts of Scripture. Where some would find themselves fixated on the subject, gravitating toward any claim of insight on the internet, *always learning, but never coming to the knowledge of the truth,* others, as in many other churches, disregarded the topic as unimportant, and gave little attention to any discussion of eschatology.

Over time, I began to realize that the problem was not as much rooted in this church as it was in the eschatological teaching available to Christians in general. When it came to eschatology, there were only a couple of hermeneutical systems known to the average Christian, and these gave relatively little substance to justify their interpretations. The underlying systems were not taught, as each church had accepted one or another system as a matter of fact, based on the conclusions of their pastor or denomination. Because of a lack of common information on the subject, most only understood a few distinctive positions, that were the conclusions of these systems, without understanding the subject matter from which they were drawn.

The eschatological ideas taught in most seminaries had historically been based on Amillenial or Dispensational systems, each with major presuppositions that dictated their interpretation of biblical prophecy. Amillennialism generally relegated all prophetic fulfillment into the past tense, with a few inconsequential future applications at the second coming; if the school even held to a literal second coming. Dispensationalism had concluded that the Church would be raptured before any eschatological predictions would come about, leading many to believe that deep study on the subject would be unprofitable. The result of either system had led the mainstream of Christianity to prejudice those who were inclined toward the topic as being unfruitful busybodies, concerned with things that were not really a priority.

Despite this prejudice, many believers were still naturally inclined toward the subject. Because these two hermeneutical systems were the only ones available, those who were inclined toward a futurist understanding of prophecy were left with the assumption that the Dispensational position was the *literal* interpretation, while the Amillenial position was just an *allegorical* element of Roman Catholic theology, that many Protestant groups had failed to reform. When the Dispensationalists accurately predicted the rebirth of the modern nation of Israel, their school of thought became the primary interpretive lens among those holding a futurist perspective.

With the Dispensationalist teaching being the dominant futurist view in the Christian discourse, their presupposition of a *Church Age,* that concluded with a rapture, followed by an unfolding *Seven-Year Tribulation,* remained largely unchallenged until the close of the 20th century. While variant positions on the timing of *the Rapture* arose to challenge this view, the dispensational hermeneutical system remained the core teaching of most seminaries with a futurist view of prophecy. As a result, the *Pre-Tribulation Rapture* proposition won out as the predominant conclusion of futurist proponents. It was within this context that those like Hal Lindsey, Tim LaHaye, and Grant Jefferies came to popularity in the latter part of the 20th century. As the Dispensationalist prediction of a *Revived Roman Empire* seemed to manifest in the European Union, and the Cold War seemed to echo their conclusions about the *Gog-Magog* invasion, the writings of these men became popular *canon* in eschatological thought. It was not until the fall of the Soviet Union in the 1990's, followed by the events of September 11th in 2001, that eschatological thought began to shift toward what it is today.

As the Cold War ended, and the growing War on Terror began to reoccupy the role of the "boogie man" that the Soviets once held, people became dissatisfied with the predictions of the Dispensationalists. A new market emerged for those offering a fresh prophetic explanation for what was occurring on the world stage. This resulted in round after round of authors claiming to have new insight, or to have predicted what was now beginning to come about in this new and tumultuous 21st century.

These new prophetic predictions had since become increasingly speculative, with their only bounds being the major presuppositions of their hermeneutical camp. As a result, the average listener was being conditioned to accept nearly any theory based on a few *fine sounding arguments,* if the theory did not disrupt their core presuppositions. This was particularly common in the Dispensationalist camp, as any theory could be given with the simple caveat, "we will be raptured before this happens," making the speculation an inconsequential form of entertainment. Because of their marketability, these theories became less theological and increasingly occult in nature. Various authors, speculating on recent news, began to occupy popular media outlets. Writers and video publishers, relying heavily on non-canonical books, conspiracy theories, and other occult ideas, were leading many into confusion. The amount of unsubstantiated theory left most in this church, like in many churches, either undiscerning or unconcerned when it came to eschatology.

To confront these challenges, our Bible study took a journey through the Scriptures, looking at prophecy as a general topic, and examining every prophecy we could find. We carefully examined the prophecies which were already fulfilled, giving attention to the original wording and apparent prediction of the prophecy before considering its fulfillment. Afterward, we took the interpretations of various prophecies, given by Jesus and his Apostles, and developed modes of interpretation to relate what was prophesied to what they interpreted. From these modes, we developed some hermeneutical boundaries as to how far one could go in their speculations, while being faithful to the form and pattern of interpretation established by the Apostolic teaching. This system—which is detailed in the appendix of this book—led us to eliminate most popular media on the subject as unreliable theory, produced for entertainment rather than serious study.

In discovering and qualifying these hermeneutical principals, I began to realize that some of the interpretive modes used in the New Testament were either ignored or disqualified, by either the Dispensational or Amillenial camp, unnecessarily hindering their understanding of prophecy. Amillennialism, largely having its basis in the writings of Origen of Alexandria, had equated any belief in a future material fulfillment of prophecy to an unhealthy attachment to the material world, as well as the reason that the Jews were motivated to persecute Jesus. In contrast, Dispensationalists held to such a strict literal interpretive method that they rejected any allegorical interpretations, to which they attributed to the *Replacement Theology* of the Roman Catholic and Mainline Protestant denominations. As I realized that the interpretive methods of each camp were at least somewhat valid, I was led to further scrutinize the premises of Dispensationalism, seeking a new hermeneutical standard.

Leaving Dispensationalism as a Hermeneutic

In studying eschatology for the past twenty years, I had explored the interpretive methods and conclusions held by numerous denominations, including Roman Catholic, Protestant Reformed, American Evangelical, and Charismatic groups. Previously, I had favored the works of Dispensationalist authors because they offered a more reasonable interpretation of unfulfilled prophecy. More than other systems of thought, they seemed to incorporate more prophetic passages, offering a cohesive explanation as to how these many prophecies would be fulfilled in a literal framework. This stood largely in contrast to the interpretations of other groups, which seemed more interested in explaining these passages away, than in trying to demonstrate either an historical or future fulfillment. Unfortunately, as I continued to explore counter-positions to Dispensationalism, I had to acknowledge the validity of the many criticisms of the system. As I began to understand these criticisms, I came to realize that the objections were not based on the futurist conclusions of the system, but in the ramifications of the system being applied toward the Gospel message.

Dispensationalism, at its core, is not simply an eschatological hermeneutic, but a theological system that carries implications toward every area of doctrine. A simple explanation of Dispensationalism is the idea that God chooses to govern humanity in different ways during different eras of time. Rather than viewing the allegorical repetition of two covenants, being demonstrated throughout the Scriptures from Genesis to Revelation, it assumes that God had offered several different covenants by which mankind was meant to live throughout history. Dispensationalism concluded that the resulting lesson of each age is to prove man's inability to obey the rules of that age, requiring God to inaugurate a new age with different rules to obey.

Dispensationalism failed to distinguish the Law Biblically as a tutor, meant to conclude all men under sin and in need of a *better covenant with better promises*. As a result, the Gospel was reduced from being the original intention of history, revealed *in the fullness of time,* to merely being the covenant of the *Age of Grace,* or *Church Age;* another *dispensation* destined to fail like all the rest. Rather than accepting the Law as being fulfilled in the death of Christ, it determined the Gospel mission to be another temporary phase, in which God had simply chosen to deal with mankind differently. Tragically, it took Jesus' teachings to his Apostles and made them part of an intermediary message, meant only to last until Paul was given a new message for the Gentiles. Dispensationalism caused confusion toward the New Testament, even leading some to conclude that Peter and Paul taught opposing gospels during the earliest days of the Church, leading them to reject the ordinance of Baptism.

The final nail in the coffin for Dispensationalism was in its conclusion on *the Rapture*. When approaching the topic as a teacher rather than a listener, I found myself utterly unable to reconcile the many logical inconsistencies of this position. The lack of any passage that places *the Rapture* before *Daniel's 70th week* made it clear that this conclusion was just another imposition of the theology onto the Scriptures, upheld by the repeated use of phrases, not used anywhere in Scripture, rather than a Biblical conclusion. While many passages existed that clearly contradicted this conclusion, Dispensationalists would annul these passages by relegating their message to another dispensation, or else by explaining them away with alternative meanings that left the texts without any coherent expression, despite lacking other texts to corroborate their supposed explanation. It became clear that the *Pre-Trib Rapture* was not the result of diligent exegetical study of the topic, but was the biproduct of an inaccurately qualified *'Church Age'*—beginning with Paul's ministry and ending with the Rapture— before the next age, centered on the nation of Israel, could begin.

New Futurist Positions

Many books, theories and commentaries have been written on *The Revelation*; some faithfully undertaken and some wildly speculative. While these can contribute to one's understanding of the book, none seem to establish a hermeneutic that explains the modes of interpretation used by Christ and the Apostles, before interpreting its contents. Without taking the time to establish such a premise, new eschatological theorists are reacting to unsubstantiated elements of Dispensational eschatology, without being able to acknowledge the elements of their interpretation that are in-fact Biblical. The resulting ideas could be much more dangerous if widely adopted.

In recent years, two primary counter-positions to the Dispensational view have risen in prominence. These positions are called *"Post-Tribulation"* and *"Pre-Wrath"* which are nearly identical in their interpretations. While doing a fair job of pointing out the many inconsistencies in the Dispensationalist conclusions, these two views fail to incorporate the many other Scriptural prophecies into their own conclusions. They fail to consider the passages of Daniel, Ezekiel, Isaiah, Hosea, Micah, Malachi, Zechariah, Jeremiah, Joel, and others that reference events surrounding the *Day of the Lord.* Additionally, like the Dispensational view, these views unnecessarily attempt to force the entire chronological narrative of *The Revelation* into *Daniel's 70th week*, obscuring the many texts and prophecies that dictate otherwise. These interpretive methods could become far more dangerous than the Dispensational view, leading many to believe the wrath of God has ended, when it has only just begun.

The consistent Apostolic teaching in the first and second centuries affirmed that the Church should be expected to face *the Antichrist*. While the *Pre-Wrath* and *Post-Tribulation* views acknowledge this, their negligent study of the other eschatological prophecies lead them to dismiss the idea of a *pseudo-Armageddon,* and the defeat of a *pseudo-Antichrist,* preceding the real *Antichrist*. While the Dispensationalists do predict this invasion of Israel before the rise of *the Antichrist*, their insistence that this must occur after *the Rapture* prohibits them from acknowledging the rise of *the Antichrist* when it occurs before their eyes. Both viewpoints utterly fail to corroborate all the prophetic texts to adequately demonstrate the rise and fall of the Antichrist within the text of *The Revelation*. In doing so, they lead their adherents to either fail to identify the Antichrist, or to unwittingly receive him as the Messiah when he arrives.

Much of the confusion between these camps is rooted in the definition of terms, causing them to base their respective views on similar terminology with differing meaning. For instance, the terms *"Pre-Tribulation," "Pre-Wrath,"* and *"Post-Tribulation"* are all technically equivalent, if one understands the proper Biblical definition of the ideas they convey. However, within their respective frameworks, they lead to very different conclusions as to the timing of *the Rapture*. This confusion can be largely attributed to the repeated use of the phrase *"the Seven-Year Tribulation,"* which is found nowhere in Scripture. The redundant use of this term, which has effectively governed the futurist discourse, should be rejected for the alternative *"Daniel's 70th week,"* as the standard terminology for this timeframe.

This work is an attempt to merge the faithful aspects of these interpretive camps into a cohesive interpretation, that gives respect to each point of view. Its purpose is to reconcile some of the varied ideas about the subject, while accepting *The Revelation* for what it is: a clear, chronological prophecy of events surrounding the second coming: *The Revelation of Jesus Christ*. This book is meant to convey an understandable narrative, beginning with the ministry of Christ and continuing with that of the Church, leading up to the catastrophic events surrounding Christ's return. While many sub-topics of the book may be considered only plausible speculation, the distinctive elements for which I would contend are as follows:

1) That *"The Revelation of Jesus Christ,"* the title of the book, represents the appearing of Christ in the clouds to rapture the Church.

2) That the Seven Letters are more than a contemporary message, but a prophetic panorama of Church history, as well as a revealed mode of distinction toward different kinds of churches that will exist until the end of the age.

3) That the Seven Seals are a panorama of *birth pangs,* beginning before *Daniel's 70th week*, comprising a *pseudo-Apocalypse,* before the coming of the *pseudo-Christ* and a *pseudo-Millennium,* beginning at the beginning of Daniel's 70th week.

4) That the Seven Years of *Daniel's* 70th *week* are revealed thematically, as both a divine wedding feast and a divine legal trial, with all the respective actors detailed throughout the narrative.

5) That the *Day of the Lord* takes place on a single day, in the middle of Daniel's 70th week, in which the seventh trumpet is sounded, the *Abomination of Desolation* occurs, the Jews flee Jerusalem, and the Church is *raptured*.

6) That the *Day of the Lord* is also *The Millennium,* a literal, material, and geopolitical reign of Christ over the nations, until Satan is released to deceive them one last time, followed by a final judgement.

Apart from these primary themes, which I am willing to defend Scripturally, any other propositions of this writing are to be considered reasoned speculations, not meant to be contentious. While prophetic theories are not meant to divide believers from fellowship, we should understand that Christ gave this body of knowledge in advance, both to prepare the Church for what we will experience as we await his return, and to guard us against the deception that will accompany these events.

The scriptures quoted throughout this text are taken from the New King James Version and the King James Version, with some minor adjustments made to modernize the language when the King James is used. Any parenthetical words inserted are based on the Textus Receptus Greek, with cross-analysis of other Critical-Text based translations. This writing has been composed in good faith toward the original meaning of the terminology, symbols, and narratives involved, toward the hope of bringing the entire Church to the table, to progress toward the same unity of thought regarding eschatology that has been pursued with those categories of theology considered to be *primary* in importance.

Acknowledgements

While this book is in many ways distinct from any other on the subject, it would be aloof to pretend that its conclusions have not been heavily influenced and clarified by the work of the many faithful workers who came before me, on whose shoulders I have been able to stand, to perhaps see a clearer picture of what may be nearer than when these men labored on the subject. To the following men, I owe a debt of gratitude, for being able to freely receive of their labors.

To Chuck Missler, whose *"Learn the Bible in 24 Hours"* series helped me to see the Bible as a divinely woven tapestry, written incorruptibly by *One Shepherd*. To Dave Hunt, whose work on apologetics helped me to remain aware of those exterior influences that have worked to supplant the simplicity of Christ. To Jacob Prasch, whose teaching on typology and symbols has helped me to see the Scriptures from a Jewish-Apostolic perspective. To Joel Rosenberg, Thomas Ice, Joe Schimmel, Alan Kurschner, Chris White, Hal Lindsey, Tim LaHaye, Billy Crone, Peter Williamson, and the many unnamed men, whose commentaries, debates, and writings have encouraged and strengthened my course of study. In the respect, that while our conclusions may diverge, our hope remains the same in our mutual longing for the soon appearing of our Lord and Savior.

To those friends who helped through prayer, encouragement, and interest. To the baristas of the Lantern Coffee Shop and Baker's Beanery in Grand Rapids, MI where I spent countless hours. To DJ Barker, Joy Hoskins, Phil Hoskins and others for their critical feedback; and to Emily Zondlak, who walked the road to self-publishing before me,

and taught me to take courage, and finish what I started. You are a treasure and a precious vessel of our Lord Jesus Christ. To all who take the time to read this work, I hope you are both blessed and challenged by this labor of love.

Yours in Christ,

Aaron Matthew Fochtman

PART 1 - THE SIGN

When considering the differing interpretive views related to the Second Coming of Christ, the distinctive groups find their disagreement in their understanding of the Olivet Discourse. Recorded in *Matthew 24*, *Mark 13*, and *Luke 21* synoptically, Jesus taught this sermon to his apostles in specific reference to their questions, not only about the destruction of the Temple, but also about *"The Sign"* of his coming at the end of the age. In understanding how he chooses to answer both questions, one can establish what Jesus expected his disciples to look for in the days leading up to his return and align these things to their corroborating witness in The Revelation.

In *Matthew 24,* Jesus alludes to three key elements, which, when aligned with his teaching in *Luke 17*, can be clearly demonstrated as occurring on a single *day* in which he is *revealed.* Considering this, one can interpret *Matthew 24* as placing *the sign* of his coming in its proper place: at the mid-point of *Daniel's 70th week,* or as Paul states: *"at the Last Trump" (1st Corinthians 15:52). "That day,"* a phrase used repeatedly in this context, is the very day in which the following events, taught by Jesus, repeated by Paul, and witnessed in *The Revelation*, will each occur:

1) The *Abomination of Desolation*, spoken by Daniel the Prophet.
2) The Jews fleeing Jerusalem into the mountains to be protected by God.
3) *The Resurrection* and *Rapture* of the Church to meet Christ in the air.

Interpreting Matthew 24

Matthew 24 should be considered the foundational passage on the second coming of Christ, to which we should seek to reconcile all other prophecies on the subject. In this passage, Jesus and his disciples are looking at the temple complex, and his disciples are marveling at its buildings. In response to their awe, Jesus tells them plainly, that the buildings will be thrown down to the very last stone. Later that night, his disciples come to him and ask him when this will happen, followed by a second question, which should be important to every disciple.

> ... *"Tell us, when will these things be? And __what will be the sign of Your coming,__ and of the end of the age?"* ~ Matthew 24:3

Jesus gives a single answer to these two questions, over which the church has divided into two interpretive camps. The *Preterist* camp, believing that most biblical prophecy has been fulfilled, suggests that this passage refers primarily to the fall of the Temple of Jerusalem in 70 AD. In contrast, the *Futurist* camp believes that this passage pertains only to things happening at the end of the age. While both camps have their arguments, with their respective merits, a better understanding of prophetic interpretation can be applied to this passage to reconcile both views, further illuminating one's understanding of prophecy in general.

Many prophecies can have a *dual fulfillment,* in which a prophetic sign is fulfilled in part at an earlier time, and then more completely in the future. This mode of interpretation was not foreign to the Jews, who would have been listening to Jesus, nor was this sense lost on the early church writers, among whom were still many Jewish believers. The influence of these traditional modes of Jewish interpretation prevailed for some time, prior to the introduction of Greek modes of interpretation, which would later come to dominate the Western Churches. The loss of this hermeneutical knowledge is at the root of the contention between these camps.

An excellent example of this Jewish mode of interpretation can be found in the prophecy of the virgin birth.

> *"Therefore, the Lord Himself will give you a sign: Behold, the virgin shall conceive and bear a Son, and shall call His name Immanuel."* ~ Isaiah 7:14

When this famous prophecy was given, it was spoken by the Prophet Isaiah to validate a promise to King Ahaz of Judah. This sign was meant to be the proof of God's promise that the enemies of Judah would be taken into captivity by the Assyrians, no longer to trouble King Ahaz. However, according to *Matthew 1:22-23*, this prophecy was fulfilled in Christ, being immaculately conceived in the virgin Mary, several hundred years after King Ahaz had died.

One could imagine similar arguments in that day as to whether this prophecy had already been fulfilled. It would not be reasonable that a sign meant to assure King Ahaz that his enemies would be removed, would be signified by a virgin birth to take place hundreds of years after his death. Most people do not try to resolve this discrepancy, taking it on faith that the Apostles were inspired by the Holy Spirit to interpret the prophecy accurately. However, this problem cannot be left unresolved, as the credibility of the Gospels, and the whole Christian teaching, depend on Jesus Christ being born of a virgin in fulfillment of this prophecy.

In the following chapter, Isaiah approaches *the prophetess,* assumed to be his wife, who conceives and bears a son. The child's name is *"Maher-Shalal-Hash-Baz,"* and conveys the meaning, *"for before the child shall have knowledge to cry 'My father' and 'My mother,' the riches of Damascus and the spoil of Samaria will be taken away before the king of Assyria." (Isaiah 8:3-4).* This child seems to fulfill the prophecy, giving assurance to the King that his enemies would be defeated. Consequently, shortly after this child was born, Assyria took the northern Kingdom of Israel and the Aramean kingdom at Damascus into captivity. As to the child's name being *Immanuel,* meaning *"God with us,"* we find that the child does in fact signify that God is with them, though not in the sense of a physical incarnation.

> *...And the stretching out of his wings will fill the breadth of Your land, **O Immanuel**....Take counsel together, but it will come to nothing; Speak the word, but it will not stand, **For God is with us**. ~ Isaiah 8:8-10*

These passages alone would seem to indicate that the prophecy had been fulfilled, with nothing more to look for in the future. The child was born, whose name signifies an imminent deliverance from Israel's enemies, demonstrating that God was with them. There does not seem to be a need for another child to be born immaculately, who is God incarnate. In fact, biblical critics have used this very misunderstanding to conclude that a virgin birth was never intended, even influencing some translators to use the alternative *"young woman"* instead of *"virgin."* However, the remainder of the prophecy will lead one to conclude that more remains to be fulfilled, which must include a Virgin Birth of God incarnate.

For unto us a Child is born, unto us a Son is given; and the government will be upon His shoulder. And His name will be called Wonderful, Counselor, Mighty God, Everlasting Father, Prince of Peace. ~ Isaiah 9:6

If one is careful to understand the various modes of interpretation used by the authors of the New Testament, one would understand that this passage has a *dual fulfillment*. In fact, many passages of Scripture, whether they are historical narratives, psalms, or express prophecies, have an immediate literal context, as well as a later prophetic implication. In most cases, these remaining references relate to Jesus Christ in his first or second coming, to the workings of Satan and *the Antichrist*, or to the *Mystery* of the Church. The authors of the Gospel would have understood this, interpreting this passage to correspond to the birth of Christ, despite having been also fulfilled in the days of Ahaz. When understanding this, we should be able to reconcile the preterist and futurist interpretations into a cohesive whole, referring both to the destruction of the temple in 70 AD, and to a more future desolation of Jerusalem and its temple near Christ's *coming* at *the end of the age;* placing the *mystery* of the Gentile Church between the two.

After the disciples ask the question, Jesus says, *"Take heed that no one deceives you"* (Matthew 24 4), suggesting that a great deception will occur around that time which will require great care to avoid. Paul would echo this very sentiment, also referring to the time preceding Christ's coming, in his letter to the Thessalonians.

> **<u>Let no one deceive you</u>** *by any means; for* **that day** *will not come unless* **the apostasy comes first***, and the man of sin is revealed, the son of perdition, who opposes and exalts himself above all that is called God, or that is worshiped, so that he sits as God in the temple of God, showing himself that he is God. ~ 2nd Thessalonians 2:3-4*

Both sayings indicate a great deception coming forth in the last days, which Paul calls *"the apostasy"* and Christ characterizes by an abundance of false Christs.

> *And Jesus answered and said to them: "Take heed that no one deceives you. For many will come* **<u>in My name</u>***, saying I am the Christ, and will deceive many."*
> *~ Matthew 24:4-5*

While many assume that this prophecy means that many people would come claiming to be Jesus Christ, which does periodically happen and will continue to happen, this is not the sweeping deception that Christ and the Apostle Paul were referring to. The statement *"in My name,"* in its biblical context, does not assume that the person is claiming to be the other person, but that the person is coming in the authority of the one in whose name they come. A more biblically consistent interpretation of this passage, might be elaborated to say,

> *"Many people will come, claiming to have been sent by Me, even calling me Christ and Lord, and yet will deceive many into following falsehood, preparing them to be deceived by Antichrist; who is the Man of Lawlessness"*

Jesus says something similar in another passage, relating to the *False Prophets* that he will judge at his second coming.

> *Not everyone who says to Me, "Lord, Lord," shall enter the kingdom of heaven, but he who does the will of My Father in heaven. Many will say to Me in that day, "Lord, Lord, have we not prophesied **in Your name**, cast out demons **in Your name**, and done many wonders **in Your name**?" And then I will declare to them, "I never knew you; depart from Me, you who practice lawlessness!" ~ Matthew 7:21-23*

The writings of the Apostles confirm this teaching, claiming that people who come in the last days will not be claiming to *be* Jesus Christ, but to deceive people into believing they are His messengers.

> *Little children, it is the last hour; and as you have heard that the Antichrist is coming, even now **many antichrists** have come, by which we know that it is the last hour.*
> *~ 1st John 2:18*
>
> *For such are **false apostles**, deceitful workers, transforming themselves into apostles of Christ. And no wonder! For Satan himself transforms himself into an angel of light. Therefore, it is no great thing if his ministers also transform themselves into ministers of righteousness, whose end will be according to their works. ~ 1st Corinthians 11:13-15*
>
> *… remember the words which were spoken before by the apostles of our Lord Jesus Christ: how they told you that there would be **mockers in the last time,** who would walk according to their own ungodly lusts. These are sensual persons, who cause divisions, not having the Spirit. ~ Jude 1:17-19*

The Apostles were unanimous in their warning that these pseudo-christs would be claiming to be sent by Him, compiling their words to deceive many. These false apostles have the dual objective, both to deceive people into licensing sin among professing Christians, and to deny that Jesus is the only way to salvation.

> *…certain men have crept in unnoticed, who long ago were marked out for this condemnation, ungodly men, (1) who turn the grace of our God into lewdness and (2) deny the only Lord God and our Lord Jesus Christ. ~ Jude 1:4*
>
> *… there will be false teachers among you, who will secretly bring in destructive heresies, even (2) denying the Lord who bought them, bringing on themselves swift destruction. And many will follow their destructive ways, because of whom the way of truth will be*

blasphemed. By covetousness they will exploit you with deceptive words; ... (1) While they promise them liberty, they themselves are slaves of corruption; for by whom a person is overcome, by him also he is brought into bondage. ~ 2nd Peter 2:1-19

Continuing in *Matthew 24*, Jesus goes on to give a series of signs, clarifying that they are *not* the sign of the end, but what he calls *"birth pangs"* or *"sorrows,"* which progress like contractions, felt by a woman about to give birth. If one were to align these signs with those in *Revelation 6*, a pattern would emerge. *Revelation 6* is a prophecy of six seals on a scroll, being opened before the end comes, corresponding with devastating signs on the earth.

*(1) For many will come in My name, saying I am the Christ, and will deceive many. (2) And you will hear of wars and rumors of wars. See that you are not troubled; for all these things must come to pass, but **the end is not yet**. For nation will rise against nation, and kingdom against kingdom. And there will be (3) famines, (4) pestilences, and (6) earthquakes in various places. All these are the beginning of sorrows. (5) Then **they will deliver you up to tribulation <thilipsis>** and kill you, and you will be hated by all nations for My name's sake. And then many will be offended, will betray one another, and will hate one another. Then many false prophets will rise up and deceive many. And because lawlessness will abound, the love of many will grow cold. But he who endures to the end shall be saved. And this gospel of the kingdom will be preached in all the world as a witness to all the nations, and then the end will come. ~ Matthew 24:5-14*

1) An archer on a white horse, going out to conquer many: This can be interpreted to be the *Spirit of Antichrist,* rather than a specific person, just as the three remaining horses represent spiritual powers, rather than individuals. This *Spirit of Antichrist* will lead those false ministers to make a mockery of the truth and lead many professing Christians into deception. His conquest is not military, but a consolidation of every false religion into a single system of devotion to the coming *Antichrist*.

2) A rider on a red horse carrying a sword, taking peace from the earth: This can be interpreted as a growing pattern of war and distress on the earth, culminating in an attempt to wipe out Israel from being a nation. Israel will be spared, but a man will arise and take the glory for the victory, impersonating the coming Messiah according to the expectation of the Jews. These wars are detailed in *Psalm 83*, *Micah 5*, *Joel 2*, *Isaiah 17* and *Ezekiel 38-39*.

3) A rider on a black horse carrying scales, bringing about economic collapse and famine: This can be interpreted as a global currency reset, as powerful nations prove the limits of their fiat economies. Drowned in debt to one another, yet unable to balance the out-of-control inflation of their respective currencies, they will have to

account for the fact that their armies, public works, and subsidy programs are insoluble, the result of which will cause their people to suffer famine.

4) A pale horse, carrying death and hades, coming to claim one fourth of the entire earth's population. This *pale* horse signifies sickliness and death as war, famine, and pestilence cause death to come in massive waves.

5) The 5th seal, after the four horses have been unleashed, represents martyrdom. This will be a worldwide persecution of faithful Christians. The *Spirit of Antichrist* will convince the world that a time of great awakening and revival is just around the corner, as soon as the divisive, fundamentalist-doomsayers (those who heed the Bible's warning) are removed from the earth.

6) While a massive worldwide earthquake is part of the 6th seal, earthquakes will begin to increase in frequency and destructiveness, continuing to increase until this great quake finally shakes the earth. Jesus makes it clear that these things will continue until he returns, but that none of them are *the sign* of his coming. Rather, these *sorrows* correspond with the Gospel reaching the ends of the earth.

After explaining this, he then gives *the sign* that he expects his disciples to look for.

Therefore, __when you see__ the 'Abomination of Desolation,' __spoken of by Daniel__ the prophet, standing in the holy place (whoever reads, let him understand), then let those who are in Judea flee to the mountains. Let him who is on the housetop not go down to take anything out of his house. And let him who is in the field not go back to get his clothes. But woe to those who are pregnant and to those who are nursing babies in those days! And pray that your flight may not be in winter or on the Sabbath. For then there will be __great tribulation,__ such as has not been since the beginning of the world until this time, no, nor ever shall be. And unless those days were shortened, no flesh would be saved; but for the elect's sake those days will be shortened. ~ Matthew 24:15

Daniel was a prophet, who was part of the captivity of the Jews to Babylon. His prophecies were all centered on a single theme known as *"the times of the Gentiles."* This would be a time that Israel would be captive to the nations, unable to live as a sovereign people in their *Promised Land,* because of their unfaithfulness toward God in the worship of idols. Daniel gives several prophecies about this era, describing the kingdoms that would dominate the world until Israel would be restored. These nations include Babylon, Persia, Greece, and Rome, followed by a mysterious kingdom arising in the last days, with a worldwide influence, ruled by a boastful man who demands to be worshipped as God. This *Abomination of Desolation* is mentioned in two of his prophecies, which signify the restoration of the Kingdom of Israel and *the Resurrection* of the dead.

> *Know therefore and understand, that from the going forth of the command to restore and build Jerusalem until Messiah the Prince, there shall be seven weeks and sixty-two weeks; [After seven weeks] the street shall be built again, and the wall, even in troublesome times. After sixty-two [more] weeks* **<u>Messiah shall be cut off</u>**, *but not for Himself. ~ Daniel 9:25*

In this first prophecy, Daniel is describing seventy weeks of years in which the Jews will be held captive to the Gentiles. Between the 69th and 70th week, there is a mysterious gap, indicating the time between Christ's first and second coming, which are presented to Daniel as surrounding two key events: the first being the death of Christ, and the second being the Abomination of Desolation.

> *And the people of the prince who is to come shall destroy the city and the sanctuary. The end of it shall be with a flood, and until the end of the war desolations are determined. Then he shall confirm a covenant with many for one week; but in the middle of the week he shall bring an end to sacrifice and offering. And* **<u>on the wing of abominations shall be one who makes desolate</u>**, *even until the consummation, which is determined, is poured out on the desolate. ~ Daniel 9:26-27*

Unknown to many, these two events represent both a real and a counterfeit *death and resurrection*, to be carried out by Christ and Antichrist respectively. The second part of the prophecy indicates a mysterious *"prince that shall come,"* who confirms a covenant for one week (or seven years). This indicates the reinstitution of the old covenant system with the temple sacrifices, which will be followed by this prince abolishing this system when he sits in the temple, claiming to be God. This was not only indicated by Paul the Apostle in *2nd Thessalonians* but also by early church writers including Irenaeus of Lyons, and Hippolytus of Rome, who wrote in the 2nd and 3rd centuries, connecting the prophecies of *Daniel*, *Matthew 24*, and *2nd Thessalonians* as relating the same events.

> *And forces shall be mustered by him, and they shall defile the sanctuary fortress;* **<u>then they shall take away the daily sacrifices, and place there the Abomination of Desolation</u>**...*Then the king shall do according to his own will:* **<u>he shall exalt and magnify himself above every god</u>**, *shall speak blasphemies against the God of gods, and shall prosper till the wrath has been accomplished; for what has been determined shall be done. He shall regard neither the God of his fathers nor the desire of women, nor regard any god; for he shall exalt himself above them all. ~ Daniel 11:31-37*

Daniel 12 will prophesy of the time after this *abomination*, which will initiate a great tribulation for the people of Israel, lasting for three and a half years.

> **At that time** *Michael shall stand up, [or arise], the great prince who stands watch over the sons of your people; And there shall be* **a time of trouble**, *such as never was since there was a nation, even to that time.* ~ *Daniel 12:1*

> *And from the time that the daily sacrifice is taken away, and the Abomination of Desolation is set up, there shall be one thousand two hundred and ninety days (three and a half years)* ~ *Daniel 12:11*

Jesus parallels the words of the angel in Daniel's vision, calling it a *"great tribulation,"* while Daniel's angel calls it *"a time of trouble."* Based on these passages, there can be no mistaking that this *Abomination of Desolation* occurs at the middle of *Daniel's 70th week*, at which time Jesus counsels the Jews in Israel to flee into the mountains.

> *...then let those who are in Judea* **flee to the mountains**. *Let him who is on the housetop not go down to take anything out of his house. And let him who is in the field not go back to get his clothes. But woe to those who are pregnant and to those who are nursing babies in those days! And pray that your flight may not be in winter or on the Sabbath. For* **then there will be great tribulation**, *such as has not been since the beginning of the world until this time, no, nor ever shall be.* ~ *Matthew 24:16-21*

In *Luke 17*, Jesus gives another prophecy related to his second coming. Jesus makes it clear that on the same day that the Jews flee Jerusalem, he will be revealed from heaven and *the Rapture* will occur.

> *As it was in the days of Noah, so it will be also in the days of the Son of Man: They ate, they drank, they married wives, they were given in marriage, until* **the day** *that Noah entered the ark, and the flood came and destroyed them all. Likewise, as it was also in the days of Lot: They ate, they drank, they bought, they sold, they planted, they built; but on* **the day** *that Lot went out of Sodom it rained fire and brimstone from heaven and destroyed them all. Even so will it be in* **the day when the Son of Man is revealed**.

> ~ *Luke 17:26-30*

> *In* **that day**, *he who is on the housetop, and his goods are in the house, let him not come down to take them away. Likewise, the one who is in the field, let him not turn back. Remember Lot's wife. Whoever seeks to save his life will lose it, and whoever loses his life will preserve it. I tell you, in* **that night** *there will be two men in one bed: the one will be taken and the other will be left. Two women will be grinding together: the one will be taken and the other left. Two men will be in the field: the* **one will be taken and the other left**. *And they answered and said to Him, "Where Lord?" So, He said to them, "Wherever the Body is, there the eagles will be gathered together."* ~ *Luke 17:31-34*

Jesus is drawing parallels between the day Noah enters the Ark, the day Lot flees Sodom, and the day that He is revealed. This is the same day that the *Abomination of*

Desolation occurs, indicating that those who flee Jerusalem will see *"one taken and the other left,"* after he appears in the clouds. While this should clearly indicate *the Rapture* occurring, we can also find that Paul corroborates this interpretation.

> *Now brethren, concerning **the coming of our Lord Jesus Christ and our gathering together to Him**, we ask you not to be soon shaken in mind or troubled, either by spirit or by word or by letter, as if from us, as though the day of Christ had come. Let no one deceive you by any means; for **that day** will not come unless the falling away comes first, and the man of sin is revealed, the son of perdition, who opposes and exalts himself above all that is called God or that is worshiped, so that **he sits as God in the temple of God, showing himself that he is God.** ~ 2ⁿᵈ Thessalonians 2:1-5*

In *Matthew 24*, Jesus also alludes to *the Rapture*, immediately after the Jews are counseled to flee Jerusalem.

> *...unless those days were shortened, no flesh would be saved; but for the elect's sake those days will be shortened. ... For as the lightning comes from the east and flashes to the west, so also will the coming of the Son of Man be. For **wherever the carcass is, there the eagles will be gathered together**. ~ Matthew 24:22-28*

Here, Christ uses the phrase *"For wherever the **carcass** is, there the eagles will be gathered together,"* where in *Luke 17* he says, *"wherever the **body** is, there the eagles will be gathered together."* In *Matthew 24*, Jesus refers to Daniel's prophecy, leading up to *the Resurrection* of the dead, while in Luke, he informs the Jews, who will be fleeing Jerusalem, what they will *see* after he is revealed. In *Matthew 24*, he uses the words *"carcass"* and *"eagles"* to indicate the resurrection of the dead, while in Luke he uses the words *"body"* and *"eagles,"* to indicate the rapture of the *"Body of Christ."* Paul will echo this, indicating the *catching up* (or <harpazo>) of the Body of Christ at this time.

> *But I do not want you to be ignorant brethren, concerning those who have fallen asleep...For the Lord Himself will descend from heaven with a shout, with the voice of an archangel, and with the trumpet of God. And **the dead in Christ will rise first. Then we who are alive and remain shall be caught up together with them in the clouds to meet the Lord in the air**. And thus, we shall always be with the Lord. Therefore comfort one another with these words. ~ 1ˢᵗ Thessalonians 4:13-18*

While Dispensationalists say that Paul is teaching some new revelation that is distinct from what Jesus taught, Paul made it clear that he was given the same Gospel by the Spirit that Peter and the other disciples were given by Christ in the flesh. Paul indicated that he also spent three years being taught by Christ in the wilderness confirming the accuracy of his Gospel by comparing it with that of the other Apostles. *(see Galatians 1:17-18, 2:1-2, 2:6-7)* Paul was not teaching some new mystery, but the same gospel that Peter had received, of which the appearing of Christ to resurrect and rapture the Church was always the conclusion.

In *Matthew 24*, Jesus finishes his answer, indicating that the *sign of his coming* was the *Abomination of Desolation*, followed immediately by his *Appearing* to resurrect and rapture the Church. He goes on to reiterate his main points, which leads some to indicate that he is continuing the narrative. However, he clearly indicates that he is returning to an earlier point in the narrative, to elaborate and emphasize earlier statements that he made, so as to make sure his disciples are not taken in this deception that will be so thorough as to deceive the whole world.

God uses a similar mode of transmitting narratives throughout Scripture. In *Genesis chapter 1*, he gives an account of the seven days of creation, while in *Genesis chapter 2*, He returns to the sixth day to elaborate on the creation of man and woman. In *Genesis 10*, He describes the division of nations by their languages, while in *Genesis 11*, He goes back to describe why, and how their languages were divided. In *Revelation 8-9*, Christ describes the signs accompanying the seven trumpets, while in *Revelation 10-11*, he will take John back in time to the *Two Witnesses*, whose testimony ends with the seventh trumpet. It should not confuse a student of Scripture when Jesus explains things this way, specifically to draw attention to certain items in more detail.

In *Matthew 24*, Jesus goes back to the deception, or *great apostasy*, that precedes his coming. He is telling them again not to be deceived into believing that Christ has come, and to wait for the sign of his appearing in the clouds. Jesus is warning them because the deception will be so thorough, that only those looking for this sign will not be taken in by the deception. He takes them back to the *great apostasy* and subsequent persecution, to describe other signs they will see before his appearing.

> Immediately ***after the tribulation*** *of those days the sun will be darkened, and the moon will not give its light; the stars will fall from heaven, and the powers of the heavens will be shaken. Then the sign of the Son of Man will appear in heaven, and then all the tribes of the earth will mourn, and they will see the Son of Man coming on the clouds of heaven with power and great glory. And **He will send His angels with a great sound of a trumpet, and they will gather together His elect** from the four winds, from one end of heaven to the other.* ~ *Matthew 24:30-31*

Some have taken this passage to mean that *the Rapture* will not take place until after the *Great Tribulation*, which takes place for three and a half years after the *Abomination of Desolation*. However, Jesus is not referring to the *Great Tribulation*, but to the *tribulation (or <thilipsis>)* brought about by false Christs <u>until</u> the *Abomination of Desolation*.

> *Then (at that time) if any man shall say unto you, "Lo, here is Christ, or there"; believe it not. For there shall arise false Christs and False Prophets that shall show great signs and wonders; insomuch that, if it were possible, they shall deceive the very elect. **<u>Behold, I have told you before</u>**. ~ Matthew 24:23*

Jesus says, *"I have told you before"* in reference to his earlier statements:

> *For many shall come in my name, saying, I am Christ; and shall deceive many…Then shall they deliver you up unto **tribulation**, **<thilipsis>** and shall kill you: and you shall be hated of all the nations for my name's sake. ~ Matthew 24:5-9*

The Scriptures are always consistent in distinguishing general tribulation, (or <thilipsis>), which occurs throughout the age, from *the great tribulation,* (or <mega thilipsis>), which tests the whole earth after the Church is raptured. This tribulation (or persecution) corresponds to the 5th seal of *Revelation 6,* while the 6th seal refers to the catastrophic signs in the heavens that come afterward.

> *And I saw when he opened the sixth seal, and there was a great earthquake; and the sun became black as sackcloth of hair, and the whole moon became as blood; and the stars of the heaven fell unto the earth, as a fig tree casts her unripe figs when she is shaken of a great wind. And the heaven was removed as a scroll when it is rolled up; and every mountain and island were moved out of their places. ~ Revelation 6:12-13*

Another point of confusion is that Christ's words, when taken as a straightforward narrative, seem to indicate that *the Rapture* occurs immediately after this 6th seal. This is the basic belief of those who hold the *Pre-Wrath* and *Post-Tribulation* views, whose adherents tend not to consider the many other eschatological prophecies that must be incorporated into this position, some even ignoring the fact that the seven trumpets begin after the 7th seal *(Revelation 8:1-2)*. While this important missing information will be reconciled with these passages later in the book, we cannot ignore these parts of *The Revelation* to maintain *Matthew 24* as a complete chronological narrative.

While this passage is difficult to interpret, we must understand that Jesus is not as interested in telling a complete chronological narrative, as he is with assuring that his disciples are not deceived. He knows that this delusion will be so persuasive that any not kept by the Holy Spirit will be deceived by its subtlety. This is because this delusion is not the cleverness of Satan in his independent will, but a sovereign act of God, meant to test the entire world, to prove who are born of His Spirit.

Studying the other prophecies that Jesus mentions, we can only draw the conclusion that he is pointing to a single day, in which the *Abomination of Desolation* occurs, the Jews flee Jerusalem, Christ appears in the clouds, the dead are raised, and the Church is raptured. Paul's teaching clearly corresponds with this conclusion, and as we will see throughout this book, *The Revelation* points to *"that day"*; a single day, in which Christ is revealed. In this book, we will compile all the prophecies about *that day* into a single chronological narrative, in order to prove this to be true.

Eschatological Position

For those theologically trained to understand eschatological categories, the conclusions of this work hold to an *already-not yet*, premillennial, and (for lack of a better term) *"mid-week"* view of *the Rapture*, systematically described as follows.

Already-Not Yet: This book attempts to reconcile the Preterist and Futurist versions of prophetic fulfillment as *already-not yet*. This is based on testimony from Jesus, suggesting that several New Covenant truths are already realized in a sense including, our new birth *(John 5:25)*, our freedom from sin *(Romans 6:18 vs. Romans 7:25)*, the government of the Church *(Matthew 16:19 vs. 2nd Timothy 2:12)*, the binding of Satan *(Mark 3:27 vs. 2nd Corinthians 4:4)*, and the Kingdom Come *(Luke 17:20-21 vs. Acts 1:6)*. In this understanding, the spiritual application of these truths is already realized by faith, while a future material application still awaits fulfillment.

Premillennial: There is little argument that the Premillennial position was held by the earliest Church scholars including those taught by the Apostles. Even Eusebius, in his 4th century Church history, though holding an Amillenial position, admitted that the first and second-hand disciples of the Apostles held this view. It is a well-documented fact that Amillennialism was the invention of Clement and Origen of Alexandria, being popularized by Eusebius and Augustine centuries later.

It should be noted that Clement and Origen's teachings were a clear merging of Christian theology and Platonic philosophy, that regarded all things material as corrupt on their material basis, rather than because of the corruption of sin. Origen took this philosophy to such an extreme that he is reported to have castrated himself, and to have relegated even marital sexual relations as a *necessary evil* rather than a sanctified pleasure. To him, the idea of a literal future kingdom with eating and drinking, was as base as fornication and to be rejected by the mature. In his view, the

Jews did not reject Christ because of their insistence on righteousness by works, but because of their insistence on a material *Kingdom Come*.

Mid-Week Rapture: Among the believers in a futurist-premillennial position, there remains the question of when in the chronology of the eschaton that one should expect *the Rapture* to take place. All futurists agree that the last period of trial, prior to Christ's return, is equated with the 70th week of Daniel's prophecy in *Daniel 9:24-27*. Futurists place *the Rapture* of the Church either before, at the end, or within this week. Two views place *the Rapture* within the week, which are the *Pre-Wrath* view, which will be contested here, and the *Mid-Week* view, which will be represented here.

While these views are often confused, the primary difference is that the Pre-Wrath view attempts to place *the Rapture* before the sixth seal, holding to the proclamation of the coming wrath made by the unbelieving *(Revelation 6:12-17)*, as revealing the actual return of Christ. They attempt to align the chronology of *The Revelation* to fit within their view of *Matthew 24*, which they read as a straight-forward chronological narrative. The view of this work does the opposite, holding *The Revelation* as a straight-forward chronological narrative, (with a single point of taking the reader back in time in *Revelation 11*), and holding to the proclamation from the *Twenty-Four Elders in Heaven (Revelation 11:15-18)* that Christ begins to pour out his wrath and to reign at the seventh trumpet, sounded in the midpoint of the week. Rather than wrestling *The Revelation* to be completely found in *Matthew 24*, it clarifies *Matthew 24*, in light of the corresponding witness in *The Revelation*.

As we approach the unveiling of the events which will transpire before Christ's coming, I feel it is important to expect a *pseudo-apocalypse*, including the downfall of an antichrist-like figure, to complete the allusion that *the Antichrist* is Christ, here to set up His Kingdom. As we will discuss in Part 5, this *pseudo-apocalypse* takes place during the seven seals, which will be demonstrated to occur before *Daniel's 70th week* begins. For those adherents to the *Pre-Tribulation* or *Pre-Wrath* views, I believe the absence of this teaching could lead to many being deceived from watching for Christ's literal appearing in the clouds for every eye to behold, and to being genuinely confused when *the Antichrist* begins to take power. This view has been put forward to equip the Church to approach these times fully aware of what is expected to transpire, and to be unmoved by any events other than the literal appearing of Christ in the clouds. In that effort, I put forward this commentary work on *The Revelation*.

PART 2 - THE REVELATION

Authorship: Written by John the son of Zebedee, the last living Apostle, while imprisoned on the Isle of Patmos under the reign of Domitian, over 20 years after the destruction of Jerusalem and the Temple. This has been testified by Irenaeus, Justin Martyr, Jerome, Eusebius, Origen, Tertullian, and every other 2nd and 3rd century witness. It is important to note that any suggestion that *The Revelation* was not written by John the Apostle, are in contradiction to the historical testimony, based on later textual criticisms that should not be considered authoritative.

The Title and Opening of the Book

When understanding the term *"The Revelation,"* one should not assume that this title is merely meant to suggest that this is one of many such types of *apocalyptic* or prophetic writings. While the term *<apokalupsis>* is often used by Paul to reference communication given to him directly by the Holy Spirit, regarding either a doctrine or an actionable command, this is not the purpose of this opening statement. In this case, *"The Revelation of Jesus Christ"* is the proper title, as well as the subject of the book. *The Revelation of Jesus Christ* is not simply a prophecy conveyed *by* the Lord, but the pivotal event for which the entire faithful Church should be waiting and hoping: *The second coming of Jesus Christ.* This terminology was used repeatedly by the Apostles.

> *Wherein you greatly rejoice, though now for a little while, if need be, you have been put to grief in manifold trials, that the proof of your faith, being more precious than gold, that perishes though it is proved by fire, may be found unto praise and glory and honor at **the revelation of Jesus Christ**: ~ 1st Peter 1:6-7*

> *Wherefore girding up the loins of your mind, be sober and set your hope perfectly on the grace that is to be brought unto you at **the revelation of Jesus Christ.** ~ 1st Peter 1:13*

> *And to you who are troubled, rest with us when the Lord **Jesus shall be revealed** from heaven with his mighty angels... ~ 2nd Thessalonians 1:7*

> *That you keep this commandment without spot, unrebukable until **the appearing of our Lord Jesus Christ**: ~ 1st Timothy 6:14*

> *And now little children, abide in Him; that **when He shall appear**, we may have confidence, and not be ashamed before him at his coming. ~ 1st John 2:28*

> *Beloved, now are we the sons of God, and it does not yet appear what we shall be, but we know that **when He shall appear**, we shall be like Him; for we shall see him as He is.*
> *~ 1st John 3:2*

We should carefully consider this opening statement before continuing further, laying aside any suggestion that this prophecy is about the past-tense destruction of Jerusalem, or a general allegory to encourage the churches amid persecution. Like many introductions in the New Testament epistles, this statement is loaded with definition and purpose, which should lay the bounds of the study going forward.

> *A) The Revelation of Jesus Christ, B) which God gave unto Him, to show unto his servants things which must shortly come to pass; and C) He sent and signified it by his angel unto his servant John: D) Who bare record of (1) the word of God, and of (2) the testimony of Jesus Christ, and of (3) all things that he saw. ~ Revelation 1:1-2*

A) *"The Revelation of Jesus Christ,"* meaning the testimony about the second coming, and the proper title of the book.

B) *"Which God gave Him to show his servants,"* meaning that it was now determined by the Father that Christ should reveal this truth to the Church.

C) *"Sent and signified it by his angel to his servant John,"* meaning that the Angel of the Lord was the one from whom John received the testimony.

D) *"Who bare the record of . . ."*

  1) *"The Word of God,"* attesting to its divine inspiration, and...

2) Things expressly given by Jesus Christ for John to record, and…

3) Things John witnessed by vision and was commanded to record.

This book goes beyond any other Scriptures to testify to its own validity. The detail used to convey the origin, nature, and authority of this testimony is required because John is the last living Apostle of the original twelve, with no other ordained witness to corroborate its authority. Its purpose is to sustain the Church in hope for the remaining delay until Christ comes.

> *Blessed is he that reads, and they that hear the words of this prophecy, and keep those things which are written therein: for the time is at hand. ~ Revelation 1:3*

Unlike any other book of the Bible, *The Revelation* makes the special claim that any who reads, hears, and keeps the words of this prophecy will be blessed, understanding that the time of *The Revelation* will soon be upon the reader. While some might argue that these statements suggest an imminent fulfillment of this prophecy, this terminology was common for the Apostles, writing in a prophetic style with a continual expectancy of Christ's *near* (as opposed to imminent) return.

> *But the **end of all things is at hand.** Therefore, be sober and watch unto prayer.*
> *~ 1st Peter 4:7*
> *Be also patient; establish your hearts: for **the coming of the Lord draws near**.*
> *~ James 5:8*

We can find allusions in the Old Testament to ethnic Israel waiting at least two thousand years until Christ would return *(see Hosea 5:14 through 6:3)*. While Jesus and the Apostles taught that we should live with a certain expectancy that Christ could return at any time, a better understanding would be that whoever would be able to both read and understand this prophecy, and also set about to guard that understanding, would be blessed, because this could only mean that *The Revelation of Jesus Christ* is near. Like the prophecies of Daniel, it is evident that the clear meaning of this prophecy would be veiled until the time of its fulfillment.

> *… Be on your way, Daniel, for the words are closed up and sealed till the time of the end.*
> *~ Daniel 12:9*

Here John testifies to three requirements to receive this blessing:

1) They must *read* this prophecy. Rather than simply read the words aloud, the implication is that one reads and studies the prophecy continually.

2) They must *hear* this prophecy. The implication is to hear with understanding, as Christ would say, *"let him who has an ear, hear,"* having the help of the Holy Spirit.

3) They must *keep* the words of this prophecy. The noun "keep" is a fortress which is used as a last defense in an ancient city; often a fortified tower kept with weapons, food, and other necessary provisions to withstand attack. The verb here implies that those who understand this prophecy should guard that understanding against confusion and deception as the day of its fulfillment draws near.

Contrary to the increasingly popular opinion in the Church, the keeping of *The Revelation* is not to be relegated to a *secondary* importance. It is a sacred promise by Christ himself that those who partake in guarding the transmission of *The Revelation* will inherit a special blessing when he appears *on that day*.

The Recipients of the Book

John begins with a formal introduction to those to whom the book would be circulated. The seven churches were the evangelistic legacy of Paul and Timothy; John having taken the oversight of these churches after the death of Paul.

> *John, to the seven churches which are in Asia: Grace be unto you, and peace, from (1) Him who was, and is, and is to come; and from (2) the Seven Spirits which are before his throne; And from (3) Jesus Christ, who is the faithful witness, and the first begotten of the dead, and the Prince of the kings of the earth. Unto Him that loved us and washed us from our sins in his own blood and has made us kings and priests unto God and his Father; to Him be glory and dominion for ever and ever. Amen. ~ Revelation 1:4-5*

In Apostolic style, John refers to the Trinity in his opening.

1) *"Him who was, and is, and is to come"* is the Father, who is represented in the eternal sense, having never subjected Himself to the bounds of time.

2) *"The Seven Spirits which are before His throne"* are the Holy Spirit, who carries out the will of God on the Earth. While this may seem strange, it is a reference to an earlier prophecy about the attributes of the Holy Spirit who would anoint the Messiah.

> *And a Shoot goes out from the stump of Jesse, and a Branch shall grow out of his roots. And the (1) Spirit of the LORD shall rest on Him, the spirit of (2) wisdom and (3) understanding, the spirit of (4) counsel and (5) might, the spirit of (6) knowledge and of the (7) fear of the LORD. And He is made to breathe in the fear of the LORD. And He shall not judge according to the sight of His eyes, nor decide by the hearing of His ears. ~ Isaiah 11: 1-3*

This prophecy alludes to the earthly ministry of Jesus, emptied of his glory and taking on the form of a bondservant. Anointed by the Holy Spirit, he carried all authority in the attribute known as *"The Spirit of the Lord,"* while possessing all humility in the attribute known as *"the fear of the Lord,"* living the life of an obedient *Son of Man.*

> *Jesus, when He had been baptized, went up immediately out of the water. And the heavens were opened to Him, and He saw the Spirit of God descending like a dove and lighting upon Him, and a voice from Heaven saying, "This is My Beloved Son, in whom I am well pleased." ~ Matthew 3:16-17*
>
> *The Spirit of the Lord is on Me, because He has anointed Me... ~ Luke 4:18*

These *"Seven Spirits"* represent the fullness of the Spirit which Christ alone was given *"without measure" (John 3:34).* The Spirit stands before the throne of God, interceding for us and dispensing the grace needed for the ministry of the Church.

3) *"And from Jesus Christ"*

"The faithful witness," who He *was,* could also be termed, *"the faithful martyr."* Jesus remained faithful, confirming both the holiness of God and the sinfulness of man by his testimony until he was put to death.

"The first begotten from the dead," who He *is,* represents that Christ was *born-again* from the dead, being called the *"firstborn of the dead" (Colossians 1:18).* While Christ was not *born-again* in the spiritual sense as we are, Christ was *born-again* in the material sense, having received a new incorruptible body. In *"the regeneration" (Matthew 19:28),* we will also be *born-again,* never again to taste death or be corrupted by sin.

"The Prince of the Kings of the Earth," is who He is to come. Where Satan had ruled as the *Prince of the power of the air,* through lies and manipulation, Christ will rule as the *Prince of the Kings of the Earth,* having supreme dominion and providing true liberty.

The Integral Statement of the Book

> *Behold, He comes with clouds; **and every eye shall see Him**, and **they also which pierced Him**: and all kindreds of the earth shall wail because of Him. Even so, Amen.*
> *~ Revelation 1: 7*

This integral statement is given to guard against *the Antichrist,* who will come in the last days. In a time of great upheaval, he will appear to be all things to all people. After this great distress in the earth, many will be convinced that the end of all things has come, and that the wrath of God has been poured out. In the aftermath, many will be told that the wrath has past, and that Christ has come. At that time, this man will be doing many great signs to convince the world the he is Christ. But as Jesus taught in *Matthew 24*, unless every eye sees Him coming in the clouds, *"do not believe it."*

The saying *"they also which pierced Him"* is in reference to the Jews who will be brought to repentance at the time of Christ's appearing. This repentance had been promised by God throughout the Old Testament, *(Deuteronomy 30:6, Psalm 22:16, Zechariah 12:10, John 19:37)*, but will not be fully realized until the Jews witness the Church being taken up, and themselves being left behind to face a *time of trouble (Daniel 12:1-2)*. As they are left behind to flee for their lives, they will finally realize that the one who was born unto them in ancient times is the very one who is now revealed unto all mankind, and the only one who is able to save them.

I am Alpha and Omega, the beginning and the ending, says the Lord, who was, who is, and who is to come, the Almighty. ~ Revelation 1:8

The Messenger of the Book

I John, who also am your brother and companion in tribulation, and in the kingdom and patience of Jesus Christ, was in the isle that is called Patmos, for the word of God, and for the testimony of Jesus Christ. I was in the Spirit on the Lord's day, and heard behind me a great voice, as of a trumpet, saying, "I am Alpha and Omega, the first and the last: What you see, write in a book, and send it unto the seven churches which are in Asia; unto Ephesus, and unto Smyrna, and unto Pergamos, and unto Thyatira, and unto Sardis, and unto Philadelphia, and unto Laodicea." ~ Revelation 1:9-11

The Protagonist of the Book

The Revelation was written during a time of persecution in which John was exiled to a prison colony. John received *The Revelation* there and was eventually set free, dying of old age in Ephesus years later. John had been given careful instructions to write the things he saw in the book. This suggests that there is deep meaning in the things he is seeing, to be interpreted and understood by the readers, adding to the narrative. Just as the Holy Spirit's ministry is divided into seven attributes, which are called, *"the Seven Spirits of God,"* this passage introduces Christ by several visual attributes representing how He governs the Church, which we will discuss in the next section.

*And I turned to see the voice that spoke with me. And being turned, I saw seven golden candlesticks; And in the midst of the seven candlesticks one like unto the Son of Man, clothed with a garment down to the foot, and girt about the breast with a golden girdle. His head and his hairs were white like wool, as white as snow; and his **eyes were as a flame of fire**; And his feet like unto fine brass, as if they burned in a furnace; and his voice as the sound of many waters. And **he had in his right hand seven stars**: and **out*** *of his mouth went a sharp two-edged sword*: and his countenance was as the sun shines in his strength. And when I saw him, I fell at his feet as dead. And he laid his right hand upon me, saying unto me, "Fear not; I am **the first and the last**: I am he that lives, and was dead; and, behold, I am alive for evermore, 'Amen'; and **have the keys of death and hades**" ~ Revelation 1:12-16

The Outline of the Book

Write 1) the things which you have seen, and 2) the things which are, and 3) the things which shall be hereafter; 4) The mystery of the seven stars which you saw in my right hand, and the seven golden candlesticks. The seven stars are the angels of the seven churches: and the seven candlesticks which you saw are the seven churches.
~ Revelation 1:17-20

Finally, Christ divides *The Revelation* into four specific elements:

1) *"The things which you have seen"* – Representing the visual elements which John himself experiences in the testimony.

2) *"The things which are"* - Representing the upcoming letters to be given to the seven churches in the present tense.

3) *"The things which shall be, hereafter"* – Representing the things to come afterward which surround the *Day of the Lord*.

4) *"The mystery of the seven stars"* – Representing the entire ministry of the Church throughout the age, which is divided into seven distinct eras.

This *"mystery"* represents the administration of the Church known as the *"ministry of reconciliation"* (2nd Corinthians 5:17). Jesus told his disciples that his death and resurrection was the *"Sign of Jonah"* (Matthew 12:38), indicating that his three days and three nights in the grave would be like Jonah's three days and three nights in the belly of the whale. Afterward, Jonah was sent to declare to Nineveh, the chief Gentile city, that it would be *"overturned"* for its sins (Jonah 3:4). Nineveh received the fear of the Lord, putting on sackcloth and ashes in repentance, to which God relented from destroying the city. Jonah was *made jealous* by this grace, leading God to instruct him on the value of His mercy, saying,

And should not I spare Nineveh…that cannot discern between their right hand and their left hand…? ~ Jonah 4:11

Nineveh is a type of the *Gentile Bride*, who heard the word of judgement and repented, delaying the wrath of God. Jonah serves as both a type of Christ, who spent three days in the belly of the earth, and of Israel, who is *made jealous* by God's mercy toward the

Gentiles. Paul is the first of the Apostles to really come to understand this mystery, which is why he becomes so zealous to evangelize the Gentiles, understanding the salvation of Israel would only come afterward.

> *For I speak to you Gentiles; inasmuch as I am an apostle to the Gentiles, I magnify my ministry, if by any means I may provoke to jealousy those who are my flesh and save some of them...For I would not, brethren, that you should be ignorant of **this mystery**, ...that blindness in part is happened to Israel, until the fulness of the Gentiles be come in.*
> *~ Romans 11:13-25*

Paul expresses this mystery again in Ephesians as the *Body of Christ*.

> *...by which, when you read, you may understand my knowledge in **the mystery of Christ**, which in other ages was not made known to the sons of men, as it has now been revealed by the Spirit to His holy apostles and prophets: that **the Gentiles should be fellow heirs, of the same Body**, and partakers of His promise in Christ through the gospel... Ephesians 3:4-6*

Paul equates this *mystery* of Christ and the Church to a *Body* and *Bride*, understanding the pattern of *Gentile Brides* held by the Old Testament types of Christ, including: Joseph, Moses, Boaz, David, and Solomon, and several others.

> *... a man shall leave his father and mother, and shall be joined unto his wife, and they two shall be one flesh. This is a great mystery: but I speak concerning Christ and the Church.*
> *~ Ephesians 5:30-32*

This mystery concludes at the seventh trumpet, when *the Bride* is taken away to a prophetic honeymoon that occurs in the midst of the week.

> *... **there should be time** (literally delay) **no longer**: But in the days of the voice of the seventh angel, when he shall begin to sound, **the mystery of God should be finished**, as He has declared to his servants the prophets. ~ Revelation 10:5-7*

> *Behold, **I show you a mystery**; We shall not all sleep, but we shall all be changed, in a moment, in the twinkling of an eye, **at the last trump**: for the trumpet shall sound, and the dead shall be raised incorruptible, and we shall be changed. ~ 2nd Corinthians 15:51*

Christ is implying that the seven churches represent this *mystery*, which is the entire ingathering of the *Gentile Bride*. These letters are *"The things which are,"* because while they represent seven historical churches at the time they were written, they also represent *"this present dispensation"* (Ephesians 1:10), and this time of *"delay"* in which God's wrath is set aside for the repentance of them that hear with faith.

PART 3 - TO THE SEVEN CHURCHES

In this section, we will review the seven letters in *Revelation 2-3* as a panorama of Church history, corroborated by three additional witnesses. These witnesses include: *The Kingdom Parables* of Jesus, recorded in *Matthew 13*; the seven churches addressed by Paul in his epistles; and the seven distinct periods of Israel's history, spanning between their deliverance from Egypt and their rejection of Christ.

Church History	Revelation Epistle	Kingdom Parable	Pauline Epistle	Israelite History
Apostolic Church	Ephesus	Seed & the Sower	Romans	Wilderness
Persecuted Church	Smyrna	Wheat & Tares	Corinthians	The Judges
Imperial Church	Pergamos	Mustard Seed	Galatians	The Kings
Papal Church	Thyatira	Woman w/ Leaven	Ephesus	Captivity
Divided Church	Sardis	Hidden Treasure	Philippians	The Silence
Marginalized Church	Philadelphia	Pearl of Great Price	Colossians	Christ Gathers
Industrialized Church	Laodicea	The Dragnet	Thessalonians	Christ Rejected

The Keys to Understanding Parables

In *Matthew 13*, Jesus gives his disciples two principals for understanding parables, which he also requires for us to interpret the seven letters in *Revelation 2-3*. These two keys will not only allow his disciples to grasp the undergirding spiritual meaning behind these parables, but will also allow them to later grasp the duality of *The Kingdom,* as an entity being both *already* and *not yet,* awaiting the material manifestation of that which is already spiritually present.

In *Matthew 13,* and in *Revelation 2-3,* Jesus repeatedly uses the phrase, *"Let him who has an ear, hear,"* which should indicate a link between his *Kingdom Parables* and his letters to the Seven Churches of *The Revelation.*

> *And the disciples came, and said unto him, "Why do you speak to them in parables?"*
> *He answered and said to them, "Because it is given unto you, to know **the mysteries of the Kingdom of Heaven**, but to them, it is not given. For whosoever has, to him shall be given, and he shall have more abundance: but whosoever has not, from him shall be taken away even that he has. Therefore, I speak to them in parables: because they, **while seeing, see not; and while hearing, they hear not, neither do they understand**."*
> *~ Matthew 13:10-13*

Jesus begins to use this phrase because of the hard-heartedness of the Jews toward him. Because of their unwillingness to hear him, he chooses to veil his remaining teaching, using this phrase to hearken back to a similar judgment in the days of Isaiah.

> *And in them is fulfilled the prophecy of Isaiah which says, "By **hearing you shall hear, and shall not understand**; and seeing you shall see, and shall not perceive: For this people's heart is waxed gross, and their ears are dull of hearing, and their eyes they have closed; lest at any time they should see with their eyes, and hear with their ears, and should understand with their heart, and should be converted, and I should heal them. But blessed are your eyes, for they see, and your ears, for they hear. ~ Matthew 13:14-16*

This reference goes back to Isaiah's commissioning by God, to prophecy unto a stubborn people who thought their security lay in their heritage, despite their willful disobedience to Him. Isaiah was convicted of this sinfulness, and because he received this conviction with contrition, God cleansed him and sanctified him unto service, foreshadowing what would occur toward the Church through Christ.

> *"... **your iniquity is taken away, and your sin is purged**." Also, I heard the voice of the Lord, saying, "Whom shall I send, and who will go for us?" Then said I, "Here am I; send me." And he said,*

*"Go, and tell this people, **"You hear indeed, but understand not; and you see indeed, but perceive not."** Make the heart of this people fat, and make their ears heavy, and shut their eyes; lest they see with their eyes, and hear with their ears, and understand with their heart, and convert, and be healed." ~ Isaiah 6:8-10*

Isaiah then prophesied of another people who would hear and obey, of which he was a type, having been purified of his sin and sent forth as a witness.

*Whom shall he teach knowledge? and whom shall he make to understand doctrine? To them that are **weaned from the milk and drawn from the breasts.** ... For **with stammering lips and another tongue** will he speak to this people, to whom he said, "This is the rest wherewith you may cause the weary to rest; and this is the refreshing: yet **they would not hear**." But the word of the LORD was unto them precept upon precept, precept upon precept; line upon line, line upon line; here a little, and there a little; that they might go, and fall backward, and be broken, and snared, and taken.*
~ Isaiah 28: 9-13

In these passages, Isaiah prophesied of how the Gentile Church would receive the Gospel after the Jews had hardened their hearts toward the Lord, demonstrated by the speaking in tongues which took place in the book of Acts. Isaiah referred to their being *"drawn from the breasts,"* representing the stewardship of the Law, which the Jews had learned *"line upon line"* and *"precept upon precept."* While the Gentiles would receive *"rest"* from the promises of the New Covenant, the Jews would reject this grace, retaining the covenant of sin and death.

Jesus first refers to the distinction between *"having ears"* and *"hearing"* in relation to John the Baptist, as he officially ends the cannon of the Law, and begins to reveal the New Covenant teaching of *The Kingdom of Heaven.*

*For this is he, of whom it is written, "Behold, I send my messenger before your face, which shall prepare your way before you." ... For all the prophets and the law prophesied until John. And if you will receive it, this is Elijah, which was to come. **He that has ears to hear, let him hear**. ~ Matthew 11:9-15*

Jesus uses this phrase to reference a prophecy by Malachi about a coming *"dreadful day of the Lord,"* in which those on the earth would either receive healing or a curse, depending on the position of their hearts toward the Law of Moses.

*Behold, **I will send you Elijah the prophet before the coming of the great and dreadful day of the LORD**: And he shall turn the heart of the fathers to the children, and the heart of the children to their fathers, lest I come and smite the earth with a curse.*
~ Malachi 4:5-6

Jesus said that John the Baptist was the Elijah who would precede this judgement, which would have been strange, because when John was asked by the Pharisees if he was Elijah, he answered, *"I am not." (John 1:19-21)*. Jesus overcomes this contradiction with two phrases, the one being *"to him who receives it"* and the other being *"to him who has ears, let him hear."* In this, he reveals that not everyone can understand that John is the Elijah to come, but only those who are *born-again*.

While Jesus explains that John is the greatest man who had ever been born, he says *"but he who is least in the kingdom of heaven is greater than he."* By this he indicated, that while John was the most righteous man to be born under the covenant of the Law, those who are *born-again* would be credited with the righteousness of Christ and would be greater than John *(Matthew 11:11)*. Therefore, of those who would receive John as this fulfillment, He said, *"...I thank thee, O Father, Lord of heaven and earth, because you have hidden these things from the wise and prudent and have revealed them unto babes." (Matthew 11:25)*. Jesus alluded to the second principal of understanding, illustrating John as being the *Elijah to come,* a prophetic fulfillment that is both *already* and *not yet* realized, to those who are *born-again* into the *Kingdom of Heaven.*

> *Then He said to them, "Therefore every scribe instructed concerning the kingdom of heaven is like a householder who brings out of his treasure things new and old."*
> ~ *Matthew 13:52*

Jesus revealed that there would be both an *old* and *new* Elijah. In their traditional understanding, the Jews expected the material return of Elijah, preceding a material judgement of God on the nations, followed by a material restoration of the Kingdom of Israel. While this expectation will be fulfilled eventually, a new spiritual fulfilment of the prophecy came first, just as it is written, *"the first shall be last, and the last shall be first" (Matthew 20:16)*. For this reason, John came *"in the Spirit and power of Elijah"* first *(Luke 1:7)*, and will come again as the *"Elijah to come" (Matthew 17:11)*.

In this, Jesus taught the difference between understanding things that are *old,* meaning according to our natural understanding, and those things that are *new,* meaning according to the spiritual understanding which he intended to unveil by the Holy Spirit. The Apostles applied this understanding, drawing the New Covenant from the Old, and *"rightly dividing the word of truth." (2nd Timothy 2:15)*, as it is written,

> *But now we have been delivered from the law, having died to what were held by, so that we should serve in* **the newness of the Spirit** *and not in* **the oldness of the letter.**
> ~ *Romans 7:6*

While this division between *old* and *new* helps to explain the application of the Gospel, and what it means to be led by the Spirit, it also serves to bridge one's understanding of the fulfillment of prophecy. Whenever God says or does something that seems contradictory to His Word, He alludes to something deeper that the hearer must discover by the Holy Spirit, always alluding to a truth revealed in the Kingdom.

- How can God tell Adam he will *"die"* on the day he eats the fruit, *(Genesis 2:17)* and allow him to live for nearly one thousand years *(Genesis 5:5)*?

- How can Jonah prophesy that Nineveh will be *"overturned"* after forty days, *(Jonah 3:4)* and yet God does not carry out the destruction of the city *(Jonah 3:10)*?

A student of prophecy cannot simply walk away from these problems. They must seek after understanding through study and in prayer. They must wrestle with these things, knowing that God is not the author of confusion and does not speak without considering the weight of His words. God's words are like nails, set in place by a master carpenter *(Ecclesiastes 12:11),* and like goads, keeping us on the narrow way. If one is patient to allow God to reveal the hidden things, we find out more about the depths of His wisdom, His love, and His mercy toward us.

In the creation, God was careful to create the day before He created the sun, moon, and stars, reserving for Himself a hidden *"day"* which He uses prophetically, representing a year, and indefinite span of time, or even a thousand years. God told Adam that he would die *"on the day"* that he ate the forbidden fruit. While Adam did die spiritually, he remained living materially for nearly one thousand years. In Adam's death, both spiritually and materially, it was foreshadowed that man would be *"born-again"* both spiritually, in regeneration by the baptism of the Holy Spirit *(Titus 3:5),* and then materially, by the resurrection at the *Day of the Lord (Matthew 19:28).*

Regarding Jonah, God was careful to choose the word *"overturned,"* when describing his intent toward Nineveh. He reserved the right to grant them repentance, overturning the spiritual rule of the city from Satan to Himself. Likewise, Jesus established that John was the *Elijah to come* to them *who can receive it,* knowing that the wrath against their sin would be spiritually applied to himself. Still, he left another *Elijah to come,* preceding the *terrible Day of the Lord* at his second coming. In this, He forecasted a mysterious *"delay,"* much like that *overturning* experience by the people of Nineveh. Just as Nineveh, the great Gentile capital, would be *overturned* spiritually in Jonah's day, and then later overturned materially, the judgement of the nations would be delayed by the preaching of the Gospel, through which the Gentiles have been granted *"repentance unto life" (Acts 11:18)*. This delay in Nineveh's judgement was not arbitrary, or some reaction by a God who changed His mind, but a deliberate intention by God to forecast what he intended toward the Gentiles, in fulfillment of His promise to bless them through the seed of Abraham.

> *And I will make your seed multiply as the stars of heaven; I will give to your descendants all these lands; and in your seed, all the nations of the earth shall be blessed; because Abraham obeyed My voice, and kept My charge, My commandments, My statutes, and My laws. ~ Genesis 26:4-5*

The Mysterious Delay

When Jesus began his ministry, he went out to the desert to be tempted by Satan. After returning, he came to his home Synagogue and read from the Scroll of Isaiah,

> *The Spirit of the LORD is upon Me, because He has anointed Me, to preach the gospel to the poor. He has sent Me to heal the brokenhearted; to proclaim liberty to the captives, and recovery of sight to the blind; to set at liberty those who are oppressed; to proclaim the acceptable year of the LORD. ~ Luke 4:18-19*

Jesus again did something strange here that begs explanation. He took a passage and read part of it, quitting mid-sentence and applying it to the current historical context.

> *He has sent Me to heal the brokenhearted, to proclaim liberty to the captives, and the opening of the prison to those who are bound; to proclaim the acceptable year of the LORD, **and the day of vengeance of our God**... Isaiah 61:1-2*

This could not be understood at the time, but *for those who are able to receive it*—that is, to receive the grace offered through Christ—the wrath has already been poured out on Jesus in our place. However, for those who reject this grace, it remains,

> *If we deliberately keep on sinning after we have received the knowledge of the truth, no sacrifice for sins is left, but only a fearful expectation of judgment, and of raging fire that will consume the enemies of God. ~ Hebrews 10:27*

Some theologians call this pattern of revelation *"already-not yet"* as it applies often to the New Covenant promises, having both a present spiritual fulfillment and a future material fulfillment. This hermeneutical key will resolve many differences in interpretation related to prophecy and its expected fulfillment. So, in Jesus' incomplete reading of Isaiah, one must understand the *mystery*, which is the delay of God's wrath in order to preach reconciliation to the Gentiles, of which Paul says,

*But we speak the wisdom of God **in a mystery**, even the hidden wisdom, which God ordained before the world unto our glory: Which none of the princes of this world knew: for had they known it, they would not have crucified the Lord of glory.*

~ 2ⁿᵈ Corinthians 2:7-8

Jesus knew that through the rejection of the Jews, he would bring salvation to all the nations under Satan's power, blinding him to those efforts that would bring about his own undoing *(Genesis 50:20)*. Jesus testified to this mystery in the synagogue, proceeding to give accounts of Gentiles being blessed instead of the Jews.

*Verily I say unto you, "No prophet is accepted in his own country. But I tell you a truth: many widows were in Israel in the days of Elijah, when the heaven was shut up three years and six months; when great famine was throughout all the land. But unto none of them was Elijah sent, save unto **Sarepta, a city of Sidon**; unto a woman that was a widow. And many lepers were in Israel in the time of Elisha the prophet; and none of them was cleansed, saving **Naaman the Syrian**."* ~ Luke 4:23-27

God did not conduct this plan without first leaving a testimony of his predetermination, as it is written, *"Surely the Lord GOD will do nothing, unless He reveals his secret unto his servants the prophets." (Amos 3:7)*. Therefore, the New Covenant epistles are the testimony of the Apostles that the plan of salvation exclusively through faith in the finished work of Jesus Christ was always the intention of the Law and the Prophets, being both *already* and *not yet* fulfilled.

- God's wrath has *already* been poured out on Christ in our place *(Isaiah 53:10)*, and *not yet* been poured out on the nations until He comes *(Revelation 11:18)*.

- We are already *born-again* through faith *(1ˢᵗ Peter 1:23)*, and not yet *born-again* until *the Resurrection (Colossians 1:8)*.

- We have *already* been saved by grace through faith *(Ephesians 2:8)* but are *not yet* saved until the end when Christ appears *(1ˢᵗ Corinthians 3:15)*.

- We are already *"seated with Christ" (Ephesians 2:5)* and are not yet with Him while we are present on the Earth *(Philippians 1:23)*.

When saying, *"To him who has ears, let him hear,"* Jesus is declaring that the message has two meanings, which are *old* and *new* or *already-not yet*. Applying this to the *Kingdom Parables* and *Seven Letters*, we can uncover a prophetic history documenting every major struggle throughout the respective histories of the Nation of Israel, and the

Gentile Church, as well as the remedy of faith which is required to overcome the challenge of each season, until Christ comes with the ultimate remedy.

The Two Witnesses of Israel and the Church

God reveals truth consistently through two or three witnesses *(2nd Corinthians 13:1)*. In history also, Israel and the Church each testify to God's salvific work toward mankind. These witnesses demonstrate how Satan persists in trying to separate man from God, and how God, being both just and merciful, works to keep us from Satan's power. They reveal how God uses Satan's evil intent to reveal the depths of God's wisdom and love toward us, showing that He is *"no respecter of persons" (Acts 10:34)* and truly desires *"all to come to repentance" (2nd Peter 3: 9)*.

To begin, we must first understand the pattern between Israel and the Church: The children of Israel were in bondage to Egypt, whose Pharaoh represented the power of Death. In Exodus, God judged Pharaoh by taking the life of his firstborn son. Israel was saved from this judgement by a lamb that was slain, to keep away the destroying angel *(see Exodus 11-12)*. God commanded Israel to sacrifice a lamb, placing the blood on the top and sides of the door, and consuming the lamb in a Passover meal, which would cause the angel of death to pass over their house. This salvation from the angel of death, foreshadowed *our* salvation from the power of death, which Christ secured for us as our Passover Lamb. In this, the salvation of Israel from the bondage of slavery foreshadowed *our* salvation from the bondage of sin.

Afterward, Israel passed through the Red Sea, foreshadowing our baptism into the death of Christ. The giving of the Law at Sinai, on Pentecost, foreshadowed the Law being *written on our hearts* through receiving the Holy Spirit as the seal of our salvation *(Acts 2)*. The emergence of the Nation of Israel, establishing its law, its government, and its worship, foreshadowed the emergence of the Apostolic Church, the New Testament Canon, and the ordinances of worship. While the Twelve Apostles mirror the Twelve Tribes of Israel, the Seventy Apostles *(Luke 10:1)* reflect the Seventy Elders of Israel *(Numbers 11:16-17)*. These seventy would evangelize the seventy Gentile nations which were dispersed at the Tower of Babel *(Genesis 10-11)*, being the original Apostles, Prophets, Pastors, Teachers, and Evangelists to the Church. This correspondence continues, between Israel unto the first coming of Christ, and the Church unto the second coming of Christ, unfolding in seven distinct eras.

[44]

The Seven Stages of the Kingdom Come

"Behold, a sower went forth to sow: And when he sowed, some seeds fell by the wayside, and the fowls came and devoured them up. Some fell upon stony places, where they had not much earth; and forthwith they sprung up, because they had no deepness of earth; And when the sun was up, they were scorched; and because they had no root, they withered away. And some fell among thorns; and the thorns sprung up and choked them. But other fell into good ground and brought forth fruit; some a hundredfold, some sixtyfold, and some thirtyfold." ~ Matthew 13:3-8

Jesus says the parable of *The Seed and The Sower* is the key to understanding *all* other parables *(Mark 4:13)*. For this reason, he goes into careful detail to explain its meaning and its implication toward other parables.

*Understand therefore the parable of the sower: (1) "When anyone hears the word of the kingdom, and **does not understand**, then comes the wicked one, and catches away that which was sown in his heart. This is he which received seed by the wayside. (2) But he that received the seed into stony places, the same is he that hears the word, and with joy receives it; yet he has no root in himself, but endures for a while: for when tribulation or persecution arises because of the word, he ends up offended **(or "falls away," per Luke 8:13).** (3) He also that received seed among the thorns is he that hears the word; but the cares of this world and the deceitfulness of riches choke the word, and **he becomes unfruitful**. (4) But he that received seed into the good ground is **he that hears the word and understands it**; which also bears fruit, and brings forth, some a hundredfold, some sixty, and some thirty. ~ Matthew 13:18-23*

Jesus lays out four types of people who hear the Gospel, detailing how they respond and the result of their response. While on the surface, it may seem like three-out-of-four types genuinely receive the Gospel, a careful understanding of the second and third type indicates that they have believed the Gospel in vain, accepting those elements that would contribute to their current nature, rather than being born-again with a new nature, able to produce the kind of fruit that accompanies salvation. These two types are discussed further in the Epistle to the Hebrews.

*(2) For it is impossible for those who were once enlightened, and have tasted the heavenly gift, and have become partakers of the Holy Spirit, and have tasted the good word of God, and the powers of the age to come, if **they fall away**, to renew them again to repentance, since they crucify again for themselves the Son of God, and put Him to an open shame.*

*(3) For the earth which drinks in the rain that often comes upon it, and bears herbs useful for those by whom it is cultivated, receives blessing from God; but if it bears thorns and briars, **it is rejected,** and near to being cursed, whose end is to be burned.*

(4) But beloved, we are persuaded of better things of you; things that accompany salvation. ~ Hebrews 6:4-9

The reason this parable is the key to understanding *all* parables is because Jesus wanted his disciples to understand that the phrase *"Kingdom of Heaven,"* is not only referring to godly things, but to ungodly as well. This kingdom is currently a warzone between the faithful and the fallen angels, in which we become a part upon being saved. In this war, Satan seeks to infiltrate and overcome the Church, as it is the priestly administration of God's kingdom. Jesus makes this even more plain in his next parable, also explaining its meaning to the Apostles.

> *The kingdom of heaven is likened unto a man which sowed good seed in his field: But while men slept, his enemy came and sowed tares among the wheat, and went his way. When the blade grew up, and brought forth fruit, then the tares also appeared. So, the servants of the householder came and said unto him, "Sir, did you not sow only good seed in your field? Why then, does it have tares?"*
>
> *He said unto them, "**An enemy has done this.**" The servants said unto him, "Would you want us to go and gather them up?" But he said, "No; because while you gather up the tares, you might also root up the wheat with them. Let both grow together until the harvest: and in the time of harvest I will say to the reapers, 'Gather together first the tares, and bind them in bundles to burn them, but gather the wheat into my barn.'"*
>
> ~ Matthew 13:24-30

Since Jesus plainly interpreted *these* parables, his explanation should govern our understanding of *the remaining* parables. These seven parables represent the progress of the Church, from the initial spreading of the Gospel to the end of the age, when the true and false are separated unto their respective judgments. They represent the effects of this incursion of false believers, and how God distinguishes true believers from false until the day of judgement. Corresponding with two other witnesses, which include the history of Israel and the seven churches addressed by Paul's epistles, one can learn how these parables coincide with the *Seven Letters to the Seven Churches,* to comprise a prophetic history of the Church from Christ's ascension until his second coming.

The First Parable: The Seed and the Sower

The subject of this first parable is the initial spread of the Gospel and the establishment of the Church. In *the Parable of the Seed and the Sower*, when the Gospel is sown, some ignore it, like those who rejected the Law and immediately took to worshipping the Golden Calf. Some believed for a time, but when tested in being commanded to take the *Promised Land*, they fell away, becoming offended at Joshua and Caleb *(Numbers 13-14)*. After God rebuked them, they wanted to try and take the *Promised Land* in their own strength and failed miserably, leaving them to wander in the wilderness until that generation had died. Many of the remainder fell into grumbling *(Numbers 21)* or fornication *(Numbers 25)* and died in the wilderness. The remainder, having been purged of the *old man,* would inherit the *Promised Land*.

Just as Israel had a commission to *go up* and take possession of the Land of Canaan, the Church had a commission to *go out* and make disciples of all nations. Just as Moses fell short of taking them into the *Promised Land*, Peter fell short in taking the Gospel out to the nations. Just as God afterward raised up Joshua to take Israel into the *Promised Land*, Christ afterward raised up Paul to bring the Gospel unto the Gentiles. Unwilling to leave Judaism behind, The Twelve failed to leave Jerusalem for decades, despite Jesus' express commands to do so. Paul even had to rebuke Peter publicly, because his cultural instincts were a public insult to the reconciliation of the Gospel. Eventually, Peter and the other Apostles came around, leaving Jerusalem and taking the Gospel from Spain to China; and from Russia to Ethiopia.

In the last portion of the parable, Jesus spoke of the harvest of the Gospel saying, *"and [they] bring forth [fruit], some a hundredfold, some sixty, and some thirty,"* indicating that the number gets smaller. The spread of the Gospel began as Peter preached, and thousands came to faith at once; but eventually this response slowed, as the Apostles came to the end of their lives. This reduction in momentum corresponds to Israel, noting that in the beginning of their nation, God fought for them, while Israel simply sat back and watched the mighty deliverance at His hand. But when they came to Canaan, God wanted them to learn to fight *(see Joshua 23),* trusting in Him to give them strength. From the time Joshua led them into the *Promised Land,* to the beginning of the Book of Judges, their victories decreased as they became comfortable among their enemies. They put some to service rather than wiping them out, while others, they quit fighting altogether, falling into coexistence, integration, and even bondage.

Just as Joshua ends with a loss of momentum, the Apostolic era ends with a loss of fervor and an inward focus. The churches had become more interested in forming catechisms and barriers to entry, than with evangelism and discipleship; the harvest slowing to a fraction of its initial pace. If the Gospel continued to spread as far and wide as it did with the Apostles, the whole world would have been reached within 100-200 years. Yet today, with our present advances in communications and transportation, there are still corners of the earth which have never heard the Good News, even 2000 years after this great commission began.

Letter 1: To the Church at Ephesus

*Unto the angel of the church of Ephesus write: "These things says He that holds the seven stars in His right hand; who walks in the midst of the seven golden candlesticks: 'I know your works, and your labor, and your patience, and how you cannot bear them which are evil; and how you have tried them which say they are apostles, and are not, and have found them to be liars; and how in your patience, for my name's sake you have labored, and have not fainted. Nevertheless, I have somewhat against you, because **you have left your first love.**'" ~ Revelation 2:1-4*

In this first letter, Christ commends the early Apostolic Church for their diligence in rooting out false apostles, yet takes issue with the fact that they are more consumed with setting up defenses against the false than with proclaiming the truth of the Gospel. Had they remembered Jesus' parables, they would know that there would always be false believers among them, and that rooting out the false and apostate should not be their consumption. They were rather to go and preach the Gospel, making disciples of all nations and teaching them to observe his commands.

Christ is not against having discernment, marking false teachers, or exercising church discipline. In the corresponding Pauline epistle to the Romans, he urges them both to *"mark them which cause divisions and offences contrary to the doctrine which you have learned; and avoid them." (Romans 16:17)*, but also to *"receive one who is weak in faith" (Romans 14:1)* and *"bear with the scruples of the weak" (Romans 15:1)*. This epistle corresponds to this era, both establishing and defending the faith; but also reminding them, in the Spirit of Christ, to be careful not to root up the *wheat* with the *tares*. As this era ends, Paul knows that heretical teachers will come, seeking to supplant the Apostolic teaching. While weeping over the thought of this *(Acts 20:28-31)*, he knows that the best defense is Christ being worshipped and proclaimed to as many as will hear.

"Remember therefore from where you have fallen, and repent, and do the first works; or else I will come unto you quickly, and remove your candlestick out of its place, unless you repent." ~ Revelation 2:5

Christ warns this church that if they continue in this practice, He would remove their lampstand, meaning that their local church would cease to exist. Consequently, the early Apostolic Church has been largely lost to us, with most of its writings and history obscured and replaced by the formalized hierarchical system it helped to create. Those churches that still attempt to maintain this ancient tradition remain the least evangelistic churches in the world, and are now being persecuted out of existence in places like Turkey, Syria, and Egypt.

Christ exhorts them by saying, *"I am He that holds the seven stars in his right hand"* alluding to prophecies given to Job and Amos, related to two constellations. In Job, when God answers him from the whirlwind, He says, *"Can you bind the cluster of the Pleiades or loose the belt of Orion?" (Job 38:31).* These two constellations represent two kingdoms: The Pleiades represent a cluster of seven stars known as *The Seven Sisters*, which are gravitationally bound to one another, while *Orion* represents the belt of *Orion, the Hunter.* One is a type of the Church while the other represents Nimrod the Hunter, a type of *the Antichrist.* God is saying to Job (in essence), *"Who but God can hold the Kingdom of God together, and who but God can take the Kingdom of Satan apart?"* In Amos, He gives the answer:

*Seek the LORD and live...**He made the Pleiades and Orion**; The LORD is His name. He rains ruin upon the strong, so that fury comes upon the fortress. ~ Amos 5:6-9*

The Didache was a common catechism used at the end of the Apostolic Era. Consider the thousands who were baptized at Pentecost *(Acts 2)*, the Ethiopian Eunuch *(Acts 8)*, or the household of Cornelius *(Acts 10)*, comparing the simplicity of their acceptance into the Church to the baptism standard of the Didache by the end of the era.

And concerning baptism, baptize this way: After reviewing all of this teaching, baptize in the Name of the Father, Son, and Holy Spirit, in living (running) water. But if living water is not available, then baptize into other water; and cold is preferred, but if not available, in warm. But if neither is available, pour water three times upon the head in the Name of the Father, Son and Holy Spirit. But before the baptism, let the overseer fast, and also the one being baptized, and all others who are able; Be sure to instruct the one being baptized to fast one or two days before. ~ The Didache (approx. 100AD)

The Didache reveals a heavier dose of scrutiny, with less joyful acceptance. It did not take long for this formality and precaution to come into the Church. Biblically, there was no precedent for a bishop being required to perform a baptism, or for requiring fasting prior, as the ordinances and offices of the Church were clearly established by Scripture. The following generations proceeded from worse to worse, making entrance into the Church more of an act of submitting to the institution than an expression of faith and hope in Christ's finished work. Yet despite this besetting error, Christ gives them this praise.

> *But this you have, that you hate the deeds of the Nicolaitans, which I also hate. To him who has an ear, let him hear. ~ Revelation 2:6-7*

Some early church writers suggested that the term *"Nicolaitans"* refers to a sect that practiced sexual immorality and open marriage; however, there is no clear evidence corroborating the existence of this sect. More likely is that the doctrine of the Nicolaitans lies in the etymology of the word. This kind of interpretive method is found in many prophecies in both the Old and New Testament, as the meanings of names and places often have specific prophetic meaning. Looking at the root words behind Nicolaitans, you find Nico (to Conquer) and Laity (the People). The doctrine of the Nicolaitans is more likely the subduing of the *common people,* through a separation and spiritual hierarchy of so-called *"clergy"* and *"laity."*

While the church leadership has real authority, able to exercise discipline in the Body toward sinful behavior, the teaching of the Apostles is clear. The Elders are to lead by example, and the Deacons are to serve by example. The priestly hierarchy, in which some people are closer to God than others and act as intermediaries, was abolished in the death of Christ when God tore the veil to the temple, making Himself equally accessible to *all* who had faith in Him, without distinction. From the Didache above, one can see the power of the *clergy* over the convert increasing, as arbitrary rules were being added prior to permitting them to being baptized.

Later, in the writings of Ignatius of Antioch, (a Bishop ordained by Peter) one can find statements that lend to a graduated hierarchy beginning to form. The Apostle Peter, though considered by many in the Church to be the chief of the Apostles, had an opposite view of the authority held by the bishop, which was a synonym for pastors or elders. He writes in his epistle to the churches in Asia minor,

> *The elders which are among you, I exhort, also being an elder, and a witness of the sufferings of Christ, and also a partaker of the glory that shall be revealed: Feed the flock of God which is among you, taking the oversight thereof, **not by constraint**, but*

willingly; not for filthy lucre, but of a ready mind; __Neither as being lords over God's__ *__heritage, but being examples__ to the flock. ~ 1ˢᵗ Peter 5:1*

The Second Parable: The Wheat and the Tares

...His disciples came to Him saying, "Explain to us the parable of the tares of the field."

He answered and said to them: "He who sows the good seed is the Son of Man. The field is the world, the good seeds are the sons of the kingdom, but the tares are the sons of the wicked one. The enemy who sowed them is the devil, the harvest is the end of the age, and the reapers are the angels.

Therefore, as the tares are gathered and burned in the fire, so will it be at the end of this age. The Son of Man will send out His angels, and they will gather out of His kingdom all things that offend, and those who practice lawlessness, and will cast them into the furnace of fire. There will be wailing and gnashing of teeth. Then the righteous will shine forth as the sun in the kingdom of their Father. He who has ears to hear, let him hear!"

~ Matthew 13: 36-43

The corresponding history of Israel, after Joshua died, there was a period of 400 years in which they were continually plagued with idolatry and oppression from their neighbors. Likewise, for nearly 300 years after the Apostles died, the Church was plagued with heretics and persecution. Eusebius, the first formal Church historian, suggested that these persecutions were the intervention of God toward a Church that had lost sight of its mission and were failing to be *salt and light* in the world.

"...increasing freedom transformed our character to arrogance and sloth...God intervenes in history to ensure that the Christian Church shall prosper."

~ Eusebius: The History of the Church, Penguin (London 1989), p 257; p 262

While this diagnosis may seem harsh and uncharacteristic of God, Christ alludes to something similar in his *Sermon on the Mount*.

You are the salt of the earth: but if the salt has lost its savor, in what way shall [the earth] be salted? [The salt] is after this good for nothing, but to be cast out, and to be trodden underfoot by men. ...Let your light so shine before men, that they may see your good works, and glorify your Father which is in heaven. ~ Matthew 5:13-16

Salt that is unsuitable for the dinner table has one other use. It can be tossed on the roads to be trampled underfoot, preventing plants from growing in the summer and ice from forming in the winter. Jesus is saying that if the Church is not proclaiming the Gospel and doing good works in his name, then the only way he can receive glory from them is by their refusing to deny him as they faithfully suffer martyrdom. Where the Church had ceased being evangelical, they proved steadfast in love, through persecution and death, shining like lights, and drawing many to Christ. By the end of the era, twenty percent of the Roman Empire had converted to Christianity, largely through the witness of these generations of martyrs.

Letter 2: To the Church at Smyrna

In his gentleness, Christ does not rebuke this persecuted church, knowing that his judgement is for their perfection and for the proving of their faith.

> To the angel of the church in Smyrna write, "These things says the First and the Last, who was dead and came to life: 'I know your works, tribulation, and poverty (but you are rich); and I know the blasphemy of those who say they are Jews and are not, but are a synagogue of Satan. **Do not fear any of those things which you are about to suffer**. Indeed, the devil is about to throw some of you into prison, that you may be tested, and **you will have tribulation ten days**. Be faithful until death, and I will give you the crown of life. He who has an ear, let him hear what the Spirit says to the churches. He who overcomes shall not be hurt by the second death.'" ~ Revelation 2:8-11

It is important to note that Satan cannot send heretics and persecutions without authorization. When trial comes, while Satan is the *agent* of that evil, it is allowed by God, to test and try those who belong to Him, in order to prove the substance.

> If there arises among you a prophet ...saying, "Let us go after other gods" ...you shall not listen to the words of that prophet ... for **the LORD your God is testing you** to know whether you love the LORD your God with all your heart and with all your soul.
> ~ Deuteronomy 13:1-3

God gives His Word, and then allows Satan to test whether the Word has been received with sincerity. In the *Parable of the Seed and the Sower*, Satan comes immediately to steal the Word that was sown. In some, Satan takes it away with little effort. In others, he brings trials and persecution, causing them to be offended and fall away. In others, he offers them carnal pleasure to make them unfruitful. Only when these efforts fail will one bear true spiritual fruit unto God.

> I hear that there be divisions among you... there must be also heresies among you, that they which are approved may be made manifest among you. ~ 1st Corinthians 11:18-19

The corresponding Pauline epistle details this testing in the church at Corinth. The Corinthians were being troubled with false teaching and carnal behavior, causing some to die as a judgement for their irreverence.

> ... many are weak and sick among you, and many sleep... if we would judge ourselves, we would not be judged. ~ 1st Corinthians 11:30

It is hard for Christians to accept that God authorizes both good and evil for His good purposes, but that same evil that judges the wicked, refines the righteous. The consuming fire that is the Lord, is deliverance for them that love Him and an everlasting torment to them that hate Him.

> *I am the LORD, and there is none else, there is no God beside me…I am the LORD, and there is none else. I form the light, and create darkness:* **I make peace, and create evil:** *I the LORD, do all these things.* ~ Isaiah 45:5-7

During this era, the true Christians would be persecuted unto death, while the heretical teachers would be left alone, or would reject Christ openly upon fear of death. Between the death of the last Apostle and the Edict of Toleration in 313 AD, ten official Roman-sponsored persecutions of the Church ensued, which are recorded in Eusebius' Church history written around 324 AD. These are the *"10 days of tribulation"* mentioned in the second epistle. Christ exhorts them not to fear death, knowing that they will be raised by Him on the last day.

Just as God raised up imperfect judges to deliver Israel from their oppressors, He raised up imperfect apologists to defend the faith from the latest heresy, and to lead the Church into faithful martyrdom. Men like Ignatius of Antioch, Polycarp of Smyrna, Papias of Hierapolis, Justin Martyr of Samaria, Irenaeus of Lyons, Hippolytus of Rome, Origen of Alexandria, and Tertullian of Carthage, each defended the truth with fervor, many of them giving their lives in martyrdom as well.

Ignatius of Antioch was faithful unto a martyr's death, yet he distinguished the office of a Bishop from that of an Elder, leaving one head of each major church, rather than the plurality of elders that God ordained for accountability and mutual submission.

Justin Martyr of Samaria defended the Gospel against the Jews of his day, but also adopted the earliest replacement theology, preparing the Church to receive a new theocratic state in place of the old Jewish theocracy.

Irenaeus of Lyons wrote masterfully against the Gnostics and other heretics of his day, but advocated the primacy of the Roman church, and produced typological teaching on the Virgin Mary that elevated her to a prominence beyond her place.

Hippolytus of Rome stood against the backsliders of his day and wrote masterfully on the Books of *Daniel* and *The Revelation,* but contributed to a later movement of the Donatists, which divided and weakened the Church.

Tertullian of Carthage defended the Trinity against the Marcionites but got caught up in the movement of the Montanists, led by ecstatic worship and possessive prophecy, similar in form to some of the modern charismatic errors.

Origen of Alexandria withstood heresies against the divinity of Christ and carried out rigorous scholarship and evaluation of the biblical texts, contributing to the purity of translation. However, he also began to adopt Greek philosophical ideas alongside the Scriptures. Mixing these ideas led him to promote celibacy, to castrate himself, and to condemn even marital sexual relationships. He went on to condemn the millennial reign of Christ as a *Jewish Fable*, discouraging the study of prophecy.

While these men seem to have failed the Church, if we look at the judges, we can see a similar pattern. Samson, who lusted after women; Barak, who cowered to lead; and Gideon, who gave up the crown, only to have his bastard son take it by murder, each failed in similar respects. God allows flawed and imperfect men to be used for His glory, but warns against exalting them beyond their appointment, as Paul says,

I applied these things to Apollos and myself, that you might learn in us not to think of men above that which is written. ~ 1ˢᵗ Corinthians 4:3

In *1ˢᵗ Corinthians 3*, Paul compares teaching to a building, and the Scriptures (the writings of the Apostles and Prophets) to its foundation. He knew that if he did not build upon that foundation with care, the result could be a loss of the reward of his labor. While a teacher would be saved if he did so in honest misjudgment, the resulting influence of his errors would lead many others into unfruitfulness and confusion. Likewise, the exaltation of men and of human philosophy would lead to a further consolidation of power, as those errors became institutionalized as orthodoxy.

After the Edict of Toleration, the peace that followed ushered in the next trial of the Church. Just as the era of the Judges ends with the people of Israel seeking a king, the era of persecution ends with the Church seeking for a patron and guardian, ultimately finding these in Constantine and in subsequent Roman Emperors.

The Third Parable: The Mustard Tree

Where the first and second parables represent the planting and growth of the Church, the third and fourth parables represent its corruption and takeover by Rome. Prophetically, Rome continues to be the Gentile power to which Israel remains captive and is the spiritual Babylon of the current age *(1ˢᵗ Peter 5:13)*.

Another parable He put forth unto them, saying, "The kingdom of heaven is like to a grain of mustard seed, which a man took, and sowed in his field: Which indeed is the least of all seeds: but when it is grown, it is the greatest among herbs, and becomes a tree, **_so that the birds of the air come, and lodge in the branches thereof_**.

~ Matthew 13:31-32

Jesus uses two distinct symbols to establish the meaning of the parable. First, he uses the symbol of a mustard seed for its smallness, which he uses in another teaching to reflect the required faith to do God's will.

And the Lord said, "If you had **_faith as a grain of mustard seed_**, *you might say unto this tree, "Be plucked up by the root and be planted in the sea," and it would obey you.*

~ Luke 17:5-6

By this symbol, Jesus is saying to the Church that all they *need* to succeed in the great commission is to trust and obey Him. However, something should be considered amiss in this saying if the mustard tree has grown to become a great tree, holding all the birds of the air. This should perplex us, as a mustard tree is a shrub, not capable by nature of holding a great many birds. This indicates that the Church has become unnaturally large. The second symbol is even more concerning.

The saying, *"all the birds of the air nest in its branches"* alludes to two other passages in the Old Testament. These passages represent two great empires: the first being the Assyrians and the second being the Babylonians. In these prophecies, a similar description of a tree is represented in the Gentile power holding the stewardship of the earth, which in the days of Jesus, was the Roman Empire.

Behold, the Assyrian was a cedar in Lebanon … Therefore, his height was exalted above all the trees of the field, and his boughs were multiplied, and his branches became long, because of the multitude of waters when he shot forth. **_All the fowls of heaven made their nests in his boughs_**, *and under his branches did all the Beasts of the field bring forth their young, and under his shadow dwelt all great nations. ~ Ezekiel 31:3-6*

…I saw and behold, a tree in the midst of the earth, and the height thereof was great. The tree grew and was strong, and the height thereof reached unto heaven, and the sight thereof to the end of all the earth. The leaves thereof were fair, and the fruit thereof much, and in it was meat for all: The Beasts of the field had shadow under it, and **_the fowls of the heaven dwelt in the boughs thereof_**, *and all flesh was fed of it. ~ Daniel 4:10-11*

In the administration of the earth, God focused on two nations, mysteriously represented by the elder nation of Babylon and the younger nation of Israel. The first is the administration of Satan over a world bound in sin, while the second is the nation of priests who are set apart by God. In this parable, it must be understood that the *"great tree"* represents the most dominant empire on the planet. Its armies are unmatched, its economy provides for the most comfort, and everyone who desires power seeks to be part of its administration. The final manifestation of this great empire is the last days *Mystery Babylon*.

> *And he cried mightily with a strong voice, saying, "Babylon the great is fallen, is fallen, and is become the habitation of devils, and the hold of **every foul spirit, and a cage of every unclean and hateful bird**." ~ Revelation 18:2*

In the Old Testament, birds were often a representation of wicked spiritual beings. The birds that seek to be part of the final *Mystery Babylon* are the demonic forces, high in the ranks of the ruling elite, manipulating and controlling mankind through this wicked city. It should be no surprise that these same spirits would seek to rise in the ranks of the Church if it were joined to the most dominant empire in the earth.

The third phase of Israel's history is represented in the monarchy of Israel. As Israel grew weary of the cycle of unfaithfulness, oppression, and deliverance by judges, they looked to have a visible king like the other nations, rejecting God from being their king *(1ˢᵗ Samuel 8:7)*. Their desire was to outsource their responsibility to trust an invisible God, relying instead on a man to represent them. The result was a nation being blessed or judged based on the decisions of one sinful man.

There were similar frustrations in the history of the Church, as the pattern of heretics and persecution wore down the resolve of many. Rather than being more encouraged in their faith as they weathered these trials, they sought to eliminate them through two measures: The first was through the adoption of a clerical hierarchy and the rule of tradition as precedent, replacing the canon of Scripture and the leading of the Spirit with traditions of men known as Cannon Law. The second was to bind the Church to the Roman state. To hold these decisions as authoritative with the backing of force, the Church sought a patron in Constantine and his successors. This compromise led to the Church becoming an apparatus of the Roman state, that would not assert its independence again for over 1000 years.

This entire period is foreshadowed in *1ˢᵗ Samuel*. Samuel's commissioning as a prophet begins with him condemning the corrupt priesthood of Eli, whose sons had been using the power of their office to abuse the people of Israel *(1ˢᵗ Samuel 2)*. This foreshadowed corrupt bishops, including men like Montanus and Arius, who because of the inordinate honor afforded to them, led multitudes astray. In Samuel, God brought about deliverance from Eli's wicked sons in a way that parallels the reign of what is today called Christendom.

In the time of Samuel, Eli's wicked sons took the Ark of the Covenant into battle, assuming to use it as a magic token to prevail against their enemies *(1ˢᵗ Samuel 3)*. Likewise, Constantine, while he was not a Christian, ordered his armies to put the sign of the cross on their shields, believing this to be a token by which to prevail. In Israel, the Philistines defeated the Israelites, taking the Ark captive and placing it before their god Dagon. There it stayed until a plague of rats and boils forced them to return the Ark, fearful of their cities being destroyed. Likewise, the Gospel was held captive by Roman Christendom until the black plague helped to release the Church from the grip of Rome.

The parallels continue in the lives of Saul and Constantine. Just as Saul sought to please all people, fearing the nation more than God, Constantine sought to allow both Christianity and Roman paganism to *coexist* in harmony, changing the Christian holidays to correspond with their pagan counterparts. Where Saul attempted to murder his own son, Constantine succeeded in murdering his. Finally, just as Saul, after chasing the witches from the land, hired a witch to summon Samuel, Constantine, who presided over the council that condemned the Arian heresy, was baptized by an Arian bishop just before he died.

Letter 3: To the Church at Pergamos

*And to the angel of the church in Pergamos write, "These things says He who has the sharp two-edged sword: 'I know your works, and where you dwell, **where Satan's throne is**. And you hold fast to My name and did not deny My faith, even in the days in which Antipas was My faithful martyr, who was killed among you, where Satan dwells."*

"But I have a few things against you, because you have those there who hold the doctrine of Balaam, who taught Balak to put a stumbling block before the children of Israel, to eat things sacrificed to idols, and to commit sexual immorality. Thus, you also have those who hold the doctrine of the Nicolaitans, which thing I hate."

*"**Repent, or else I will come to you quickly and will fight against them with the sword of My mouth**. He who has an ear, let him hear what the Spirit says to the churches. To him who overcomes I will give some of the hidden manna to eat. And I will give him a white stone, and on the stone a new name written which no one knows except him who receives it." ~ Revelation 2:12-17*

In this letter, Christ commends the church for standing fast in the face of martyrdom and holding fast to His name. It is important to note that for its errors, the early

Roman Catholic church was still essentially Christian in doctrine. Still, Christ tells them that they dwell *where Satan's throne is,* as the Roman Empire that they had joined for protection was the very administration of Satan that had murdered their brethren.

They hold to *"the teachings of Balaam,"* a wicked prophet who used sorcery for divination and took money from Balak, the King of Moab, to curse Israel *(Numbers 24).* When God made it impossible for him to curse the nation, he advised the King of Moab to send his women among them to seduce them into forbidden sin, moving God to judge them *(Numbers 25).* This foreshadowed how Roman Paganism would eventually come to corrupt the church, making them unfruitful and causing them to come under discipline from the Lord.

Some of them hold to *"the doctrine of the Nicolaitans."* When Constantine adopted the church as his own, the first thing he did was to give them the same *tax-exempt status* which was afforded to the pagan priests, as their service led to support of the Roman state and increased the tourist trade. Some of the clergy were put on the national payroll, and were even made tax collectors and governors, literally ruling over the people. The power and financial rewards of holding church offices would lead to various thugs nesting in the church, eventually leading to church offices being bought and sold, as the church became the administration of the Roman Empire.

In the corresponding Pauline epistle, the Galatians were warned against the encroachment of the Judaizers, a growing sect that was working to convince the Gentile converts that they must now go through circumcision and keep the Law of Moses in order to be perfected for salvation. Similarly, the Roman Catholic hierarchy worked to convince the Church that they needed to submit to various sacraments and ordinances, which they invented from the Talmud, attempting to make themselves a new kind of Levitical priesthood. Paul rebuked the Galatians for obeying these men, reminding them where their faith originated.

> *This only I want to learn from you: Did you receive the Spirit by the works of the law, or by the hearing of faith? Are you so foolish? Having begun in the Spirit, are you now being made perfect by the flesh?* ~ Galatians 3:2-3

Paul unveils the motives of these charlatans, demonstrating that while they claim to bring them closer to God through their rituals, they are actually pushing them further from God, so that *they* can become the intermediary, exercising power over the faith of those they have deceived.

They zealously court you, but for no good; yes, they want to exclude you, that you may be zealous for them. ~ Galatians 4:17

Christ's warning to them is to repent of trusting in the world as a partner with shared goals, or even as an ally against a common enemy. He wants the Church to understand that they represent a holy power outside of this world, which will not be accepted by them because of their love of sin.

Do not think I came to send peace on earth: I came not to send peace, but a sword. ~ Matthew 10:34

Blessed are you, when men shall hate you, and when they shall separate you from their company, and shall reproach you, and cast out your name as evil, for the Son of Man's sake...Woe unto you, when all men shall speak well of you, for so did their fathers to the False Prophets. ~ Luke 6:22-26

Christ is telling this church, which is allied with the world empire, that if they do not repent, he will come and fight against them with *"the sword of his mouth,"* the very means by which he defeats *the Antichrist*. He is telling them that this error will lead them to seek this same protected status with *the Antichrist* when he comes to power and will ultimately leave them facing Christ as an enemy when he comes.

Finally, to the meek among this church, Christ is giving them a message to encourage them. He says he will give them *"hidden manna"* and a *"white stone with a new name on it,"* which *"no one knows"* but the individual who receives it. In this, he is reminding them of the personal and intimate nature of their salvation, assuring them that no other intermediary can be placed between them and His love, which they received by faith. In Galatians, Paul will also echo this sentiment towards those being overcome by the Judaizers saying,

Stand fast therefore in the liberty by which Christ has made us free, and do not be entangled again with a yoke of bondage. ~ Galatians 5:1

The Fourth Parable: The Woman with Leaven

*Another parable He spoke to them: "The kingdom of heaven is like **leaven**, which a woman took and hid in three measures of meal till it was all leavened." ~ Matthew 13:33*

The fourth era represents the dark ages of Roman Catholicism, including the Papal system, the Eucharistic heresy, and the worship of Mary and the saints. This system, while abounding in charitable works, was a complete return to paganism, veiled in a Christian facade. To understand this, we must explore the three symbols in this next parable.

In both the Old and New Testament, leaven symbolizes the corruption of sin. The reason for this is because of its effect on bread, creating the appearance of increasing the substance while it devours the bread to create a gaseous void. During his ministry, Jesus compared the produce of leaven to that of the religious leaders.

> Then Jesus said unto them, "Take heed and beware of **_the leaven_** of the Pharisees and of the Sadducees." ~ Matthew 16:6

Likewise, Paul exhorts the Corinthians to understand the spiritual meaning behind the Jewish Feast of Unleavened Bread, and to understand the message as they partook in the Lord's Supper.

> Your glorying is not good. Do you not know that a little leaven leavens the whole lump? **_Purge out the old leaven_**, that you may be a new lump, as **_you are unleavened_**. For even Christ our Passover is sacrificed for us: Therefore, let us keep the feast, not with old leaven, neither with the leaven of malice and wickedness; but with the unleavened bread of sincerity and truth. ~ 1st Corinthians 5:6-8

Paul and Jesus each use leaven as a symbol for hypocrisy, false doctrine, and apostasy, applying it to the Judaizers who correspond with the previous era, warning them that "a little leaven leavens the whole lump" (Galatians 5:7-9). Likewise, in this parable, the "whole" is leavened through a woman putting leaven in three loaves of meal. To understand why, we must return to the corresponding history of Israel. Knowing that Israel would eventually demand a king, God forewarned them in Deuteronomy against what He knew would corrupt their king.

> When you shall say... "I will set a king over me, like as all the nations that are about me...Neither shall he multiply wives to himself, that his heart turn not away..."
> ~ Deuteronomy 17:14-17

Just as Adam chose to hearken to the voice of his wife rather than the voice of God (Genesis 3:17), God knew that intermarriage with pagan women would eventually lead to pagan corruption. While God had already forbidden this intermarriage in the Law of Moses, He gave an additional warning regarding the king, knowing the common practice of forming treaties and alliances with nations through intermarriage.

After David achieved peace from Israel's enemies, the kingdom was passed to Solomon, who disobeyed every command given for a king (Deuteronomy 17), multiplying hundreds of wives from the nations around him and eventually incorporating every form of pagan worship into the kingdom of Israel. Similarly, within a generation of Christianity becoming the state religion of Rome, the Imperial

Church would follow the politics of the emperor, leading to immediate corruption in the ministerial offices. As the Roman Empire became weakened by barbarian incursions and the mounting threat of the Islamic Caliphate, the Bishops of Rome would ally with the Frankish kings in the West, forming a new *Holy Roman Empire* and adopting the pagan title of *Pontifex Maximus,* which was previously held by the Caesars.

Just as the ten tribes of Northern Israel began to hate the idolatry of Solomon and the excessive burden of his rule, the Eastern and Western churches would become divided with two major points of contention. The first issue was iconoclasm, which was a zeal in the East to eliminate the many images and icons that were increasingly becoming objects of worship. The Papal church strongly opposed this, even going so far as to change the Ten Commandments, removing the prohibition against graven images. The second issue was Papal supremacy, in which the Roman Catholic church began to assert that the Bishops of Rome were inheritors of the office of Peter, holding supreme judgement over the rest of the Church. Just as the ten tribes split from the two tribes in Israel, the five centers of early Christianity split from Rome in the *Great Schism,* to form the Eastern Orthodox church.

The final element of the parable is the *"three measures of meal,"* alluding to the days of Abraham when he ate with the Lord.

> *And the LORD appeared unto him…he lifted up his eyes and looked, and lo, three men stood by him: … And Abraham hastened unto Sarah, and said, "Make ready quickly* ***three measures of fine meal****, knead it, and make cakes upon the hearth."*
> *~ Genesis 18:1-6*

In this passage, Abraham is meeting the Lord on their way to judge Sodom and Gomorrah. He asks Sarah to prepare three measures of meal for them as a fellowship meal to bless them. This passage mysteriously alludes to *The Trinity*, while the fellowship meal foreshadows the communion meal of bread and wine, offered as a remembrance of what Jesus did on the cross. This meal, prior to being called the *"communion"* was called the *"thanksgiving meal,"* from which we get the name *Eucharist*.

The Roman Catholic system denies that Jesus died once for all sin and that forgiveness is offered freely to all who trust in Him, receiving a seal of redemption that cannot be undone. Rather, it teaches that the Eucharist is a reincarnation of Christ into the bread, sacrificed daily like the Old Testament sacrifices to make continual atonement for sins. It is taught that the only sure way for one to maintain salvation is in the continual confession to a Roman Catholic priest, in order to receive an infusion of grace through this meal. The *thanksgiving* for what Christ finished at the Cross was replaced with a continual sacrificial meal, meant to maintain one's salvation. The Roman Catholic Eucharist offering involves the worship of a disk-shaped wafer, while the cup of the Lord's blood is withheld from the people. This is the very *"leaven of the Pharisees and Sadducees"* of which Christ says, *"does not enter in, and hinders those who would enter" (Luke 11:52).*

In the corresponding Pauline epistle to the Ephesians, he focuses on the mystery of *the Body* and *Bride of Christ*, represented in the Church.

> *And He put all things under His feet and gave Him to be head over all things to **the church, which is His Body**, the fullness of Him who fills all in all. ~ Ephesians 1:22*

This epistle focuses on the unity and authority of *the Body*, which is the *Bride of Christ*, destined to reign with Him. It emphasizes how the true church is united by one Spirit and one baptism and is given the ministerial offices to support and defend that unity, emphasizing how a true husband can never hate his own body.

> *... who loves his wife loves himself. For **no one ever hated his own flesh**, but nourishes and cherishes it, just as the Lord does the church. For we are members of His Body, of His flesh and of His bones. ~ Ephesians 5:28*

The application of this epistle is that no husband other than Christ can preserve this unity or be *one flesh* with the Church. The defilement of the communion meal, which is the remembrance of the spiritual truth that we are members of *One Body* that was broken for us, is an outward reflection of this spiritual error. The resulting schism reveals the impossibility of the church to remain united, while still married to Rome.

Letter 4: To the Church at Thyatira

> *And to the angel of the church in Thyatira write, 'These things says the Son of God, who has eyes like a flame of fire, and His feet like fine brass: "I know your works, love, service, faith, and your patience; and as for your works, the last are more than the first. Nevertheless, I have a few things against you, because **you allow that woman Jezebel**, who calls herself a prophetess, to teach and seduce My servants to commit sexual immorality and **eat things sacrificed to idols.**"' ~ Revelation 2:18-20*

Christ, whose eyes are a flame of fire, is omniscient in his judgement. He knows this Roman Catholic system abounds in charitable works, providing education, orphanages, hospitals, and adoption services; a tradition which began in the early church and continues unto this day. It is not for this that Christ faults them, but for the toleration of that sin of Jezebel, which is the corruption of worship and practice in the assembly. To understand Jezebel, and the consequences of her corruption, one must return to the corresponding histories of Israel and the Church.

After the division of Israel, both kingdoms continued in Solomon's errors to varying degrees, just as both halves of the Imperial church continued in similar errors of worship and practice. In Israel, the archetype of this error involved King Ahab of Israel marrying Jezebel, the princess of Sidon. Ahab became completely dominated by Jezebel, allowing her to kill nearly every prophet in Israel while making the priests of Baal ministers in their place. This corruption not only degraded the Kingdom of Israel, but also nearly destroyed the Kingdom of Judah as their daughter Athalia nearly succeeded in killing off the entire Davidic line. *(see 2nd Kings 8 & 11)*

Just as Jezebel and Ahab replaced the God-ordained worship practices with the false worship of Baal, the Roman Catholic system adopted a false worship early after its inception. Constantine immediately began replacing the biblical Jewish feasts with Pagan rites, built around the annual solstice calendar. At the Council of Ephesus, a generation later, Mary was elevated to be called, "The Mother of God" and whoever resisted this was deemed heretical. Eventually, Mary would come to be called "The Queen of Heaven," the very title given to the likes of the Egyptian Isis *(Jeremiah 7:8)* and the Greek Artemis of Ephesus, the very city where the idol makers had persecuted Paul *(Acts. 19: 23-41)*.

While the Eastern and Western church initially split over these practices, both eventually returned to the worship of images and relics; the worship of various saints and Mary; the dark and arbitrary use of pilgrimages and repetitive ritual; and to a dead liturgical practice that made no room for the Holy Spirit. Various martyrs were made the object of worship as the patrons of cities, prayer requests, and craft guilds. The polytheistic pagan system was nearly complete, with a pantheon of gods for every occasion and a mother goddess at the head. Where the Roman Catholic system had the initial appearance of Christ taking dominion, the actual result was the Church coming into pagan captivity.

Veiled behind the Eucharistic sacrifice is the Monstrance, which reflects the image of Baal. Assyrian Archeologists have unearthed a similar idol in which a sun symbol sits on top of a crescent moon, to which hands were raised in adoration. In fact, the Roman Catholic mass carries out this very ritual, with the bread being formed into a sun-disk shape, sitting inside a golden sunburst on top of a small crescent moon, which upholds the disk. Rome's spiritual counterpart in Islam mirrors this symbol, venerating the crescent moon, which sit atop their temples to cradle the rising sun.

God's judgement on Israel was to allow their pagan neighbors to take them into captivity, forcing them to worship the false gods with whom they chose to coexist. Just as the two parts of Israel would become captive to Assyria and Babylon respectively, the two parts of Christendom would become captive to Islam in the East, and to the Frankish kings in the West. What began as a spiritual captivity would eventually manifest in the Caliphate seizing Constantinople in the East, and Napoleon seizing Vatican City in the West. This false Christian worship will eventually become merged with Islamic worship to reunite the Roman Empire in the worship of Antichrist. Christ promises two forms of tribulation to those who remain in this system and refuse to repent of its errors.

> *"And I gave her time to repent of her sexual immorality, and she did not repent. Indeed, I will cast her into a sickbed, and those who commit adultery with her, into **great tribulation**, unless they repent of their deeds. **I will kill her children with death**, and all the churches shall know that I am He who searches the minds and hearts. And I will give to each one of you according to your works." ~ Revelation 2:21-23*

They will go through *"great tribulation."* Those who remain in this corrupted church will not be raptured, but will instead give their testimony through the martyrdom they compromised to avoid. That *"her children"* would be killed is indicative of Jezebel representing the *Mother of Harlots*, whose children form *Mystery Babylon* which will ultimately be destroyed during the *"great tribulation."*

> *"Now to you I say, and to the rest in Thyatira, as many as do not have this doctrine, who have not known the depths of Satan, as they say, I will put on you no other burden."*

After this, Christ gives a caveat to those who attend a church and unknowingly carry out this false worship. On them he places *"no other burden,"* not holding them accountable for this ignorance, but instead exhorting them to hold fast to the salvation that they already possess.

> But **hold fast what you have** till I come. And he who overcomes, and keeps My works until the end, to him **I will give power over the nations and he shall rule them with a rod of iron**; They shall be dashed to pieces like the potter's vessels–as I also have received from My Father; and I will give him the morning star. He who has an ear, let him hear what the Spirit says to the churches. ~ Revelation 2: 25-29

Christ's final words to Thyatira address the root cause of the error. He says the overcomer *shall* rule with Him, *"even as he has received from the father."* The desire for the Church to Christianize the world through politics rather than through faithful suffering caused them to fall into a captivity to fruitless works and ritual. Christ promises that if they embrace that suffering, which he also suffered in the will of the Father, that they will be rewarded with a true Kingdom when he returns. Where their marriage to the world government resulted in the Church being broken into pieces, Christ's return will result in the world government being broken into pieces to be ruled by himself and his *Bride*.

As the last two parables represented the church becoming corrupt in their relationship with Rome, the next two parables represent the Church becoming rejuvenated through the separation of Church and State, and the work of reformation, ongoing unto the present day. The next two parables can only be understood when interpreted as a pair. Their pairing is not a redundant message, but a subtle inference to the fact that while the first element would be necessary to liberate the Church, a second element would be necessary to bring her to perfection.

The Fifth Parable: The Treasure in the Field

Again, the kingdom of heaven is like unto treasure hidden in a field; which when a man has found, he hides, and for joy thereof goes and sells all that he has, and buys that field.
~ Matthew 13:44

Just as the Ark of the Covenant was finally released from the Philistines after being broken by a plague of boils, brought on by rats *(1ˢᵗ Samuel 6:4)*, the Gospel would be set free from the captivity of Roman Catholicism after the Bubonic plague. During the Black Death, John Wycliffe suggested that the plague was God's judgement on

Europe because of an unholy clergy, being condemned for his views. Before he was executed, he would publish the first English-language Bible, creating an appetite in Western Europe for the Word of God in the common tongue. His teachings would influence John Hus to preach against the Papacy, also being put to death for his courage. His words would inspire Martin Luther to confront the corruption of Rome at a time where diverging political interests would help foster the Reformation.

During the life of Martin Luther, the Papal system had nearly eradicated the concept of grace, having reduced the Apostolic faith to a system of complete spiritual bondage, with the common believer working tirelessly to maintain a state of salvation, only to die expecting hundreds, thousands, or even millions of years in purgatory. Worse than this was that the Roman clergy would allow the laity to purchase reduction from this purgatory with money, causing hypocrisy to reign among the rich and hopeless desperation among the poor.

Martin Luther was blessed with the burden of his sin, to which he was counseled by an elder monk to search the Scriptures for relief. In doing so, he discovered the doctrine of *grace by faith, apart from works,* the good news of the Gospel which had been long hidden. His discovery made him repulsed by the works-based practices of the Roman system and his public protest would encourage multiple regional churches to also reject the power of Rome. The desire among the European kingdoms to establish national independence would prevent Rome from silencing these theologians, launching the Protestant Reformation that would spread across Europe.

Sadly, many of these church groups were lax in their zeal to return to a pure biblical faith, and merely reformed to an earlier version of Roman Catholicism; their respective states maintaining the theocratic errors of the early Imperial Church. Many of these churches, still beholden to national governments, were merely a miniaturized version of what they had left behind, while their theology, still laced with Greek philosophy and dead ritual, merely reverted to the earlier days of Roman Christendom. Christ's fifth letter reveals these shortcomings.

Letter 5: To the Church at Sardis

*And to the angel of the church in Sardis write, "These things says He who has the seven Spirits of God and the seven stars: 'I know your works, that you have a name that you are alive, but you are dead. **Be watchful** and strengthen the things which remain, that are ready to die, for I have not found your works perfect before God. Remember therefore* *how you have received and heard; hold fast and repent. Therefore, **if you will not watch, I will come upon you as a thief**, and you will not know what hour I will come upon you.*

*You have a few names even in Sardis who have not defiled their garments; and they shall walk with Me in white, for they are worthy. He who overcomes shall be clothed in white garments, and I will not blot out his name from the Book of Life; but **I will confess his name** before My Father and before his angels. He who has an ear, let him hear what the Spirit says to the churches.'" ~ Revelation 3:1-6*

This letter is all about denominations and what must come about for these groups to become unified as the *Bride of Christ*, fit to be raptured in the last days. Christ reminds them of his attribute as having the seven spirits and seven stars. Just as Christ made his sovereignty known to the church at Ephesus, he is reminding the denominational churches that there is but one Church, and one Name by which she is called; not of their distinctive denominations, but of Jesus Christ alone.

Christ quickly rebukes the church, noting their hypocrisy in having *"a name that they are alive"* while being spiritually dead. This speaks to many denominations that sprang from the Reformation, quickly becoming the very state institutions full of false converts that Roman Christendom once was. While many of these held the theological distinctive of salvation *by grace alone through faith alone*, many other errors of the Roman Catholic system were left unchallenged. Christ warns them that if they do not continue to reform these things, he will *"come upon them like a thief,"* meaning that they will also be found aligned against Him when he comes to destroy the *Kingdom of Antichrist*. Christ gives them two exhortations: the first relating to his coming and the second relating to their doctrine.

First, he reminds them to *"watch."* This term is specifically eschatological, as it hearkens back to his warnings in *Matthew 24.*

Watch therefore, for you do not know what hour your Lord is coming. But know this, that if the master of the house had known what hour the thief would come, he would have watched and not allowed his house to be broken into. Therefore, you also be ready, for the Son of Man is coming at an hour you do not expect." ~ Matthew 24: 2

Every single mainline denomination, (those that originally split from the Roman Catholic Church), maintained the Amillenial teaching of Origen and Augustine. It was not until Darby and the Plymouth Brethren, 300 years later, that any Western churches began to study this teaching and obey this command to *"watch."* In this letter, Christ is specifically reminding the Church of their responsibility to know and understand eschatological prophecy. While he comes at an hour they do not expect, he expects them to know the signs of his coming and always be watching for them.

After this, Christ gives another piece of counsel that is perhaps more fundamental than the first. He commands them to *"remember how you have received and heard,"* indicating that they are not going to the Scriptures themselves and allowing the Holy Spirit to teach them as they *"hear with faith" (Galatians 3:2)*. Christ is counseling them to remember the church before Christendom, before the Ecumenical Counsels and denominational creeds, when the Scriptures and the Spirit ruled the church. Christ is reminding them of a church that had no members through cultural induction, when every person that joined the church did so at the cost of their reputation, rather than to advance their social standing. Christ says that there are *"some names that have not defiled their robes,"* which means that not every denomination of Christianity is inherently unfaithful, but that a true faith needs to be personal and responsible to Him alone. He promises the overcomer that if they adhere to this truth, he will confess *"their name"* (as opposed to the name of their church group) to the Father, thus assuring them of their salvation.

The corresponding period in Israel's history is known as the *Post-Exilic Period*. After Cyrus allowed the Jews to return to Jerusalem, to rebuild the city and the Temple, Ezra read the entire law aloud, inspiring national zeal to return to obedience. Later, after the Greeks conquered the Persians, Antiochus Epiphanes violated the temple, prompting the Maccabees to lead a revolt against him. While they broke with this oppression, they immediately began to ally with the Romans and the Spartans against him, leading to their eventual captivity to Rome. Their faith was reduced to a matter of national pride rather than personal conviction, and eventually broke down into several different sects, each one believing they represented the true faithful Israel. For all the effort among these groups to claim the superiority of their belief system, their ways did not produce a common faith in Christ at the time of his first coming.

As each group remained focused on building up the predominance of their influence, they all failed to discern the signs of his coming. This was demonstrated when the Magi, a pagan group once influenced by the prophet Daniel, came looking for the Christ child, while the many Jewish sects seemed uninterested and unaware of his coming. Corresponding to Sardis, Christ assures them that their churches are not false, but merely incomplete. While they have more to learn and understand, he wants them to know that the missing elements of their obedience are found among the other denominations. Just as Christ is sovereign over the breakup of Christendom, he is also sovereign over the reunification of the Church *in Spirit and in Truth*. In the corresponding Pauline epistle, he counsels the Philippians to rest in Christ, as he fulfills his promise to bring them to perfection.

> *I thank God upon every remembrance of you, always in every prayer of mine, making request for you all with joy, for your fellowship in the gospel from the first day until now,* ***being confident of this very thing: that He who has begun a good work in you will complete it until the day of Jesus Christ****. ~ Philippians 1:3-6*

Paul counsels them to strive toward unity, not at the expense of sound doctrine, but in mutual patience in understanding, trusting that Christ will sort out the true from the false and bring their doctrine to clarity. The unity that they are appointed to will only come about as his sovereign hand guides them through both the Scriptures, and the trials that will serve to differentiate between the true and false believers.

> *Some indeed preach Christ even from envy and strife, and some also from good will: ...What then? Only* ***that in every way, whether in pretense or in truth, Christ is preached; and in this I rejoice****, yes, and will rejoice. ~ Philippians 1:15-18*

> *Therefore, if there is any consolation in Christ, if any comfort of love, if any fellowship of the Spirit, if any affection and mercy, fulfill my joy by* ***being like-minded****, having the same love, being of one accord, of one mind. ~ Philippians 2:1-2*

> *Therefore, let us, as many as are mature, have this mind; and* ***if in anything you think otherwise, God will reveal even this to you****. Nevertheless, to the degree that we have already attained, let us walk by the same rule, and let us be of the same mind.*
> *~ Philippians 3:15-16*

The counsel of Christ is not for these denominations to submit to one of the groups; nor is it for individuals to continually break away, until the Church is reduced to an endless multiplication of fellowship gatherings with no institutional authority. Rather, His counsel is to remember that every good gift comes from God, to rejoice wherever Christ is preached, and to consider the grace given toward other denominations, knowing that there are *a few names that have not soiled their garments*. He reminds them that they are not the only church with apprehension of the truth, and that they should hold fast to their convictions, while being willing to listen to others in the greater *Body of Christ*.

The Sixth Parable: The Pearl of Great Price

Again, the kingdom of heaven is like unto a merchant man, seeking goodly pearls: Who when he had found one pearl of great price, went and sold all that he had and bought it.
~ Matthew 13:45

The second parable of an indispensable treasure represents the remaining need for the Church to be brought to perfection. While the doctrine of *salvation by grace through faith alone* is the foundational teaching of the Gospel, there is one thing that remains, which every denomination must receive. While many believe that missing element is *their* particular doctrinal distinctive, which the other denominations lack, what they all require to bring about their perfect maturity are the fires of testing, which will lead them to rely on Christ alone as their confidence.

The corresponding era of the history of Israel was in the time of John the Baptist and the earthly ministry of Jesus Christ. During this time, those who sought to be faithful were broken and oppressed. By the Romans, they were overtaxed and abused, and by their religious leaders, they were burdened with legalistic ritual and left untaught in the truth. When Christ came, he did not tell any sect, *"This group has it right,"* but instead went to the known sinners and rejects, picking from every denomination and from those with no camp at all. He pitied them, as their teachers were more interested in self-preservation than in shepherding them.

And Jesus, when he came out, saw many people, and was moved with compassion toward them, because they were as sheep not having a shepherd: and he began to teach them many things. ~ Mark 6:34

Jesus began to gather the nobodies, the rejects, and the misfits to make them into new creatures, rebuilding a world upside-down, where the one who is *forgiven much, loves much*. Through their weakness, he built a kingdom where the least would be the greatest, saying to them,

… But it shall not be so among you: but whosoever will be great among you, shall be your servant: And whosoever of you will be the greatest, shall be servant of all. For even the Son of Man came not to be ministered unto, but to minister, and to give his life a ransom for many." ~ Mark 10:42-44

Letter 6: To the Church at Philadelphia

*And to the angel of the church in Philadelphia write: "These things says He that is holy, He that is true, **He that has the key of David**, He that opens, and no man shuts it; and shuts, and no man opens it; I know your works: 'behold, I have set before you an open door, and no man can shut it: for you have a little strength, and **have kept My word, and have not denied my name**. Behold, I will make them of the synagogue of Satan, which say they are Jews, and are not, but do lie; behold, I will make them to come and worship before your feet, and to know that I have loved you. Because you have kept the word of my patience, **I also will keep you from the hour of temptation**, which shall come upon all the world, to try them that dwell upon the earth. Behold, I come quickly: hold fast to what you have, so that no man takes your crown.'" ~ Revelation 3:7-10*

*Him that overcomes will I make a pillar in the temple of my God, and **he shall go no more out**: and I will write upon him the name of my God, and the name of the city of my God, which is the New Jerusalem, which comes down out of heaven from my God: and I will write upon him my new name. He that has an ear, let him hear what the Spirit says unto the churches. ~ Revelation 3:11-13*

Christ knows how hard it will be to follow Him in purity in the last days. He reminds the faithful church that though they seem to be making little impact, and having little influence or popularity, that their hope is secure. He encourages them to look to what matters and to remember the purpose of their calling, reminding them simply to *keep his Word* and to *not deny his name*. He is allowing a new kind of "World Church" to form, absorbing all the wealthy, healthy, and beautiful people.

> *...turning the grace of our God into lasciviousness, and **denying the only Lord** God, and our Lord Jesus Christ. ~ Jude 1:4*

Christ knows that in the purification of the Church, it will not be a matter of doctrinal minutiae or of quantifiable measures of success. As the era ends, this church, whose name means *brotherly love,* will discover that their brothers and sisters are a remnant drawn from every denomination, just as Jesus' original disciples were drawn from every sect. As the hypocrites amass into a World Church, that will deny the exclusivity of Christ and the simplicity of His Word, these believers will realize that they are only here to *finish the race* and simply testify to the truth, no matter the cost.

In the corresponding Pauline epistle, he reminds the Colossians to look to his example, as he continues *"making up what is lacking in the sufferings of Christ." (Colossians 1:24).* He warns them about being led astray by being judged in immaterial matters. He reminds them to look to Christ alone and their heavenly reward, encouraging and bearing with one another in love, just as Christ warns the Philadelphians not to let anyone *"rob you of your crown."*

> *Let no one cheat you of your reward, taking delight in false humility and worship of angels, intruding into those things which he has not seen, vainly puffed up by his fleshly mind… ~ Colossians 2:18*

Paul is not talking about a loss of salvation, but a loss of rewards, being deceived by false measures of humility and spirituality that are imposed on the mainstream church. Christ warns of false miracle-workers in this era, and a wicked generation that *seeks after a sign.* He knows that these means will not cause the last remaining Gentiles to come to faith, but that they will be convicted by witnessing the faithful obedience of the elect as they turn away from the comforts of this world and face the shame of rejection with their heads held high.

Christ mentions the *"Key of David,"* a phrase hearkening back to a prophecy of Isaiah, relating to the removal of the wicked steward Shebna, who counseled Israel to *"eat, drink, and be merry, for tomorrow we die." (Isaiah 22:13).* In this prophecy, the *Key of David* is taken from him and given to the righteous Eliakim, whose name means *"resurrection of God."* The stewardship of Shebna represents the rule of Satan in the earth, which is near to being ended as Christ prepares to rapture his Bride. He reminds this church to stand fast in the hope that he has saved them through their faith and to not be discouraged.

Finally, Christ makes a promise to them to *"keep them from the hour of trial."* This church will be tested and tried to the ends of their faith, but he will not allow them to fail. Though they will be tested through apostasy, worldwide upheaval, and the rise of Antichrist, in the end, before the world is tested by being demanded to worship the Beast and his image, they will be removed to *the New Jerusalem* in the Rapture.

> *Immediately after the tribulation of those days … they shall see the Son of Man coming in the clouds of heaven with power and great glory. And He shall send his angels with a great sound of a trumpet, and they shall gather together his elect from the four winds, from one end of heaven to the other. ~ Matthew 24:29-31*

The Seventh Parable: The Dragnet

*Again, the kingdom of heaven is like unto a net, that was cast into the sea, and gathered of every kind: Which when it was full, they drew to shore and sat down, and **gathered the good into vessels, but cast the bad away**. So shall it be at the end of the world:*

the angels shall come forth, and sever the wicked from among the just, and shall cast them into the furnace of fire: there shall be wailing and gnashing of teeth.

~ Matthew 13:47-50

In the seventh parable, the message is simple. Jesus is coming to make a distinction. All the world will be within the grasp of his net, yet only those He calls *"good"* will be kept. The purpose of this parable is to relate a time coming to separate the *wheat* from the *tares*. To this last church era, Jesus gives a message of fear for them that will witness this *catching away* and be found left behind. He wants them to know that they are aware of this because there is still hope for them.

Corresponding with the history of Israel, this passage represents the final disposition of Israel toward Christ at his first coming. In the end of his life, all the various sects joined together against Him. The Sadducees and Pharisees, as well as Pilate and Herod, found unity in their mutual hatred of the *Son of Man*. Likewise, in this final era of Church history, the final hour will be marked by a unification of the world against the true Church.

Letter 7: To the Church at Laodicea

*And to the angel of the church of the Laodiceans write, "These things says the Amen, the Faithful and True Witness, the Beginning of the creation of God: 'I know your works, that you are neither cold nor hot. I could wish you were cold or hot. So then, **because you are lukewarm, and neither cold nor hot, I will vomit you out of My mouth**. Because you say, "I am rich, increased in goods, and have need of nothing" – and do not know that you are wretched, miserable, poor, blind, and naked, I counsel you to buy from Me gold, refined in the fire that you may be rich; and white garments, that you may be clothed, that the shame of your nakedness may not be revealed; and anoint your eyes with eye salve, that you may see; for as many as I love, I rebuke and chasten. Therefore, be zealous and repent.' '**Behold, I stand at the door and knock**. If anyone hears My voice and opens the door, I will come in to him and dine with him, and he with Me. To him who overcomes I will grant to sit with Me on My throne, **as I also overcame** and sat down with My Father on His throne. He who has an ear, let him hear what the Spirit says to the churches.' ~ Revelation 3:14-22*

Christ warns this final church, which has been led to believe that comfort, success, large churches, and peace with the world is the measure of godliness. In his ministry, Jesus preached the opposite:

But woe unto you that are rich! for you have received your consolation. ... Woe unto you, when all men shall speak well of you! for so did their fathers to the False Prophets.

~ Luke 6:24-26

Christ warns them that the world will be so overtly wicked at this point that if a believer is found acceptable, it is because their testimony is nonexistent. They do their best to cover it up, or to keep themselves so separate from the world that they bear no witness that can be accounted for. This disposition is foreshadowed in the Song of Solomon, when the Shulamite lies in bed while Solomon knocks at the door. She does not want to answer the door because she has taken off her robe and washed her feet, expressing that she does not want to discomfort herself *(Songs 5:2-3)*. By the time she feels moved with desire to open for him, she goes to the door to find that he has departed. This passage foreshadows Christ, knocking at the door of the Laodicean church, beckoning the faithful to *"come out of her."* Those that finally do will be saved by fire as they at last give their testimony through faithful martyrdom.

> ***I opened to my beloved; but my beloved had withdrawn himself*** *and was gone:* ***my soul failed when he spoke****: I sought him, but I could not find him; I called him, but he gave me no answer. The watchmen that went about the city found me.* ***They smote me, and they wounded me****; the keepers of the walls* ***took away my veil from me****.*
> ~ *Songs 5:6-7*

As Jesus said in *Matthew 5:10-16*, those who have lost their saltiness will give their testimony by the loss of their lives. In their final hours, Laodicea, and *Mystery Babylon* will be one and the same, as Christ cries, *"come out of her my people" (Revelation 18:4)*. Christ reminds this church, that *"whomever He loves, He rebukes and chastens."* For those who finally face the persecution they avoided, their reward will be eternal life.

> *And fear not them, which kill the body but are not able to kill the soul: but rather fear him, which is able to destroy both soul and body in the lake of fire.* ~ *Matthew 10:28*

The corresponding Pauline epistles remind the Thessalonians what will occur before *the Rapture (1ˢᵗ Thessalonians 4:13-18)* and that this will not occur until the *Abomination of Desolation* occurs *(2ⁿᵈ Thessalonians 2:3-4)*. While these words may not prepare them to be taken up in *the Rapture*, they will assure that they understand what has happened when it has passed. Like the Apostles who scattered, or Peter who denied Jesus three times, these Laodicean Christians will find courage in their final hour. They will find the strength to face the persecution that they avoided, and to not shrink back from death. These last souls will complete the *Gentile Bride of Christ,* who will be raised to life when He sets up his kingdom, to *"reign with Him for a thousand years." (Revelation 20:4)*.

PART 4 – THE TRIAL BEGINS

The Revelation is broken up into three distinct portions by Christ: The first is *"the things which you have seen,"* signifying all the visionary elements, not specifically relating a narrative. The second is *"the things which are,"* signifying the present age, represented in the seven letters to the seven churches. The third is *"the things which shall be hereafter,"* representing the narrative surrounding Christ's appearing in the clouds and the *Kingdom Come*. It is this third portion that will cover the remainder of *the Revelation* from chapter 4 onward.

The Judgement Sits: Revelation 4 Interpreted

*After this I looked, and behold, a door was opened in heaven: and the first voice which I heard was as it were of a trumpet talking with me; which said, "Come up here, and I will show you **things which must be hereafter**." ~ Revelation 4:1*

Some will speculate that this *voice like a trumpet* signifies the very voice of the archangel *(1ˢᵗ Thessalonians 4:16)*, which Paul says will precede *the Rapture*, assuming this to be proof that *the Rapture* has occurred and noting the absence of the word *"Church"* in the rest of the book as additional proof. This is an ignorance that permeates the Pre-Tribulation rapture camp, which is based on an inconsistent interpretation, which they are obligated to account for.

The absence of the word *"Church,"* does not prove that the Church has been raptured, any more than the absence of the word *"Israel,"* in Chapters 8-21, means that Israel is somehow missing from the narrative. As the narrative speaks primarily in symbol, one should be able to see that symbols like the *"martyrs"* in chapter 6, the *"great multitude from every tribe, nation, and tongue"* in chapter 7, and the ascending *"prayers of the saints"* in chapter 8, each represent the Gentile Church. One should understand that *"the harvest"* in chapter 14 is the very harvest of the Church, mentioned in *Matthew 13:30,* while the return of the *"wife of the lamb"* in chapter 19 is the same as Christ coming *"with all of his saints,"* mentioned in *Zechariah 13:5.* There is plenty of evidence to prove that the Church is still on the earth until Christ appears.

In *Revelation 4,* John is caught up into the throne room of heaven, departing from the realm of Earth into the realm of the Spirit, which is eternal and unrestrained by time. Having received the testimony of the seven letters to the seven churches, John will receive the corresponding heavenly events, also beginning with the resurrection of Christ and proceeding to *The Revelation* at the end of the age.

> *And immediately **I was in the spirit**: and behold, a throne was set in heaven, and one sat on the throne. And He that sat was to look upon like a jasper and a sardine stone: and there was a rainbow round about the throne, in sight like unto an emerald.*
>
> *~ Revelation 4:2-3*

That John was *in the spirit* precludes that he is witnessing *the Rapture.* Paul also teaches of one caught up to heaven in *2nd Corinthians* but makes a distinction between being caught up bodily and being caught up *"in the spirit."*

> *I knew a man in Christ above fourteen years ago, (whether in the body, I cannot tell; or whether out of the body, I cannot tell: God knows;) such a one caught up to the third heaven. ~ 2nd Corinthians 12:2*

Paul is not fully sure whether this one was caught up into heaven physically, meaning *in the body,* or *in the Spirit,* which is *out of the body.* Paul knows that a born-again believer is always seated in heaven, even while physically present on the earth, explaining that upon our physical death, we will be immediately present in heaven.

> *And [He] has raised us up together, and made us sit together in heavenly places in Christ Jesus: ~ Ephesians 2:6*
>
> *...to be absent from the body is to be present with the Lord. ~ 2nd Corinthians 5:8*

In this passage of *the Revelation,* John is *"in the Spirit,"* as opposed to being taken up bodily, proving that this cannot be *the Rapture,* since *the Rapture* necessarily involves a bodily resurrection.

> And round about the throne were four and twenty thrones: and upon the thrones **I saw four and twenty elders sitting**, clothed in white raiment; and they had on their heads, crowns of gold. And out of the throne proceeded lightning and thundering and voices: and there were seven lamps of fire burning before the throne, which are the seven Spirits of God. ~ Revelation 4:4-5

These *Twenty-Four Elders* allude to a prophecy by Daniel representing a delegation of elders charged with judgement in the Kingdom of God.

> I beheld till the **thrones were set down**, and the Ancient of days sat, whose garment was white as snow, and the hair of his head like pure wool: his throne was like the fiery flame, and his wheels as burning fire. A fiery stream issued and came forth from before him: and ten thousand ten-thousands ministered unto him, and ten thousand ten thousands stood before him: **the judgment was set**, and **the books were opened**.
> ~ Daniel 7:9-10

In ancient times, when a king would convene for judgement, or to go to war, or to pass on the inheritance of the kingdom, he would have his lords sitting beneath him. These nobles might give counsel to the situation, but the judgement of the king would be binding. We still model this in the modern courtroom, where the judge relies on the counsel of twelve jurors. This pattern can be traced back to the twelve tribes of Israel, which are also reflected here. This court of judgement is already seated in heaven, just as we are seated with Christ. The first twelve are the twelve sons of Israel, who have an eternal inheritance in their name *(Ezekiel 48)*, while the second twelve are the twelve Apostles, of whom it was said,

> ... you who have followed Me will also sit on twelve thrones, judging the twelve tribes of Israel. ~ Matthew 19:28

The purpose of this judgement is to put the stewardship of Satan on trial. In *Daniel 7: 1-8,* Satan's kingdom is represented by four great beasts through which he exercises dominion in the earth. These beasts contrast four heavenly beasts, which administer the creation of God.

> And before the throne there was a sea of glass like unto crystal: and in the midst of the throne, and round about the throne, were **four beasts full of eyes before and behind**. And the first beast was like a lion, and the second beast like a calf, and the third beast had a face as a man, and the fourth beast was like a flying eagle. And the four beasts had each of them six wings about him; and they were full of eyes within: and they rest not day and

night, saying, Holy, holy, holy, Lord God Almighty, which was, and is, and is to come. And when those beasts give glory and honor and thanks to him that sat on the throne, who lives for ever and ever ~ Revelation 4:6-9

These four beasts represent the powers of God in their administration over the forces of the creation, just as the *Twenty-Four Elders* represent the judgement of God in their administration of His Kingdom.

The four and twenty elders fall down before him that sat on the throne, and worship him that lives for ever and ever, and cast their crowns before the throne, saying, "You are worthy, O Lord, to receive glory and honor and power: for you have created all things, and for your pleasure they are and were created." ~ Revelation 4:10-11

This judgement is a legal proceeding, in which the dominion of earth will be taken from Satan, whose agent is *the Antichrist,* and given to the Church, whose head is Christ. This reflects the end of Daniel's four beasts, which rule the earth prior to Christ's eternal kingdom. This judgement begins in *Revelation 4*, and continues until *Revelation 20*, when every person is judged according to what is written in the books.

*But **the judgment shall sit**, and **they shall take away his dominion**, ...the greatness of the kingdom under the whole heaven shall be given to the people of the saints of the Most High, whose kingdom is an everlasting kingdom...~ Daniel 7:26-27*

While there are several books used in this judgement, this first book contains the legal framework by which Satan's stewardship of the Earth will be taken away, justifying his imprisonment and final destruction.

The Seven Sealed Scroll: Revelation 5 Interpreted

*And I saw in the right hand of Him who sat on the throne **a scroll written inside and on the back, sealed with seven seals.** Then I saw a strong angel proclaiming with a loud voice, "Who is worthy to open the scroll and to unseal its seals?" And no one in heaven or on the earth or under the earth was able to open the scroll, or to look at it.*
~ Revelation 5:1-3

In this passage, the key to understanding the scroll is that it is written upon on both sides. This scroll is first foreshadowed in *Ezekiel 2-3* (which will be examined later, when it is finally opened) but whose contents and purposes are explained in *Zechariah 5*. The scroll has a judgement which is written on the front and back, representing a curse by which Satan will be judged because of two sins he commits.

*Then I turned, ... and looked, and behold a flying scroll... Then said he unto me, "This is the curse that goes forth over the face of the whole earth: for every one that commits thievery shall be cut off as **on this side** according to it; and every one that commits*

[78]

*perjury shall be cut off as **on that side** according to it. I will bring it forth, says the LORD of hosts... ~ Zechariah 5:1-3*

To properly understand this judgement, one must first understand *"dominions"* or *"principalities."* These are realms of authority which are designated by God to the stewardship of the one to whom He has given dominion. All creation is under God's dominion, but He delegates sub-dominions to Angels or Man according to His will. The Bible refers to these as *"principalities"* when Paul says,

> *For we wrestle not against flesh and blood, but against principalities, against powers, against the rulers of the darkness of this world, against spiritual wickedness in high places. ~ Ephesians 6:12*

Many of these principalities have spiritual powers over them, enforcing the bounds of their dominion. These are angelic beings over various facets of power, authority, and even physical location. For instance, *"Death"* is a power, while *"Hades"* (which is also called *"Sheol"* or *"The Grave"*) is its principality. Death and Hades are considered a type of prison, having bars and gates *(Jonah 2:6)*, and preventing any from escaping *(Isaiah 14:17)*. One cannot enter Hades except by the power of Death, and one must sin to be given over to Death. Since sin comes through belief in lies, and Satan is the father of these lies, he has dominion over all sinners through the power of Death and Hades, over which he was given authority.

In the beginning, God said of Adam's kind, *"let them have dominion over all the earth."* *(Genesis 1:26)*. Earth was originally created to be the dominion of Adam. So, Adam was a prince, and his principality was the Earth, which in Hebrew is called, <Adamah>, or *"Adam's Land."* Adam had complete authority over the earth, and the ability to do with it whatever he willed with one exception: *The Tree of the Knowledge of Good and Evil* was holy unto the Lord, separated unto Him alone. When Adam ate of the fruit, he gave over dominion of the earth to Satan, who was the Cherub who had served as a covering and steward of the Earth.

> *You were in Eden, the garden of God...You were the anointed cherub who covers; I established you... you walked back and forth in the midst of fiery stones. ~ Ezekiel 28:13*

Satan was placed in guardianship over man whenever God was not present on Earth. It was for this reason that he walked back and forth *in the midst of the fiery stones.* He was appointed to watch over man, and if they sinned, to block their way to God, preventing them from entering His presence with sin upon them and being destroyed.

While Satan was an instrument of discipline, created for holiness, he had his own agenda, which unbeknownst to him, God knew from the beginning.

> You were perfect in your ways from the day you were created, until iniquity was found in you. **By the abundance of your trading You became filled with violence within, and you sinned**; Therefore, I cast you as a profane thing out of the mountain of God; And I destroyed you, O covering cherub, from the midst of the fiery stones. Your heart was lifted up because of your beauty; You corrupted your wisdom for the sake of your splendor; I cast you to the ground, I laid you before kings, that they might gaze at you.
> ~ Ezekiel 28:15-17

This *abundance of trading* began when Satan reasoned that if he could tempt mankind to exchange the truth for a lie and to disobey the Lord, then his temporary stewardship could become a permanent one. He saw the Earth as a dominion through which he could multiply his power to contest with God. He saw the Earth as a place from which he could reign through deceit and ascend to equality with God.

> ... "I will ascend into heaven, I will exalt my throne above the stars of God; I will also sit on the mount of the congregation on the farthest sides of the north; I will ascend above the heights of the clouds, I will be like the Most High." ~ Isaiah 14:13

Satan's trading included an elaborate array of promises to various angelic powers, making the corruption of mankind their mutual interest. Through his trade, he seduced mankind to give up the Earth through sin, leading the Lord to block their way to the *Tree of Life*.

> So, He drove out the man; and He placed cherubim at the east of the garden of Eden, and a flaming sword which turned every way, to guard the way to the tree of life.
> ~ Genesis 3:24

Because mankind was withheld from the *Tree of Life*, they were destined to die. This fear of death made man even more prone to the temptations of sin, knowing that their life was short, as they had no promise of another life after this one. It was for this reason that Paul said,

> If the dead do not rise, "Let us eat and drink, for tomorrow we die!"
> ~ 1st Corinthians 15:32

Man could only hope to attain their desires in this life, and in doing so, covetousness became the motive by which all men were driven.

> ...I saw that for all toil and every skillful work of man is because of envy of his neighbor.
> ~ Ecclesiastes 4: 4

Then, when desire has conceived, it gives birth to sin; and sin, when it is full-grown, brings forth death. ~ James 1:15

Satan continued to rule over men by his lies because they were all captive to sin through *"the fear of death" (Hebrews 2:15)*. He maintained this captivity by the threat of death, over which he had dominion, driving men through their desperation. Satan reasoned that God could not judge him unless he destroyed the entire Earth, and because of this, he could keep forever what he was only meant to steward, as long as he could keep men captive to sin.

While God must punish all sin in accordance with His justice, He will also judge Satan for willfully leading mankind into sin in order to usurp their dominion. While many have found the Old Testament laced with God's intention to save mankind through the sacrifice of Jesus Christ, most do not realize that His intention to punish Satan for this usurpation is also prophesied. God first revealed His knowledge of Satan's motives in *Genesis 30,* which was shown in a type, when Jacob tricked Laban in order to acquire his flock.

> *Let me pass through all your flock today, removing from there all the speckled and spotted sheep, and all the brown ones among the lambs, and **the spotted and speckled among the goats; and these shall be my wages**. So, my righteousness will answer for me in time to come, when the subject of my wages comes before you: every one that is not speckled and spotted among the goats, and brown among the lambs, **will be considered stolen**, if it is with me. ~ Genesis 30:32-33*

Jacob, whose name means *"supplanter" (Genesis 27:36),* feigned service to Laban while secretly usurping all his flocks. Because Jacob's wages consisted of all the spotted and speckled sheep, he enticed the spotted and speckled sheep to mate with the strongest in the flock, eventually producing a heard that was entirely spotted and speckled. Just as mankind became the property of Satan through sin, Laban's sheep became the property of Jacob through breeding. Only a sinless man could qualify to take back the stewardship of Earth, and for this reason, Satan made sure to tempt every man to sin. Just as Jacob could not be considered a thief unless he was found with a spotless lamb, Satan could not be considered a thief unless he took a sinless man captive to Death.

God planned to give mankind a sinless man, who would save them from the power of sin and death, and regain the stewardship of Earth, which He also foreshadowed in Joseph. In the same way that Adam was given dominion over the Earth, Joseph was given dominion over the entire house of Potiphar, with one exception: Potiphar's wife, who was in his house, was holy unto Potiphar, and was forbidden. It is for this reason, that when she tried to seduce Joseph, he said:

> *There is no one greater in this house than I, nor has he kept back anything from me but you, because you are his wife. How then can I do this great wickedness, **and sin against God**? ~ Genesis 39:9*

Joseph's temptation was the same as Adam's: to forget being thankful for all God had given and to reach for the one thing that was forbidden. Joseph passed the test, being a type of Christ, who resisted all temptation by Satan. Like Christ, he was falsely accused, yet vindicated and elevated to take authority over a greater dominion, able to save both Israel and the Gentiles from famine. Where Joseph gained authority over Egypt, Christ gained authority over all Heaven and Earth. Christ will return to take hold of this dominion once the offer of grace has been preached throughout the earth.

This transition of stewardship is mysteriously prophesied in Isaiah, when the stewardship of Jerusalem is taken from the wicked Shebna and given to righteous Eliakim, whose name means *"resurrection of God."* This prophecy reveals how Satan is an unfaithful steward, who counts mankind as a wall of defense from his well-deserved judgement; a means to maintain a throne that was never his.

> ***You numbered the houses of Jerusalem, And the houses you broke down to fortify the wall***...*And in that day the Lord GOD of hosts called for weeping and for mourning, for baldness and for girding with sackcloth. But instead, joy and gladness, saying, **"Let us eat and drink, for tomorrow we die!"** Then it was revealed in my hearing by the LORD of hosts, **"Surely for this iniquity there will be no atonement for you, even to your death,"** says the Lord GOD of hosts. Thus says the Lord GOD of hosts: "Go, proceed to this steward, to Shebna, who is over the house, and say: 'What have you here, and whom have you here, that you have hewn a sepulcher here, as he who hews himself a sepulcher on high, who carves a tomb for himself in a rock?...He will surely turn violently and toss you like a ball into a large country; There you shall die, and there your glorious chariots shall be the shame of your master's house. **So, I will drive you out of your office, and from your position he will pull you down**.'"*
> ~ Isaiah 22:14-19

God's intention in eternal judgement is to punish Satan, for corrupting his wisdom and turning his office into a means to sacrifice others to his own ambition. While man was tempted in ignorance, Satan plotted with full knowledge of the holiness of God.

> *You defiled your sanctuaries by the multitude of your iniquities, by the iniquity of your trading. Therefore, **I brought fire from your midst and it devoured you**, And I turned you to ashes upon the earth in the sight of all who saw you. All who knew you*

among the peoples are astonished at you; **<u>You have become a horror and shall be no more forever</u>**. ~ *Ezekiel 28:18*

God calls the lake of fire a place *"prepared for Satan and his angels" (Matthew 25:41)*, but for those who were deceived by him, Jesus said,

Father forgive them; for they know not what they do. ~ *Luke 23:34*

This is the fundamental difference between men and angels: Men are eternal souls in temporary bodies, while angels are eternal souls in eternal bodies. For them, there is only one kind of death, with no forgiveness for sin, because they sin with full knowledge of God. However, mankind is created in ignorance, able to die and be born-again, both spiritually and physically. God created mankind this way because he knew that mankind would be tempted to fall into sin and would need to be saved. God created mankind to be redeemable, not only to destroy the purposes of Satan, but to turn what Satan intended for evil to good, making an opportunity to reveal His mercy toward mankind.

Still, we must remember that every instance of temptation and trial committed by Satan is authorized by God. Because God is just, He will not judge Satan for wicked motives without having expressed a command which Satan intentionally disobeyed. Where God gave the Law to condemn Israel, He also gave a curse in the *"scroll that went forth over the whole earth."* This scroll contains a universal judgement for the one who commits two specific sins. Just as Christ would have two comings, Satan would have two agents through whom he would commit these sins.

At his first coming, it was no coincidence that Jesus chose Judas, a known thief, to be the *man of perdition* who would betray him. Satan had legal authority to commit all sinners to Death and Hades, but he did not have authority to falsely imprison one that *knew no sin*. Through Judas, he committed a sin called *"manstealing" (1ˢᵗ Timothy 1:10)*, which is the same as *kidnapping*. In this offense, Satan became the thief, fulfilling the first clause of the curse. When *the spotless lamb* was found in Satan's prison, He was considered stolen, causing Satan to lose authority. Christ now holds the keys of Death and Hades, freeing the believers from the fear of death by this assurance:

...on this rock I will build My church, and the gates of Hades shall not prevail against it.
  ~ *Matthew 16:18*

The second clause of the scroll will be fulfilled in the last days, when *the Antichrist*, commits the sin of perjury. When the temple is rebuilt, he will stand in the Most

Holy Place and claim to be God. When he does this, the penalty contained in this scroll will be applied to Satan, and all who remain willingly under his dominion through the love of sin.

> *I will bring it forth, says the LORD of hosts, and it shall enter into the house of the thief, and into the house of him that swears falsely by my name: and it shall remain in the midst of his house,* **and shall consume it** *with the timber thereof and the stones thereof.*
> *~ Zechariah 5: 4*

Just as God promised to Satan prophetically, that he would consume him from within by fire *(Ezekiel 28:18)*, this curse promises to consume the house of the thief and the perjurer. The entire Earth is appointed to be burned. In the end, Satan, with all who obey him, will be consigned to the lake of fire for eternal judgement.

> *But* **the judgment shall sit**, *and they shall take away his dominion,* **to consume and to destroy it** *unto the end. ~ Daniel 7:26*

Thankfully for us, God was not willing to carry out this doom before giving us a covering from this fiery judgement. Where Satan sought to grasp the dominion through thievery and deceit, sacrificing the lives of mankind unto himself, Jesus regained the dominion through laying down his life as a sacrifice to save mankind.

> *And the key of the house of David will I lay upon his shoulder; so,* **He shall open, and none shall shut; and He shall shut, and none shall open**. *And* **I will fasten him as a nail in a sure place**; *...In that day, ... shall the nail that is fastened in the sure place be removed, and be cut down, and fall; and* **the burden that was upon it shall be cut off**: *for the LORD has spoken it. ~ Isaiah 22:22-25*

The Lamb that was Slain

> *And I wept much, because no man was found worthy to open and to read the book, neither to look thereon. ~ Revelation 5:1-4*

In this vision, the absence of the Son should be conspicuous. From this eternal perspective, mankind has failed, as no man is found worthy to regain the sovereignty over the Earth, which was forfeited to Satan in the fall. The weight of this despair is felt by John as he weeps at the burden of this reality. Without one who is worthy to take the dominion from Satan, mankind is trapped under his dominion to be consumed by fire with him in the end. After the scroll is highlighted, Christ makes his appearance, having fulfilled his earthly ministry, prevailing to make propitiation for mankind, making a way for them to pass through the fire. Living his earthly life without sin unto death, though he was condemned by perjury, he was vindicated and raised to life to live and reign forevermore.

> *And one of the elders said unto me, "Do not weep: behold, the Lion of the tribe of Judah, the Root of David, has prevailed to open the book, and to unseal its seven seals." And I looked and saw in the midst of the throne and of the four beasts, and the elders, stood **<u>a Lamb as it had been slain</u>**, having seven horns and seven eyes, which are **<u>the seven Spirits of God sent forth into all the earth</u>**. And He came and took the Book out of the right hand of him that sat upon the throne. ~ Revelation 5:5-7*

After his resurrection, Christ attained the High Priesthood and needed to go to the Father to offer up his own body and blood on the altar.

> *... "Touch me not; for I have not yet ascended to my Father: but go to my brethren, and say unto them, I ascend unto my Father, and your Father; and to my God, and your God." ~ John 20:17*

> *For such a high priest became us, who is holy, blameless, undefiled, separate from sinners, and made higher than the heavens; who needs not daily, as those high priests, to offer up sacrifice, first for his own sins, and then for the people's: for this he did once, when **<u>he offered up himself</u>**. ~ Hebrews 7:26-27*

Christ became our intercessor, after which the Seven Spirits of God, representing the Holy Spirit that had rested upon him without measure, now proceeded from Christ to be poured forth to dwell in us.

> *... I tell you the truth; It is expedient for you that I go away: for if I go not away, the Comforter will not come unto you; but if I depart, I will send him unto you. ~ John 16:7*

The Worship of the Lamb

> *And when He had taken the book, the four beasts and twenty-four elders fell down before the Lamb, having every one of them harps, and golden vials full of odors, which are the prayers of saints. And they sung a new song, saying, **<u>"You are worthy to take the book, and to open the seals thereof: for you were slain</u>**, and have redeemed us to God by your blood out of every kindred, and tongue, and people, and nation; And have made us unto our God, kings and priests: and we shall reign on the earth." And I beheld, and I heard the voice of many angels round about the throne, and the Beasts and the elders: and the number of them was ten thousand times ten thousand, and thousands of thousands; saying with a loud voice, "**<u>Worthy is the Lamb</u>** that was slain to receive power, and riches, and wisdom, and strength, and honor, and glory, and blessing. And every creature which is in heaven, and on the earth, and under the earth, and such as are in the sea, and all that are in them, I heard say, "Blessing, and honor, and glory, and power, be unto him that sits upon the throne, and unto the Lamb for ever and ever." And the four beasts said, "Amen." And the four and twenty elders fell down and worshipped him that lives for ever and ever. ~ Revelation 5: 8-14*

[85]

PART 5 - THE BIRTH PANGS

"These are the beginning of sorrows." ~ Matthew 24:8

In this next section, we will look at what Jesus called *"The beginning of Sorrows"* (or <odin>), literally meaning *"Birth Pangs."* These will correspond both with the opening of the seven seals on the scroll and the completion of the ingathering of the Gentiles, after which the Spirit is poured out on the remnant of Israel. These events manifest in the groaning of the earth under the weight of sin, which will continue until the *Abomination of Desolation*. When this groaning reaches its climax, two events will also occur in the same day, which are *the Rapture* of the Church to the Jerusalem above and the fleeing of the remnant of Israel from the Jerusalem below.

1st Seal	2nd Seal	3rd Seal	4th Seal	5th Seal	6th Seal	7th Seal
Apostasy	Wars	Famine	Death	Martyrs	Quaking	Trumpets

Like many of the major themes of Bible prophecy, there is an *already-not yet* pattern to these birth pangs, which must be understood to differentiate between what has been fulfilled and what will be fulfilled in the future. It is important to examine this symbol throughout Scripture and to understand its meaning, so as not to make unsound predictions about *Revelation chapter 6*. Before examining the narrative, it is important to note who is giving birth. For understanding, we must examine the first woman and her labor, as these *birth pangs* fulfill the most ancient prophecy given to Eve, *"the mother of all the living"* (Genesis 3:20).

> *To the woman He said, I will greatly multiply **your sorrow** in your conception; in **sorrow** you shall bring forth children; ~ Genesis 3:16*

Looking beyond the plain narrative, Adam and Eve were also each a type of grace and works. After they sinned, Adam was given a judgement of living by hard labor. Though toiling all his life, he would die and return to the dust, representing the failure of our works to produce life *(Genesis 3:17-19)*. However, Eve was given a judgement of sorrows unto conception, representing grace producing a *new man* or *inner man* in the sinner. The new man would be revealed through travail, representing the suffering of chastisement, resulting in a new body and a hope for the future. While Adam's judgment represents the death of the *old man,* Eve's judgement represents the eternal life of the *new man,* foreshadowing the difference between those born of the flesh in sin and those born of the Spirit by grace.

Spiritually, these *travails* also represent the earth groaning under the curse of sin, while the *birth* represents the revealing of the children of God, who are Eve's spiritual children throughout the earth. Just as the seed of Abraham is one *"Seed"* in Christ but many in *His Body (Galatians 3:16),* the seed of Eve, is both one *Son* and many *Children.*

> *Notwithstanding she (Eve) shall be saved in childbearing, (through Christ) if they (her children) continue in faith and love and holiness with sobriety. ~ 2ⁿᵈ Timothy 2:15*

This motherhood of Eve would be spiritually transferred to Jerusalem, which was also called Zion, *"the mother of us all"* (Galatians 4:26).

> **Before she travailed**, she brought forth; before her pain came, she was delivered of **a man child**. Who has heard of such a thing? … Shall the earth be made to bring forth in one day? Or shall a nation be born at once? For **as soon as Zion travailed, she brought forth her children**. ~ Isaiah 66:7-8

In this passage, one should notice that Zion brings forth a man child *"before she travailed,"* and then brings forth her children *"as soon as she travailed."* This represents the two advents of Christ, revealing that in his first coming, Zion delivered him in a time of peace, but in his second coming, her children will be brought forth in a time of great travails in the earth.

> *For the earnest expectation of **the creature waits for the manifestation of the sons of God.** … Because the creature itself also shall be delivered from the bondage of*

corruption into the glorious liberty of the children of God. For we know that the whole **creation groans and travails in pain together until now**. ~ Romans 8:19-22

Eve's children are being revealed as they are *born-again* through faith, ultimately to be *born-again* at their glorification, which is the transforming of our corruptible bodies into the incorruptible likeness of Christ. Paul describes this revelation of the children as our coming to faith, ultimately fulfilled during a time when the earth breaks out in intense *birth pangs* as the fullness of the Gentiles comes in *(Romans 11:25)*. These *birth pangs* climax with *The Revelation*, when *the Resurrection and the Rapture* occur.

> *In a moment, in the twinkling of an eye,* **at the last trump***: for the trumpet shall sound, and the dead shall be raised incorruptible, and we shall be changed. For this corruptible must put on incorruption, and this mortal must put on immortality. So,* **when this corruptible shall have put on incorruption***, and this mortal shall have put on immortality, then shall be brought to pass the saying that is written, "Death is swallowed up in victory. O death, where is your sting? O grave, where is your victory?"* ~ 2nd Corinthians 15:52-53

At that time, the earth will give birth as it gives up the *"dead in Christ"* to the Jerusalem above, while at the same time, those of the Jerusalem below also come to faith in Christ. At this moment, the two will share one faith and *"all Israel will be saved"* *(Romans 11:26)*, as Micah also says,

> *Therefore, He shall give them up, until the time that she who is in labor has given birth. Then the remnant of his brethren shall return to the children of Israel.* ~ Micah 5:3

Understanding this prophetic theme as dictating the narrative, we should look to Jesus' testimony in *Matthew 24,* and to other prophetic mentions of *"labor pains,"* or *"giving birth,"* to understand the complete picture that God is forecasting.

> *For many will come in My name, saying, "I am the Christ," and will deceive many. And you will hear of wars and rumors of wars. See that you are not troubled; for all these things must come to pass, but the end is not yet. For nation will rise against nation, and kingdom against kingdom. And there will be famines, pestilences, and earthquakes in various places.* **All these are the beginning of sorrows**. ~ Matthew 24:5-8

Looking at Jesus' words, we see that the *"beginnings of sorrows"* include false christs, persecutions, famines, pestilences, earthquakes, and death, which already began in the days of the Apostles and progress unto the present day.

> *Little children, it is the last hour; and as you have heard that the Antichrist is coming, even now many antichrists have come, by which we know that it is the last hour.*
> ~ 1st John 2:18

Who shall separate us from the love of Christ? Shall tribulation, or distress, or persecution, or famine, or nakedness, or peril, or sword? As it is written, "For your sake we are killed all day long; we are accounted as sheep for the slaughter."
~ Romans 8:35-36

In the coming days, when the birth pangs become rapid and increasing in severity, then the birth of the children of Zion is near and the *Resurrection and the Rapture of the Church* will come soon afterward; another element that is *already* and *not-yet*.

Unsealing the Scroll: Revelation 6 Interpreted

This scroll, containing the statute by which Satan will be judged, will be opened before he commits the second offense. The signs corresponding with the seals being unsealed are not the wrath of God, but the *"sorrows"* which Jesus testified are *"not the end" (Matthew 24:8)* and will occur as the gospel is preached throughout the earth.

The First Seal: The Mystery of Lawlessness

*And I saw when the Lamb opened one of the seals, and I heard, as it were the noise of thunder, one of the four beasts saying, "Come and see." And I saw and behold a white horse: and **he that sat on him had a bow**; and a crown was given unto him: and he went forth conquering, and to conquer. ~ Revelation 6:1-2*

Corresponding with the first seal is the conquest of the *Spirit of Antichrist*. This horseman is not specifically revealing the man known as *"The Beast"* any more than the other horses are representative of a single man. Rather, this is the *"mystery of lawlessness"* which Paul says is *"already at work" (1ˢᵗ Thessalonians 2:7)*. This is the spirit of error and apostasy in the earth, working to consolidate every false religion into a single lie; the same to which John had testified, *"we know that Antichrist is coming, and even now, many antichrists have come" (1ˢᵗ John 2:18)*.

The Antichrist is foreshadowed throughout the Old Testament as the primary agent of Satan in the earth. The first type of Antichrist was Cain, who proceeded to offer up the fruit of his own works. In envy, he persecuted faithful Abel, stalking him into the field and killing him. For this reason, *the Antichrist* is a hunter and a man of the field, who persecutes the shepherd. Through Cain's children came trade, cities, weapons, and all opposition to humble living, working to escape the labor that God ordained in His mercy. As evil continued to grow in the earth, Cain's descendant Lamech turned the grace of God into a license for immorality, saying,

*Then shall they know that I am the LORD their God, ...Neither will I hide my face any more from them: for **I have poured out my spirit upon the house of Israel**, says the Lord GOD. ~ Ezekiel 39:28-29*

*And it shall come to pass afterward, that I will pour out my spirit upon all flesh; and your sons and your daughters shall prophesy; your old men shall dream dreams; your young men shall see visions: ... **in those days will I pour out my spirit**.*

~ Joel 2:28-29

*"Do not harm the earth, the sea, or the trees till we have sealed the servants of our God on their foreheads." And I heard the number of those who were sealed. **144,000 of all the tribes of the children of Israel were sealed**: ~ Revelation 7:3-4*

Aligning these prophecies will demonstrate how this war will lead up to the beginning of *Daniel's 70th week*, which will begin after this outpouring of the Spirit. It is important to note that the language of *Joel* makes it clear, that this battle is "***before** the Day of the Lord" (Joel 2: 31),* demonstrating that it cannot be the wrath of God. While this war will conclude with an unbelieving remnant fleeing underground to avoid the wrath of God, this similarity is the intended purpose of this war, causing the unbelieving to believe this lie and the false peace to follow.

One should consider this war, and the nations involved, as this is perhaps the clearest sign that the time is near. Two passages are crucial to understanding how this war begins, and how *the Antichrist* first reveals himself in the context of this conflict. The first passage is *Psalm 83*, written in the days of King David, while the second is in *Micah 5,* in a prophecy related to the birth pangs of Israel.

Psalm 83: The War on Terror

*...Keep not silence O God; do not be speechless and be not still O God. For lo, your enemies roar; and those who hate You have lifted up their head. They take shrewd counsel against **Your people**, and plot against **Your hidden ones**. ~ Psalm 83:1-3*

First, Asaph alludes to two groups: *"Your People,"* indicating the Nation of Israel, and *"Your hidden ones,"* alluding to the Gentile Church, a people that were hidden in a mystery throughout the Old Testament. This signifies that this Assyrian enemy would be against both Israel and the Church in the time that this prophecy unfolds.

*... "Come and **let us cut them off from being a nation,** so that the name Israel may be remembered no more." For with one heart they have plotted together; they have made a covenant against You. The tents of Edom and the Ishmaelites; of Moab and the Hagarites; Gebal, Ammon, and Amalek; the Philistines with the people of Tyre; and **Assyria has joined with them**; they have helped the sons of Lot...~ Psalm 83:4-8*

This list of nations should provoke curiosity, as there was never an ancient time when all these nations were in an alliance against Israel. At the time this prophecy was written, not only was Assyria not mentioned as a threat, but the King of Tyre was an ally and friend of King David and Solomon, supplying the master foreman and the wood for the building of the temple. This conspiracy to destroy Israel has been underway for some time and is now unfolding even as we speak. These people represent several cities and regions, that seem to have alliances that transcend national boundaries and ethnic relationships. These groups represent offshoots from the Muslim Brotherhood, whose original charter called for the destruction of Israel. If these cities were traced to the terrorist groups rooted in them, they would include Al Qaeda, Hamas, Hezbollah, and ISIS. Recently ISIS has sought to consolidate all of them into a revived Caliphate, having its capital in the original Assyrian territory.

> *Do to them as to Midian, as to Sisera, as to Jabin at the torrent Kishon; who perished at Endor; they became as dung for the earth. Make their nobles like Oreb, and like Zeeb; yea, all their princes like Zebah, and like Zalmunna; who said, "Let us take possession for ourselves of the houses of God." ~ Psalm 83:9-12*

In this passage there are two subtle allusions to the rise of *the Antichrist,* which have their source material in the Book of Judges. The first allusion is to Sisera *(Judges 4),* the general whom Jael kills by driving a tent peg through his head. This *mortal headwound* foreshadows the wound by which *the Antichrist* dies, while being killed by a woman, signifies his being killed without the agency of man.

> *I saw one of his heads as it were wounded to death ~ Revelation 13:3*
> *...but he shall be broken without [a man's] hand. ~ Daniel 8:25*

The second allusion is to the story of Gideon. In this story, Gideon is offered the kingdom for delivering Israel from the Midianite kings. Gideon declines, but goes on to judge Israel, eventually passing the authority to his seventy sons. These seventy sons signify the nations in the Table of Nations *(Genesis 10),* foreshadowing a New World Order after this war. Gideon had a bastard son named Abimelech, who rose up and slaughtered his seventy brothers, foreshadowing how *the Antichrist* will subdue the nations just as Nimrod had before they were divided. Abimelech also received a *mortal headwound* while attacking a city, when its people took refuge in a strong tower. A rock was thrown from the tower by a woman, striking Abimelech, who said to his armor bearer, *"Draw your sword and slay me, so men do not say of me, "A woman killed him."* *(Judges 9:54).*

These signify that *the Antichrist* will first show himself within the context of this war, eventually resulting in a New World Order which will be usurped by him. While *Psalm 83* prophesies the onset of this war, *Micah 5* details its expansion.

Micah 5: The War Expands

Now gather yourself in troops daughter of a troop; one sets a siege against us; they shall strike the Judge of Israel with a rod on the cheek. And you, Bethlehem Ephrathah, you who are least among the thousands of Judah, out of you, He shall come forth to Me, to become Ruler in Israel, He whose goings forth have been from of old, from the days of eternity. ~ Micah 5:1-2

Because of the prophetic verse about the Messiah coming from Bethlehem, many scholars assume the whole of *Micah 5* is about him. However, the next passage clearly prophesies God hardening the Jews until Christ is preached to the ends of the earth, just as Paul teaches in *Romans 9-11*.

Therefore, He will give them over __until the time the one giving birth has given birth__; then the rest of His brothers shall return to the sons of Israel. And He shall stand and feed in the strength of Jehovah, in the majesty of the name of Jehovah His God, and they shall rest. For now, __He shall be great to the ends of the earth__. ~ Micah 5:3-4

The next verses mysteriously represent *the Antichrist*, being received as the *"Man of Peace,"* for delivering Israel from an Assyrian enemy who enters the land of Israel.

And this One [or Man] shall be [our] peace. When Assyria shall come into our land; and when he shall walk in our palaces, then we shall raise against him __seven shepherds and eight principal men__. And they shall assault the land of Assyria with the sword, and the land of Nimrod at her own entrances. And he shall deliver us from Assyria when he comes into our land, and when he treads within our border. ... Your hand shall be high above your foes, and all your enemies shall be cut off. ~ Micah 5:5-9

The only other use of this idiom, *"seven, even eight"* is in signifying *the Antichrist*, who becomes an eighth through a *pseudo-resurrection*.

Here is the mind which has wisdom...And there are __seven kings__: five are fallen, and one is, and the other is not yet come; and when he comes, he must continue a short space. And the Beast that was, and is not, even he is __the eighth, and is of the seven, and goes into perdition__. ~ Revelation 17:9-11

The seven men, of which one is also the eighth, are seven kings that come to support Israel against this Assyrian invader, which are likely those involved in the present conflict in Syria and Iraq, fighting against ISIS in alignment with Israel's interests.

... "The fourth beast shall be the fourth kingdom upon earth, which shall be diverse from all kingdoms, and shall devour the whole earth, and shall tread it down and break it in

[95]

*pieces. And **the ten horns out of this kingdom are ten kings that shall arise**: and another shall rise after them; and he shall be diverse from the first, and **he shall subdue three kings**." ~ Daniel 7:23-24*

Currently, ten of the most powerful nations in the world are fighting a proxy war in Syria, all of them under the guise of "fighting a war on terror" against ISIS and other groups. These nations have varied goals, with seven of them supporting Western economic interests and the other three supporting Eastern economic interests. If the Western alliance were to prevail, they would remove three kings (Russia, Iran, and China) from being in the land, literally *"subduing"* and *"plucking them up" (Daniel 7:8)*. While this may not be the intended interpretation of this passage, it is a notable coincidence, which may at least foreshadow the geopolitical conquests of *the Antichrist* in the last days.

It is indicated by the words *"we shall raise,"* that it is not the Lord doing the saving, but Israel in their own manipulations, being helped by this *"man of peace."* The remainder of the passage indicates that afterward, the Lord will humble Israel, causing them to forsake the work of their hands before executing judgement on the nations around them.

> *And it shall be **in that day**, says the LORD, I will cut off your horses out of your midst, and I will destroy your chariots. And I will cut off the cities of your land and throw down all your strongholds. … and you shall never again worship **the work of your hands**. And I will pluck your shrines out of the midst of you; so, I will destroy your cities. And **I will execute vengeance in anger and fury on the nations**, such as they have not heard.* ~ Micah 5:10-15

As of 2019, this war in Syria has raged now for eight years, as the culmination of the War on Terror and the Arab Spring. This ongoing war began with the Iraq war in the 1990s, and has since overturned nearly every government in the Middle East and North Africa that would traditionally ally with Russia, China, and Iran against Western interests. Every nation targeted has been overthrown except for Syria, whose capital Damascus is prophesied to be permanently destroyed. *Ezekiel 38* gives the context in which this will come about.

Ezekiel 38: Israel Invaded

The interpretation of *Ezekiel 38* is contended, because like many prophecies in the Old Testament, it has a dual fulfillment. This war occurs immediately before *Daniel's*

70th week, later repeating itself at the end of the Millennium, as it is recorded in *Revelation 20*.

> *Now the word of the LORD came to me, saying, "Son of man, set your face against Gog, of the land of Magog, the prince of Rosh, Meshech, and Tubal, and prophesy against him, and say, 'Thus says the Lord GOD: "Behold, I am against you, O Gog, the prince of Rosh, Meshech, and Tubal.* **<u>I will turn you around, put hooks into your jaws</u>**, *and lead you out, with all your army, horses, and horsemen, all splendidly clothed, a great company with bucklers and shields, all of them handling swords." ~ Ezekiel 38:1-4*

Some scholars believe that Turkey will lead this invasion, because many of these ancient nations have cities named for them in Anatolia. However, it should be noted that Ararat in Eastern Turkey was the place where Noah's Ark came to rest; where Noah's descendants originally lived and many of them likely had cities named after them. At the time this prophecy was written, Eastern Turkey was called Assyria, while Western Turkey was called Grecia. Since Ezekiel and Daniel mention these nations in other prophecies and neither of them are mentioned in this prophecy, it is unlikely that Turkey will be included in this invasion.

Also, regarding *"Rosh,"* there is contention as to whether this is a proper name because this word is often translated *"chief"* in the Old Testament. One should note that Benjamin had as son by this name *(Genesis 46:21)*, and multiple translations support Rosh being a national people including the Greek Septuagint (LXX), published in a time near to this prophecy being given. It is supported by ancient Assyrian archeology that a people known as the *Rosh* existed to the north of Assyria in the time of their kingdom.

Regarding the identity of these nations: Magog is the predecessor of Mongolia, which made up the northern horse-riding tribes, once called Scythians. The descendants of Magog spanned from Korea in the East, once called "Goguryeu," to Hungary in the west, where the descendants of Attila the Hun finally settled. Being the chief nation in the North during the time of Ezekiel, their influence grew to encompass what is now primarily called Russia. Rosh is the ancient name for the Rus, who inhabited Ukraine, and from where the name "Russia" comes, while the descendants of Meshech founded Moscow. Finally, Tubal is the ancient name for Tbilisi, the capitol of Georgia, that sits just beneath the modern Russian border.

> *Persia, Cush, and Put are with them, all of them with shield and helmet; Gomer and all its troops; the house of Togarmah from the far north and all its troops-many people are*

with you. Prepare yourself and be ready, you and all your companies that are gathered about you; and be a guard for them. ~ Ezekiel 38:5-6

Regarding the remaining nations: Persia is Iran, Cush is Sudan, and Put is Libya. Gomer fathered the Armenians, being the eldest grandson of Noah and inheritor of the land surrounding the Ark. Finally, the house of Togarmah occupied the Central Asian lands of the Turkish peoples, whose core nation was once called Turkmenistan. These nations, though unrelated in culture and ethnic heritage, will find a common enemy in the western powers. These nations have traditionally been armed by Russia, and will ultimately fall in as supporting armies, when their coalition tries to take over the Middle East against the Western coalition of NATO.

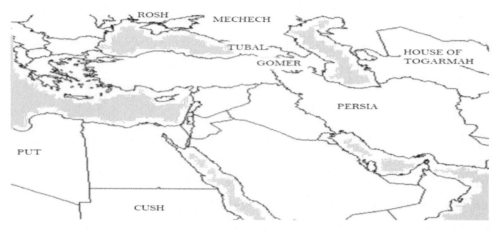

Opposing these nations will be a western coalition, which will be allied with Israel and Saudi Arabia. Because World War III will have global implications, their capacity to support Israel will be extremely limited.

> *... In the latter years you will come into the land of those brought back from the sword and gathered from many people on the mountains of Israel, which had long been desolate; they were brought out of the nations, and now all of them dwell safely..."On that day it shall come to pass that thoughts will arise in your mind, and you will make an evil plan: You will say, "I will go up against a land of unwalled villages; I will go to a peaceful people, who dwell safely, all of them dwelling without walls, and __having neither bars nor gates, to take plunder and to take booty__, to stretch out my hand against the waste places that are again inhabited, and against a people gathered from the nations, who have acquired livestock and goods, who dwell in the midst of the land."*
>
> __*Sheba, Dedan, and the merchants of Tarshish, with all their young lions*__ *will say to you, "Have you come to take plunder? Have you gathered your army to take booty, to carry away silver and gold, to take away livestock and goods, to take great plunder?"*
> *~ Ezekiel 38:8-13*

[98]

While the primary target of this invasion is clearly Israel, another prophecy in Jeremiah suggests that Saudi Arabia may also be a target of this invasion, although requiring the conquest of Israel to be successful.

> *Flee, get afar off, dwell deep, O you inhabitants of Hazor (Saudi Arabia), … Arise, get you up unto the wealthy nation,* ***that dwell without care, says the LORD, which have neither gates nor bars****, which dwell alone. And* ***their camels shall be a booty, and the multitude of their cattle a spoil****: and I will scatter into all winds them that are in the utmost corners; and I will bring their calamity from all sides thereof, says the LORD.* ~ Jeremiah 49:30-32

Also mentioned are *Tarshish and its young lions*. Tarshish was a Japhetite people, who had cities on the far side of the Mediterranean, with whom Tyre would trade in Ezekiel's day. Their trade goods show that they were predecessors of England, who were known to trade in tin, as well as the other minerals listed here.

> *Tarshish was your merchant by reason of the multitude of all kind of riches; with silver, iron, tin, and lead, they traded in your fairs.* ~ Ezekiel 27:12

If Tarshish represents England, its merchants, or *"young lions,"* are its former colonies in the United States, Canada, and Australia. While this prophecy focuses on Israel, they will have allies; though these allies may be too busy with their own battle fronts to come to the aid of Israel as this war progresses.

> *So, son of man, prophesy and say to Gog, says the Lord Jehovah: "In that day when My people of Israel dwell securely, shall you not know it? And you shall come from your place out of the recesses of the north, you and many peoples with you, …* ***It shall be in the latter days****, and I will bring you against My land, so that the nations may know Me when I shall be sanctified in you, O Gog, before their eyes."*
>
> *So, says the Lord Jehovah: "****Are you he of whom I have spoken in former days, by the hand of My servants the prophets of Israel****, who prophesied in those days and years, that I would bring you against them?"* ~ Ezekiel 38:14-18

The reference by the Lord to having mentioned Gog by other prophets confirms that this is the same northern army spoken of in *Joel chapter 2*. Joel indicates that the army involved in this invasion is the largest to be seen for years to come. This army invades at the peak of human population prior to the Millennium. While Armageddon is also a great battle, it will occur after more than half the population of Earth is killed, meaning that the armies will be relatively small in comparison.

> *…* ***for the Day of the Lord comes, for it is near at hand****; A day of darkness and of gloominess, a day of clouds and of thick darkness, as the morning spread upon the*

mountains: ***a great people and a strong; there has not been ever the like, neither shall be after it, even to the years of many generations****. ~ Joel 2:1-2*

God is making it clear that He is causing this great army to come against Israel, to lead them to repentance and reliance on him, just as in *Joel 2.*

And the LORD shall utter His voice before His army: for his camp is very great: for He is strong that executes His word: for the Day of the Lord is great and very terrible; and who can abide it? ~ Joel 2: 11

Just as ancient Nineveh repented at the preaching of Jonah in hopes that God might relent from judging them, the remnant of Israel also becomes humbled at this invasion and calls for a solemn fast, in hopes that God might spare them.

Therefore also now, says the LORD, turn you even to me with all your heart, and with fasting, and with weeping, and with mourning: And rend your heart, and not your garments, and turn unto the LORD your God: for he is gracious and merciful, slow to anger, and of great kindness, and will repent of the evil. ***Who knows if He will return and repent****, and leave a blessing behind him; even a meat offering and a drink offering unto the LORD your God?*

Blow the trumpet in Zion, sanctify a fast, call a solemn assembly: Gather the people, sanctify the congregation, assemble the elders, gather the children, and those that suck the breasts: ***let the Bridegroom go forth of his chamber, and the Bride out of her closet****. ~ Joel 2:12-16*

The saying, *"let the Bridegroom go forth from his chamber, and the Bride out of her closet,"* takes care to designate separate rooms for the bride and bridegroom. This is not a wedding chamber, where the marriage is consummated, but separate rooms for a bride and bridegroom, to prepare for a wedding ceremony. By the Spirit, Israel is calling for the unification of the prophetic *Bride* and *Bridegroom*, which must occur before they are finally saved. This signifies the gathering for a wedding, which is another major theme of *The Revelation*. This prophetic symbol, indicates that the time of this war, is right before *Daniel's 70th week*, which will be demonstrated to encompass a week-long prophetic *wedding feast*. God will respond to Jerusalem's cry, and initiate their salvation, which will unfold as God removes their enemies and pours out His Spirit on them in the aftermath of this war.

Isaiah 17: The Destruction of Damascus

The destruction of Damascus will be a flash point, which causes the regional war to grow into a global nuclear conflict. While the prophecy does not indicate who destroys Damascus, it is clear that the results of its destruction will correspond with the remainder of the war in *Ezekiel 39*.

> *Behold, 1) Damascus is taken away from being a city, and it shall be a heap of ruins. 2) The cities of Aroer are forsaken... And 3) the fortress shall cease from Ephraim, and 4) the kingdom from Damascus, and the rest of Syria. They shall be as the glory of the sons of Israel, says the LORD of hosts. ~ Isaiah 17:1-3*

There are four distinct elements to the fulfillment of this prophecy:

1) Damascus must become a *heap of ruins,* never to be rebuilt.

2) *The cities of Aroer,* in the region north of Amman, Jordan, *will also be forsaken,* suggesting an evacuation.

3) *The fortress will cease from Ephraim,* suggesting a withdrawal of fortified settlements in the West Bank.

4) *The kingdom from Damascus,* will become *the glory of Jacob* suggesting that Syria and its territories will be annexed by Israel, being controlled as they were in the days of Solomon.

The only scenario that would make these prophecies a reality and that is a nuclear attack on Damascus and the Golan, causing an impassable blockade of nuclear radiation. Israel will be threatened by a great Northern Army, the likes of which the world has never known. Damascus would be the supply point for a northern attack on Israel, while the attack would be made through the Golan. In this desperate situation, Israel or an ally will employ this tactic to deter the invasion of Israel.

> *... in that day, the glory of Jacob shall be made thin, and the fatness of his flesh shall become lean. And it shall be **as reaping of the harvest grain***, *and his arm reaps the ears. And it shall be as he who gathers ears in the Valley of the Rephaim (the West Bank).* ***Yet gleaning grapes shall be left in it****... and his eyes shall have respect to the Holy One of Israel. And he shall not look to the altars, the work of his hands... Isaiah 17:4-7*

The sheaf of wheat symbolizes a map of Israel without the West Bank. If such a tactic were employed, the prevailing winds would take the fallout east and south, evacuating Syria, the West Bank, and Northern Jordan, pushing out the invaders as the area becomes devastated by radiation.

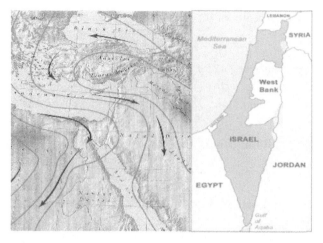

*In that day his strong cities shall be like a forsaken branch, and an uppermost branch; which they left because of the sons of Israel; and it will become a ruin... Woe to the multitude of many people, who make a noise like the noise of the seas; and to the rushing of nations who make a rushing like the rushing of mighty waters! The nations shall rush like the rushing of many waters; but God shall rebuke them, and they shall flee far off, ... **This is the lot of those who plunder us**, and the lot of those who rob us.*

~ Isaiah 17:9-14

Ezekiel 39: Global Nuclear War

*And you, son of man, prophesy against Gog, and say, "Thus says the Lord GOD: 'Behold, I am against you, O Gog, the prince of Rosh, Meshech, and Tubal; and **I will turn you around and lead you on, bringing you up from the far north**, and bring you against the mountains of Israel...You shall fall on the open field; for I have spoken,' says the Lord GOD. 'And **I will send fire on Magog and on those who live in security in the coastlands**. Then they shall know that I am the LORD.*

~ Ezekiel 39:1-6

The remainder of Ezekiel's prophecy suggests that nuclear war unfolds between Magog, representing modern Russia, and *them that dwell carelessly in the coastlands*. The Bible testifies that the earliest settlers in *"the coastlands"* were the children of Javan. Tarshish, a son of Javan, will ally with Israel in this war and represents England and her colonies, most likely representing the United States.

*And the sons of Javan (Greece): Elisha and **Tarshish** and Kittim and Dodanim. **By these were the coasts (or isles) of the nations divided** in their lands, everyone after his tongue, after their families, in their nations.* ~ Genesis 10:4

More likely it will not be Israel, but one of the seven allies from *Micah 5* that will initiate this nuclear conflict. Looking to *Ezekiel 39*, it is most likely that this ally is the

United States of America. This may begin with an attack on Damascus and then escalate to a full nuclear exchange between the two nations. This passage ends identically to *Isaiah 17*, with Israel plundering those who would plunder them.

> *Behold, it is coming, … This is the day of which I have spoken. And the inhabitants of the cities of Israel shall go out and shall set on fire and burn the weapons, both the shields and the bucklers, the bows and the arrows, and the javelins, and the spears. And **they shall burn them with fire seven years**, so that they shall take no wood out of the field, nor cut down any out of the forests, for they shall burn the weapons for fire. And **they shall plunder those who plundered them**, and rob those who robbed them, says the Lord Jehovah.* ~ Ezekiel 39: 8-10

The remainder of the passage indicates that this army which invades Israel will become a waste of radiated bones and will require a dedicated group of professionals to clean up the radiation for seven months after the war ends.

> *"And it will be in that day I will give to Gog a place there, a grave in Israel, the valley of those who pass by, east of the sea. And it shall stop the noses of those who pass by. And there they shall bury Gog and all his multitude. And they shall call it, The Valley of the Multitude of Gog. And the house of Israel shall bury them, to cleanse the land, seven months. And all the people of the land shall bury…And men shall separate those who continually pass through the land, burying those who passed through, who remain on the face of the earth, to cleanse it. At the end of seven months they shall search. And as they pass, those who pass through the land, and any man sees a bone, then he shall build a post beside it, until the buriers have buried it in The Valley of the Multitude of Gog. And also, the name of the city is Hamon-Gog. And they shall cleanse the land…So says the Lord Jehovah.* ~ Ezekiel 39:7-16

After the war, a treaty will be made for seven years involving a surrender of nuclear material to peaceful purposes. Israel seems to give up the West Bank as an independent state, dividing the land *(Joel 3:2)*, while most of it residents, along with those of the Gaza strip and southern Lebanon, are relocated to Saudi Arabia, likely to be employed in the construction of Neom. At the signing of this peace treaty, which will include provisions to rebuild the temple and reinstitute the sacrificial system, *Daniel's 70th week* will commence, initiating the final salvation of Israel.

The Return of the Jews from America

In *Isaiah 18*, a mysterious nation is mentioned *"beyond the rivers of Cush, whose lands the rivers divide."* This land is described as having many similarities with ancient Cush, but is unnamed because it does not represent Cush, but the United States of America which did not yet exist.

*Woe to the land shadowed with buzzing wings, which is beyond the rivers of Cush, which sends ambassadors by sea, even in vessels of reed on the waters, saying, "Go, swift messengers, to **a nation tall and smooth of skin**, to a people terrible from their beginning onward, a nation powerful and treading down, whose land the rivers divide."*
~ Isaiah 18:1-2

This *"land of whirring wings"* may represent planes and helicopters, which were first produced in the United States. The United States is divided East and West by the Ohio and Missouri Rivers, emptying into the Mississippi River in the same way that the White Nile and the Blue Nile begin in Ethiopia and South Sudan to meet in North Sudan, forming the Nile River that flows through Egypt.

The American natives were known for being exceptionally tall, averaging 5 feet 8 inches in the 1700s, making them the tallest people in the world at that time. They were also known for being smooth skinned, most of them having no facial or body hair. However, the Hebrew words <mashak> and <mowrot> can also mean, *"spread out"* and *"independent,"* a good representation of the American people. Like the ancient Cushites had papyrus ships, the Native Americans were known for their birch-bark canoes, made of a paper-like covering which they also used for writing material. The American nation became a leading naval power, sending out ambassadors worldwide and being known and feared throughout the world.

*All people of the world and dwellers on the earth, you will see as one lifts up a **banner** on the peaks. And you will hear as the blowing of a trumpet. For so the LORD said to me, I will take My rest, and I will look on in My dwelling place, like a clear heat in the sunshine, like a cloud of dew in the heat of harvest.* ~ Isaiah 18:3-4

The Americans proved to be a people who were *terrible from their beginning onward,* arising in rebellion and conquest. They subjugated the native tribes and created a slave caste in the name of "manifest destiny," while at the same time raising a banner of "liberty" under which all the nations were invited to gather.

*For before the harvest, when the bud is perfect, and the sour grape is ripening in the flower, then He will cut off the sprigs with pruning hooks and take away and cut down the branches. **They shall be left together to the birds of the mountains, and to the Beasts of the earth**; and the birds shall summer on them, and all the Beasts of the earth shall winter on them. In that time shall be brought to the LORD of hosts the present from a tall and smooth people, terrifying, from its beginning and onward; a mighty and trampling nation whose land the rivers have divided, to the place of the name of the LORD of hosts, Mount Zion.* ~ Isaiah 18:5-7

This prophecy claims that this nation will bring a gift to the Lord in the land of Israel *"before the harvest,"* at a time when their branches are cut and they are left to *"the Beasts of the earth and the fouls of the air."* This seems to suggest that America will be weakened and withdrawn from its lofty place, given to the Beasts of the earth (The last days superpowers), and *the fouls of the air* (demonic powers) before *the harvest (the Rapture).* The gift that they will bring to the *"place of the names of the Lord of Hosts,"* likely represents the six million Jews that still reside in the United States, finally returning to their homeland in Israel.

> *Therefore so says the Lord Jehovah: And I will return the captivity of Jacob, and will have mercy on the whole house of Israel, and will be jealous for My holy name; after they have borne their shame and all their sins, by which they have sinned against Me, when they dwell securely in their land and no one terrifies; **when I have brought them again from the peoples, and gathered them out of their enemies' lands**, and am sanctified in them, in the sight of many nations; then they shall know that I am the LORD their God, who exiled them among the nations. But I have gathered them to their own land and **have not left any of them there**. Nor will I hide My face from them anymore, for I have poured out My Spirit on the house of Israel, says the Lord Jehovah.*
>
> *~ Ezekiel 39:21-29*

Both Joel 2 and Ezekiel 39 reflect a complete regathering of Israel back to the Promised Land, and an outpouring of God's Spirit upon them. However, it should be noted that this repentance is not a wholesale salvation of the entire ethnic people. While many will come to faith at this victory and the subsequent preaching of the 144,000, many will put their trust in the Antichrist as he fulfills the expected accomplishments of the Messiah on their behalf. The outcome of this war is foreshadowed by Isaiah during the reign of Hezekiah, at a time when Jerusalem was invaded by a great northern army from Assyria. Hezekiah compares his distress to birth pangs and pleads for mercy, knowing that Jerusalem cannot save themselves apart from a deliverance at the hands of the Lord.

> *And it came to pass, when king Hezekiah heard it, that he rent his clothes, and covered himself with sackcloth, and went into the house of the LORD. And… Hezekiah said, "This day is a day of trouble, and of rebuke, and of blasphemy: for **the children are come to the birth**, and there is not strength to bring forth." ~ Isaiah 37:14*

Hezekiah cries out to God for deliverance, to which God responds by sending an Angel to strike the Assyrian army and to deliver Jerusalem *(Isaiah 37).* After this, the King of Babylon sends envoys to Hezekiah, feigning peace and goodwill. Hezekiah shows the envoys his treasuries rather than giving glory to God and for this reason, Isaiah prophesies that the Jews will go into captivity to Babylon *(Isaiah 39)*.

> *I will put my hook in your nose, and my bridle in your lips, and I will turn you back by the way by which you came:* ~ *2nd Kings 19:28*
>
> *And I will turn you back, and put hooks into your jaws, and I will bring you forth, and all thine army… ~ Ezekiel 38:4*

The figure of hooks links this Assyrian invasion to invasion of the great Northern Army of *Ezekiel 38* and *Joel 2*. The army of God's judgement, which He turned away from Jerusalem in the days of Hezekiah, will return to invade Israel in the latter days. God is foreshadowing that after Israel is delivered from this great Northern Army, its leaders will fail to give glory to God, and through this arrogance, they will invite *the Antichrist* into their land, ultimately falling into bondage to him.

The Collateral Damage: The 3rd, 4th, and 5th Seals

While the first two seals describe the spiritual and military overturning of the Earth, the next three seals will demonstrate the collateral damage that will occur. These consequences are a worldwide economic collapse, the death of one fourth of mankind, and the martyrdom of Christians throughout the nations.

> *When He opened the third seal, I heard the third living creature say, "Come and see." So, I looked, and behold, a black horse, and he who sat on it had a pair of scales in his hand. And I heard a voice in the midst of the four living creatures saying, "A quart of wheat for a denarius, and three quarts of barley for a denarius; and do not harm the oil and the wine." ~ Revelation 6:5-6*

Several major factors will be contributing to the economic collapse in these times: The crashing fiat economies of the world, deliberate destruction of resources by enemies at war, natural disasters and plagues exhausting emergency resources, and the storing of supplies to support a remnant that will hide away underground. Droughts, fires, floods, and the feeding of armies will lead the world to such a state of famine that an entire days' wages will barely be enough to buy a daily ration of food.

> *When He opened the fourth seal, I heard the voice of the fourth living creature saying, "Come and see." So, I looked, and behold, a pale horse. And the name of him who sat on it was Death, and Hades followed with him. And power was given to them over a fourth of the earth, to kill with sword, with hunger, with death, and by the beasts of the earth.*
> *~ Revelation 6:7-8*

While the casualties will accumulate to one fourth of the world's population, many will be the result of persecution; not be a natural byproduct of war, but a deliberate measure of the governments of the world, seeking a scapegoat for the war.

> And when he had opened the fifth seal, I saw under the altar the souls of them that were slain for the Word of God, and for the testimony which they held: And they cried with a loud voice, saying, "How long, O Lord, holy and true, **<u>will you not judge,</u>** and avenge our blood on them that dwell on the earth?" And white robes were given unto every one of them; and it was said unto them, that **<u>they should rest yet for a little season</u>**, until their fellow servants also and their brethren, that should be killed as they were, should be fulfilled. ~ Revelation 6:9-11

Coinciding with the Letter to the Church of Philadelphia, the perfection of the saints will come through the faithful witness of the persecuted as they are martyred throughout the world. Liberal churches, who affirm an interreligious equality, will seek exemption from persecution. In fear and hypocrisy, they will betray faithful Christians, either by their silence or by delivering them over to execution.

> Then they will deliver you up to tribulation and kill you, and you will be hated by all nations for My name's sake. Many will be offended, will betray one another, and will hate one another. Then many false prophets will rise up and deceive many, and because lawlessness will abound, the love of many will grow cold. ~ Matthew 24:9-12

The Sixth Seal: The End of the War

The war is halted by a great shaking of the earth. This shaking will be accompanied by signs in the heavens which will lead many to believe that the wrath of God has come. For those who hate the appearing of Christ, they will assume that He has come and flee to underground strongholds. Undiscerning Christians will believe these are the final signs of the apocalypse and may believe the deception to follow.

> And when He had opened the sixth seal, I looked, and behold, there was a great earthquake. And the (1) sun became black as sackcloth of hair, and the moon became like blood. And the (2) stars of heaven fell to the earth, even as a fig tree casts her untimely figs when she is shaken by a mighty wind. And (3) the heaven departed like a scroll when it is rolled together. And (4) every mountain and island were moved out of their places.

> And the kings of the earth, and the great men, and the rich, and the chief captains, and the mighty men, and every bondman, and every freeman, hid themselves in the dens, and in the rocks of the mountains. And they said to the mountains and rocks, "Fall on us, and hide us from the face of Him sitting on the throne, and from the wrath of the Lamb; for the great day of His wrath has come, and who will be able to stand?"

> ~ Revelation 6:12-17

Looking at the four signs here, it appears that a great planetary object will pass by the earth, causing the effects of both a solar and lunar eclipse at the same time. It will also cause a meteor showers or satellites to fall from the sky and the poles to shift, moving all the landmarks of earth from their alignment to the stars, *"moving them from their place."* Isaiah 24 parallels this time when the Gospel is preached throughout the earth during a time of worldwide famine and deception in the earth.

> *Behold, the LORD makes the earth empty, and makes it waste, and **turns it upside down**, and scatters abroad the inhabitants thereof… Therefore, the curse has devoured the earth, and those who dwell in it are desolate. Therefore, the inhabitants of the earth are burned, and few men are left. ~ Isaiah 24:1-6*

> *From the ends of the earth we have heard songs: "Glory to the righteous!" But I said, "I am ruined, ruined! Woe to me! The treacherous dealers have dealt treacherously, Indeed, the treacherous dealers have dealt very treacherously."*

> *The earth is violently broken; the earth is split open; the earth is shaken exceedingly. The earth shall reel to and fro like a drunkard and shall totter like a hut; Its transgression shall be heavy upon it, and it will fall, and not rise again. ~ Isaiah 24:16-20*

Just as in *Revelation 6*, in this prophecy the Sun turns dark, the Moon turns red, and the elite of the earth gather underground to hide from the Lord during a great shaking of the earth.

> *And it shall be in that day, the LORD shall punish the host of the high place on high, and on the kings of the earth on the earth. And they shall be gathered as prisoners are gathered in a dungeon. And they shall be shut up in the prison, and after many days they shall be judged. Then **the moon shall blush, and the sun shall be ashamed**, when the LORD of hosts shall reign in Mount Zion, in Jerusalem, and gloriously before His elders. ~ Isaiah 24:21-23*

This event is foreshadowed in *Joshua 10*, when a great sign in the heavens is followed by the kings of Canaan hiding in caves.

> *Then Joshua spoke to the LORD…**And the sun stood still, and the moon stood still**, until the people had avenged themselves on their enemies. … And the sun stood still in the midst of the heavens and did not hasten to go down about a whole day. And there was no day like that before it or after it, that the LORD listened to the voice of a man. For the LORD fought for Israel. ~ Joshua 10:12-14*

> *And Joshua returned, and all Israel with him, to the camp at Gilgal. But **these five kings fled and hid themselves in a cave at Makkedah**. … Joshua said, "**Roll great stones on the mouth of the cave and set men by it in order to keep them**.*
> *~ Joshua 10:15-18*

In the days of Joshua, after the Sun and Moon stood still for a whole day, an astronomical change was recorded in all the earth. Prior to this event all the ancient calendars of the known world that once calculated a 360-day year suddenly lost their accuracy, and to this day, the year is calculated at 364 ¼ days. Some similar event may occur here, causing the earth to return to a 360-day year, allowing for the pinpoint accuracy of all the prophecies related to *Daniel's 70th week*.

Before *Daniel's 70th week* begins, God will pour out his Spirit on the remnant of Israel that were brought to repentance at this war. Like the Apostles at Pentecost, 144,000 young men will be sealed and sent out to preach the gospel throughout Israel until Christ comes. The next chapter will show that these witnesses are the groomsmen of the Lamb who will follow the Bridegroom wherever He goes.

PART 6 - THE WEDDING PARTY

When God first foretold that Israel would be sent into captivity, He assured them that their salvation would come in three steps:

> And it shall come to pass, when all these things are come upon you...you shall return unto the LORD your God and shall obey His voice. Then the LORD your God will turn your captivity...and (1) **_will return and gather you from all the nations_**, whither the LORD your God has scattered you...(2) And the LORD your God **_will circumcise your heart_**, ... to love the LORD your God with all your heart, and with all your soul, that you may live. (3) And the LORD your **_God will put all these curses upon your enemies_**, and on them that hate you, which persecuted you. ~ Deuteronomy 30:1-7

The *circumcision of the heart* is the sealing of the Holy Spirit when one is *"born again"* (Romans 2:29). For Israel, this occurs *after* they are regathered into the Land, but *before* God punishes their enemies, ending their captivity to the Gentiles.

> Be glad then, sons of Zion, and rejoice in the LORD your God. For He has given you the former rain according to righteousness, and He will cause the rain to come down for you, **_the former rain and the latter rain_** in the first month...And it shall be afterward, **_I will pour out My Spirit on all flesh_**. And your sons and your daughters shall prophesy; your old men shall dream dreams; your young men shall see visions. And also, I will pour out My Spirit on the menservants and on the maidservants in those days.
> ~ Joel 2:18-19

This *"former and latter rain,"* is a mysterious idiom representing the bookends of the ingathering of the Gentiles, starting with the great outpouring of the Holy Spirit on the believing Jews at Pentecost, and ending with the outpouring of the Spirit on believing Israel in the last days. This idiom is found repeatedly in Scripture, being given exclusively to Jewish audiences, while being omitted from any epistles written to the Gentile churches.

> *... if you will listen carefully to My commandments which I command you today, to love the LORD your God and to serve Him with all your heart and with all your soul, **I will give the rain of your land in its due season, the former and the latter rain**, that you may gather in your grain and your wine and your oil.*
> ~ *Deuteronomy 11:13-14*
>
> *Come and let us return to the LORD.... **After two days** He will bring us to life; in the third day He will raise us up, and we shall live in His sight. Then we shall know, if we follow on to know the LORD. His going out is prepared as the morning; and **He shall come to us as the rain, as the latter and former rain to the earth**.* ~ *Hosea 6:1-3*
>
> **Ask rain from the LORD in the time of the latter rain**. *The LORD shall make storm clouds, and He gives them showers of rain, grass to everyone in the field.*
> ~ *Zechariah 10: 1*
>
> *... be patient brothers, until the coming of the Lord. Behold, the farmer waits for the precious fruit of the earth and has long patience for it, until **He receives the early and the latter rain**. You also be patient, establish your hearts, for the coming of your Lord draws near.* ~ *James 5: 7*

This *latter rain* reflects the final repentance of Israel before the coming of the Lord. According to *Hosea 6*, this occurs *"after two days,"* which indicates a time exceeding two thousand years from Christ's ascension (29-33 AD). Like the original disciples at Pentecost, these servants are sealed by the Holy Spirit for redemption.

> *And after these things I saw four angels standing on the four corners of the earth, holding the four winds of the earth so that the wind should not blow on the earth, nor on the sea, nor on any tree. And I saw another angel ascending from the east, having the seal of the living God. And he cried with a loud voice to the four angels, to whom it was given to hurt the earth and the sea, saying, "Do not hurt the earth or the sea or the trees until **we have sealed** the servants of our God in their foreheads." ~ Revelation 7:1-3*

Here, a dangerous error has been put forward by the Dispensationalists. Because they assume that *the Rapture* has already occurred, they must make sense of *Revelation 7*, which represents an innumerable host of Gentile saints who *"come out of tribulation."* To reconcile this passage, they invent a second group called, "Tribulation Saints" who

[112]

are convinced by this mysterious disappearance at the rapture to accept Christ, being afterward led by these 144,000 Jewish believers.

One should note that there was never a teaching in Scripture, or in the early church, of a *"great harvest"* after *the Rapture*. While this may sound ideal, there is no Scripture to suggest that the 144,000 evangelize anyone outside of ethnic Israel. In fact, Scripture states that the Jews will not be redeemed until *"**after** the fulness of the Gentiles come in" (Romans 11:25)*. It should be considered indicative of the fact that *the fullness of the Gentiles* is completed that these Israelites are being sealed.

Rather than a *great harvest*, Christ warned of evil growing worse, bringing about a *great apostasy* and trials in the church until the very end. He does not promise to pour out His Spirit again on the nations after they have rejected the Gospel. Rather, He sends on them a great delusion, so that they will believe the lie and are gathered to worship *the Antichrist*. This *apostasy* was taught repeatedly by Jesus and the Apostles *(Matthew 24:4; 2nd Thessalonians 2:3; 2nd Peter 2; Jude 1:11-12 & 1st John. 2:18-19)*.

Biblically speaking, there is only one *"great harvest,"* which is the offer of salvation, through preaching the Gospel to the Nations. Remembering the seventy nations in the original Table of Nations of *Genesis 10*, Jesus sent seventy Apostles after the initial twelve, to foreshadow his intent to evangelize the Gentiles.

> *…**the Lord appointed seventy others**, And He sent them two by two before His face into every city and place where He was about to come. Then He said to them, **"The harvest truly is great**, but the laborers are few. Therefore, pray to the Lord of the harvest that He may send forth laborers into His harvest." ~ Luke 10:1-2*

Jesus sent out the original twelve, knowing that they would be rejected by Israel, and immediately sent out seventy as well, to signify his sovereignty over their being sent to the Gentiles. This was always his plan, knowing that a day would come, after the Gentiles were grafted in, that he would again send out ministers to reap the harvest of Israel. So, when he sent out the twelve, he gave them the prophecy:

> *…when they persecute you in this city, flee into another; for truly I say to you, "In no way shall you have finished the cities of Israel until the Son of Man comes."*
> *~ Matthew 10:23*

This prophecy, involving disciples evangelizing the cities of Israel until Christ comes, will be fulfilled by the 144,000 after *the fulness of the Gentiles come in*. While they are busy about their work and before they have gone to all the cities of Israel, the Lord will come to rapture them along with the Church as the *great harvest* is completed.

> *They sang as it were a new song before the throne, before the four living creatures, and the elders; and no one could learn that song except the hundred and forty-four thousand who __were redeemed from the earth__.* ~ Revelation 14:3

> *And another angel came out of the temple, crying with a loud voice to Him who sat on the cloud, "Thrust in Your sickle and reap, for the time has come for You to reap, for __the harvest of the earth is ripe__."* ~ Revelation 14:15

Remember, that according to Ephesians, two things apply to those who have come to a saving faith. The first, is that they have been sealed for redemption by the Holy Spirit *(Ephesians 1:14)*, and second is that they are *"seated in heaven" (Ephesians 2:6)*. Their appearing in heaven in John's vision does not necessarily mean that they have been raptured. Understanding these things helps to clarify the true meaning of *Revelation 7* for what it represents, not a second great harvest, but a royal wedding party, who will engage in a week-long wedding feast throughout *Daniel's 70ᵗʰ week.*

Revealing the Wedding Party

The whole Bible is a story of a wedding, from its first marriage in *Genesis 2*, to its final marriage in *Revelation 21*. The whole Gospel is about the injured marital relationship of Adam and Eve being redeemed in Christ and the Church. It is by this wedding that the Kingdom of Israel makes peace with the Kingdom of the Gentiles. This wedding, involving a Jewish King and a *Gentile Bride*, is replete throughout the Bible and leads us to *Daniel's 70ᵗʰ week*, the Seven Day Wedding Feast that was foreshadowed in the stories of Jacob and of Samson.

The pattern of the *Gentile Bride* joining the sovereign of God's people begins in Genesis. A type of the *Bride* is found in Sarah, who, being the half-sister of Abraham, was both sister and *Bride*, like the Shulamite, who Solomon called *"My Sister, My Bride" (Songs 4:9)*. Sarah is the first type of the Church, who being adopted of the father and having been begotten of the Spirit, is at once both the sister of Christ and the *Bride of Christ*. After this, Abraham was separated from the Nations and two great kingdoms were formed, being later called, "Israel" and the "Nations" (or the "Jews and Gentiles"). One represented the people who were set redeemed unto the Lord, while the other represented those held captive to Satan.

After this, the heir of the holy people would always go to the nations to secure a *Bride*. First, in *Genesis 24, the Servant* (Eliezer) left the camp, at the request of *the Father* (Abraham), to gather a *Bride* (Rebekah), for *the Son* (Isaac), sealing her with a nose ring, and leading her to the *Promised Land,* where she entered the son's house and consummated the marriage, thus becoming his wife. In a type, it was shown that the Holy Spirit, the Servant of the Godhead, would collect, seal, and lead the *Bride* to *the Son,* to finally consummate the marriage at *the Rapture.* Because of this, Paul said, *"I have betrothed you to One Husband" (2nd Corinthians 11:2).*

After this, twins were born to Isaac and Rebecca, and because Jacob was persecuted by Esau, he fled to the Gentiles and there bargained for a *Bride.* Just as Christ came first for Israel, but found no fruit there, Jacob first worked for Rachel, but was given Leah instead. After Jacob had married her and had consummated the marriage, he was told by her father, *"finish her week, and you may have her sister also" (Genesis 29:27).* Leah, whom Jacob knew during the week, would be his *Bride* from whom most of his sons came, a type of the Gentile Church. Rachael, for whom he had come first, would only bear children at the very end. Similarly, Christ came first for the children of Israel, but would not be received until the very end, after He consummates his relationship to the *Gentile Bride* during *Daniel's 70th week.*

After being rejected by his brethren, Joseph would receive a *Gentile Bride (Genesis 41:45).* Her Children, representing the Church, would be adopted into Israel *(Genesis 48:5),* becoming more numerous and occupying the largest part of the *Promised Land.* Moses also, who fled from Egypt, would receive a *Gentile Bride (Exodus 2:21),* by whose Father he would be instructed not to rule alone, but to appoint others *to co-rule (Exodus 18:17-27).* These were the seventy elders, after the seventy sons of Israel who went into Egypt *(Exodus 24:1),* another type of the Gentile Church who will rule with Christ throughout the Millennium.

After this, Rahab the harlot would foreshadow the redeemed *Gentile Bride,* who believed the witness of the two spies and hung the scarlet from her window *(Joshua 6),* receiving not only her life, but marriage to Salmon, who would father Boaz and the line of David *(Matthew 1:5).* Likewise, Ruth was redeemed by Boaz, though she was a Moabite and forbidden from the tribes of Israel *(Deuteronomy 23:3-6),* becoming the great-grandmother of David. Later David, who being persecuted from Israel, also gathered a wife from a Gentile King *(1st Chronicles 3: 2).* Finally, Solomon, despite having hundreds of wives, found true love in the Shulamite, a black skinned foreigner from Kedar, loving her beyond the daughters of Jerusalem *(Songs 1:5)*. Each of these foreshadow Christ, eternally destined to have a *Gentile Bride*.

Now Samson, who *"defeated his enemies more in his death than in his life"* *(Judges 16:30)*, was in this way a type of Christ. Samson also married a Gentile, a Philistine woman, which was by the Lord *(Judges 14:4)*. When he asked for her, he was given a feast by his father, and by custom, thirty men were gathered to be his companions. In the story, Samson challenged these men with a riddle. After the 4th day, the companions sought out his bride for the answer, now calling her *"the wife of Samson"* *(Judges 14:15)*. Just as Jacob would know his *Gentile Bride* in the midst of the week, so would Samson consummate his marriage in the midst of the week after the exchange of vows at the beginning. Understanding Samson's wedding feast is the key to understanding the 144,000 and their relationship to Christ and the Gentile Church during *Daniel's 70th week*.

A Hebrew wedding ceremony has three distinct stages even unto the present day:

1. **The Exchange of Vows**: In every culture, a public profession of intent to marry and remain faithful is made before witnesses, with some authority, being a father, king, judge, or ship's captain, to confirm the marital covenant. These vows must be exchanged in the presence of two witnesses to be valid.

2. **The Consummation:** While the vows would provide the intent, the covenant would not be ratified unless sealed with blood. For this reason, God designed women to bleed at the loss of their virginity. God intended every covenant to be confirmed by blood, foreshadowing Christ's blood poured out for us. The witnesses would guard the wedding chamber, observing the brides "tokens of virginity" as a witness to the union and the proof that the bride was a virgin.

3. **The Marriage Supper:** What we might call, "the reception dinner," is the introduction of the two as one; Husband and Wife, which the witnesses "receive" as one person. The wife would take the name of the Husband, foreshadowing being given a new name by Christ when we are born-again.

For convenience, we reverse the order of the honeymoon and the reception in modern weddings, but in ancient times, the proof of the bride's virginity was displayed publicly and given to the parents of the bride, so that in cases of annulment, they could prove by law that they provided their daughter as a virgin *(Deuteronomy 22:13-21)*. If the bride was not found to be a virgin, she would be stoned to death under the Law. Even in western weddings, the throwing of the flowers and the removing of the garter are both representations of the bride and groom announcing the bride's loss of virginity to her husband.

In the case of a royal wedding, a bride not being found a virgin could be a serious offense, potentially leading to war between nations that would have considered this wedding to be the bond of peace between them. In the story of Samson, the thirty companions were given by the Philistine father as careful insurance against such an offense. In *Revelation 7*, the 144,000, like the thirty companions of Samson, are the young virgin companions of the groom. Here is the first element of the wedding party as we see them sealed for this purpose.

If one were to search the Scriptures, the rest of the wedding party would be found. Just as the *Groom* has his *groomsmen* guarding the sanctity of the wedding, the *Bride* had her *bridesmaids;* young virgins who help to prepare and adorn her. Christ calls his original Jewish disciples, *"children of the Bridechamber" (Matthew 9:15),* as they are the ones who prepare the *Gentile Bride.* Likewise, John the Baptist calls himself *"the friend of the Bridegroom" (John 3:29),* being a near relative and the *Best Man.* The Father officiates the wedding while the Lamb is the *Groom.* Finally, the *Bride* appears; the party growing silent as the wedding begins. But before we move on to *the Bride,* being presented at the beginning of the wedding week, we must notice something. One of the Tribes is missing from the party.

The Lost Tribe of Dan

Most would breeze through this section, not bothering to notice the most important element. Understanding that Jesus is the Son of David, King of the Jews, his witnesses would come from every tribe, honoring the unity of the tribes, as this wedding would have national implications for all of Israel. Yet in this scenario, one tribe is inconspicuously absent.

And I heard the number of those who were sealed, one hundred and forty-four thousand, having been sealed out of __every tribe__ of the sons of Israel. Out of the tribe of Judah, twelve thousand were sealed. Out of the tribe of Reuben, twelve thousand were sealed. Out of the tribe of Gad, twelve thousand were sealed. Out of the tribe of Asher, twelve thousand had been sealed. Out of the tribe of Naphtali, twelve thousand were sealed. Out of the tribe of Manasseh, twelve thousand were sealed. Out of the tribe of Simeon, twelve thousand were sealed. Out of the tribe of Levi, twelve thousand were sealed. Out of the tribe of Issachar, twelve thousand were sealed. Out of the tribe of Zebulun, twelve thousand were sealed. Out of the tribe of Joseph, twelve thousand were sealed. Out of the tribe of Benjamin, twelve thousand were sealed. ~ *Revelation 7:4-9*

Unknown to many, there are actually thirteen tribes of Israel, as Jacob adopted Joseph's two sons near his death *(Genesis 48)*. Still, when the tribes are listed, God holds the number twelve intact, always naming twelve of the thirteen. Most of the time, the tribe of Levi is not listed, as they were the priestly class and not allowed to join the army or own land. However, in the Book of Chronicles and the Book of Revelation, the tribe of Dan is omitted. In Chronicles, Dan himself is mentioned and the city that bore is name, but nothing is recorded of his descendants. This suggests that the tribe of Dan has no part in the Kingdom of Israel, foreshadowing that Dan is the tribe from which *the Antichrist* comes. While the omission is subtle, the intent is clear when studied carefully.

Between the two wives of Jacob, Rachael was his first love, yet could not conceive, while Leah, having born multiple sons, failed to earn his love. Because of this, Rachael committed the same act that Sarah did, offering up her handmaid to bear her children. In this, Dan was the firstborn after the likeness of Ishmael, who was also a type of *the Antichrist*. Rachael believed the child to be the product of God judging her with infertility and named him Dan *(Genesis 30:6)*, which means, *"Judgement."* As Dan was the firstborn son of the favored wife, he might have prevailed as the ruler of the house of Jacob.

Leah would finally give up trying to earn Jacob's love, calling her fourth son Judah, meaning *"Praise" (Genesis 29:35)*, and deciding instead to praise the Lord for giving her so many sons. Judah, after laying down his life for his brother Benjamin, *(Genesis 44:33-44)* prevailed in the eyes of Jacob, and was given the rule of his brothers, alongside his brother Joseph. When Jacob prophesied what would come upon his sons in the latter days, of Judah he prophesied that the Messiah would come from his descendant David. But when he prophesied of Dan, he said,

Dan shall judge his people, as one of the tribes of Israel. **Dan shall be a serpent by the way***, an adder in the path, that bites the horse's heels, so its rider **falls backward**. I have waited for Your salvation, O LORD.* ~ *Genesis 49:16*

Jacob prophesied of Dan ensnaring Israel by confirming the Old Covenant, which will be fulfilled in *the Antichrist,* indicating that Israel will be *"waiting for salvation"* when this happens. Moses also prophesied of Dan saying,

Dan is a lion's whelp. *He shall leap from Bashan. ~ Deuteronomy 33:22*

By this, Moses would indicate his impersonation of Christ, who would come from Judah *(Genesis 49:9)*. For these reasons, the early church writers, Hippolytus of Rome and Ephrem the Syrian, both believed that *the Antichrist* would descend from Dan.

> *…Then that worthless and abominable dragon shall appear…When therefore the end of the world comes, that abominable, lying and murderous one is born from the tribe of Dan. ~ Ephrem the Syrian - On the Last Times (around 350 AD)*

> *"Dan," he says, "is a lion's whelp" and in naming the tribe of Dan, he declared clearly the tribe from which Antichrist is destined to spring. For as Christ springs from the tribe of Judah, so Antichrist is to spring from the tribe of Dan… What, then, is meant by the serpent but Antichrist, that deceiver who is mentioned in Genesis, who deceived… out of the tribe of Dan, then, that that tyrant and king, that dread judge, that son of the devil, is destined to spring and arise, the prophet testifies when he says, "Dan shall judge his people, as (he is) also one tribe in Israel"*

> *~ Hippolytus of Rome – On Christ and Antichrist (around 210 AD)*

While the Bible tells us nothing about Dan himself, his first descendant referenced is Aholiab, who along with Bezaleel of Judah, was gifted to build the tabernacle *(Exodus 31 & 36)*. In Judges, the Danites entice a grandson of Moses to set up a counterfeit religion, after sacking a city in Sidon *(Judges 17-18)*. The last Danite mentioned in Scripture is the son of a Danite woman and a man of Tyre. His name is Hiram, and he is sent by the King of Tyre to build Solomon's Temple *(2nd Kings 7:13-14 & 2nd Chronicles 2:13)*. This foreshadows the Antichrist, rebuilding Solomon's Temple.

When Deborah and Barak rallied the tribes to defeat the Midianites *(Judges 5:17)*, Deborah records the victory in song, marking those who would not come to his aid, saying of Dan, *"why did Dan remain in ships?"* The Danites would continue to trade with Tyre and eventually sail with the Greeks, mingling with them and disappearing from Israel *(Ezekiel 27:19)*. Just as Moses came from the House of Pharaoh, and finally revealed himself to be a Hebrew, *the Antichrist,* coming from Grecia, will eventually reveal himself to be a judge of Israel, helping them to rebuild their temple before deceiving them by claiming to be their Messiah and God.

Returning to the wedding assembly, we can see who is finally being indicated here, arrayed in white on her approach toward the Lamb,

After these things I looked, and lo, a great multitude, which no man could number, <u>__out__</u> <u>__of all nations and kindreds and people and tongues, stood before the throne and__</u> <u>__before the Lamb, clothed with white robes__</u>, with palms in their hands. And they cried with a loud voice, saying, "Salvation to our God, sitting on the throne, and to the Lamb." And all the angels stood around the throne, and the elders, and the four living creatures, and they fell before the throne on their faces, and worshiped God saying, "Amen! Blessing and glory and wisdom and thanksgiving and honor and power and might be to our God forever and ever. Amen." ~ Revelation 7: 9-12

This announcement indicates that the *fullness of the Gentiles* has come to faith and will be raptured before the *great tribulation* begins. Carefully observing the present-tense and future-tense language below, reveals that these are *already-not yet* in heaven.

And one of the elders answered, saying to me, "Who are these who are arrayed in white robes, and from where do they come? And I said to him, Sir, you know. And he said to me, "<u>__These are the ones who come out of great tribulation__</u> and have washed their robes, having whitened them in the blood of the Lamb. Therefore, <u>__they are__</u> before the throne of God, and <u>__they serve Him__</u> day and night in His temple. And Him sitting on the throne will dwell among them. <u>__They will__</u> not hunger any more, nor thirst anymore, nor will the sun light on them, nor any heat. For the Lamb who is in the midst of the throne <u>__will feed them__</u> and will lead them to the fountains of living waters. And <u>__God__</u> <u>__will__</u> wipe away all tears from their eyes. ~ Revelation 7:13-17

We will see this exact pattern again, immediately after *the Rapture* in *Revelation 15*, regarding those left behind, during the *great tribulation*. They are shown in heaven as those who refused the *Mark of the Beast* and will be later resurrected in *Revelation 19*. Just as chapter 15 indicates their salvation and chapter 19 indicates their glorification, we can understand *Revelation 7* reflects the completion of *the Bride* and *Revelation 14* represents *the Rapture* and glorification of *the Bride*.

The Wedding Week will unfold as follows: First the wedding party is gathered *(Revelation 7)*. Then, after the vows are exchanged, *the Bride and Groom* are escorted by the witnesses to the wedding chamber *(Revelation 14)*. Finally, after the *Bridegroom* emerges, the *Wife of the Lamb* re-emerges *(Revelation 19)*, having been united to Him. While the symbols may change, the two subjects are the same. In *Revelation 7*, there is the Lamb, and the *multitude from every tribe nation and tongue*. In *Revelation 14*, they are The *Son of Man* on the cloud and the *harvest*. In *Revelation 19*, they are the *Wife of the Lamb* and the Lord of Glory on the white horse.

The Wedding Parables

The wedding parable of *Matthew 22* also represents the unbelieving Jews and the Gentiles, who would come to the wedding feast. First, God sends the prophets to Israel to prepare them for the wedding, but they reject these servants.

> *And Jesus answered and spoke unto them again by parables, and said, "The kingdom of heaven is like unto a certain king, which made a marriage for his son. And sent forth his servants to **call them that were bidden** to the wedding: and **they would not come**.*
> ~ *Matthew 22:1-3*

Then, Christ sends His Apostles, calling Israel to the wedding, but they reject them as well. For this offense, God destroys their city, Jerusalem.

> *Again, he sent forth other servants, saying, 'Tell **them which are bidden**, Behold, I have prepared my dinner: my oxen and my fatlings are killed, and all things are ready: come unto the marriage. But they made light of it, and went their ways, one to his farm, another to his merchandise: And the remnant took his servants, and entreated them spitefully, and slew them. But when the king heard thereof, he was wroth: and he sent forth his armies, and destroyed those murderers, and burned up their city.*
> ~ *Matthew 22:4-7*

Finally, the Holy Spirit sends the Apostles to the Gentiles, compelling them to come, demonstrating the universal call of the Gospel to all mankind.

> *Then he said to his servants, "The wedding is ready, but they which were bidden were not worthy. **Therefore, go into the highways, and as many as you shall find**, bid to the marriage." So those servants went out into the highways, and gathered together all as many as they found, **both bad and good**: and the wedding was furnished with guests.*
> ~ *Matthew 22:8-10*

While many are called to the wedding, only those who have *put on Christ* will be welcome, while those who are *"wretched, miserable, naked, and blind"* are spewed out. While thinking themselves worthy to attend the feast by virtue of invitation, they refuse the wedding garments that appropriate their place at the table.

> *And when the king came in to see the guests, he saw there a man which had not on a wedding garment: And he said unto him, "Friend, **how did you come in here not having a wedding garment**?" And he was speechless. Then said the king to the servants, "Bind him hand and foot, and take him away, and cast him into outer darkness; there shall be weeping and gnashing of teeth." For many are called, but few are chosen.*
> ~ *Matthew 22:11-14*

This election is again mirrored in the parable of the ten virgins in *Matthew 25*:

*Then the kingdom of heaven shall be likened to ten virgins who took their lamps and went out to meet the Bridegroom. Now five of them were wise, and five were foolish. Those who were foolish took their lamps and **took no oil with them**, but the wise took oil in their vessels with their lamps. But while the Bridegroom was delayed, they all slumbered and slept. ~ Matthew 25:1-5*

In the parable of the ten virgins, the subject is also the salvation of the Church and the rejection of the lukewarm. All of them are given lamps, representing the testimony of the risen Lord. They all believe and consider themselves to be Christians; however, only half of them take oil with their lamps, representing the seal of the Holy Spirit. Of these, many will *"have a form of godliness but deny its power" (2nd Timothy 3:5)*, merely giving assent to Christ, but not abiding in Him. Jesus prophesies of a time when the church will not be taught to watch for the Lord's coming, represented in the sleeping virgins.

*And at midnight a cry was heard: "Behold, the Bridegroom is coming; go out to meet him!" Then all those virgins arose and trimmed their lamps. And the foolish said to the wise, "Give us some of your oil, for our lamps are going out." But the wise answered, saying, "No, lest there should not be enough for us and you; **but go rather to those who sell, and buy for yourselves**." And while they went to buy, the Bridegroom came, and those who were ready went in with him to the wedding; and the door was shut. Afterward the other virgins came also, saying, "Lord, Lord, open to us!" But he answered and said, "Assuredly," I say to you, I do not know you. "Watch therefore, for you know neither the day nor the hour in which the Son of Man is coming."*
~ Matthew 25:6-13

As Christ tells the Laodiceans to *"buy for yourselves gold, tried in the fire…,"* the foolish virgins are counseled to *"buy for yourselves"* oil for their lamps. As the Laodiceans are *"spewed out,"* so are these foolish virgins rejected. Christ is not saying they will be saved by watching for His appearing, but that if they are sealed by the Holy Spirit, they *will* hope for His appearing and be aware when it is near. In Jesus' final parable of a wedding feast, he refers to those who will be met by Him when he returns from the wedding, to take part in the final marriage supper.

…if that servant says in his heart, "My master is delaying his coming," and begins to beat the male and female servants, and to eat and drink and be drunk, the master of that servant will come on a day when he is not looking for him, and at an hour when he is not aware, and will cut him in two and appoint him his portion with the unbelievers.
~ Luke 12:45

Of the three types of people mentioned in this parable, the first are those who claim to know Christ, but live unto their own kingdoms, gathering wealth and power unto themselves at the expense of others *(Luke 12:1)*. Rather than fearing God, they fear man, and will join in the persecution to save themselves *(Luke 12:4-5)*. Rather than confess Christ as the only way of being saved, they will deny Him in compromise with the world *(Luke 12:8)*. All of this is connected to the fact that they are not watching for His coming, which is evidence that the Holy Spirit has not sealed them for redemption. These will be rejected from salvation in the end.

> *And that servant who knew his master's will and did not prepare himself or do according to his will, shall be beaten with many stripes. ~ Luke 12:47*

The next group refers to those who come out of Laodicea at the last hour, who had been sealed with the Holy Spirit to *"know his will"* but were lax in their obedience and did not let their lights shine before men. These will be *"beaten with many stripes,"* representing their martyrdom at the hands of *the Antichrist*.

> *But __he who did not know__, yet committed things deserving of stripes, shall be beaten with few. For everyone to whom much is given, from him much will be required; and to whom much has been committed, of him they will ask the more. ~ Luke 12:48*

Finally, the last group refers to the last days Israelites that come to faith in the end; who being enemies of the cross, *"did it ignorantly and in unbelief"* (1st *Timothy 1:13*). These will suffer trials, but not the martyrdom of those who come out of Laodicea.

While the weeklong *Wedding Feast* is a subject of *Daniel's 70th week*, the final *Marriage Supper* is the dividing line between the saved and the lost. The *Marriage Supper* is not *the Rapture*, but the final reception banquet, in which *the Bride and Groom* are reintroduced as Husband and Wife *(Revelation 19: 7)*. This event should be the hope and expectation of every saint, as it is synonymous with the Lord's reign. To be thrown out of this feast is to be rejected from God's presence for eternity.

The wedding party is gathered to officially complete the 6th seal, and at the opening of the 7th seal, *Daniel's 70th week* will begin. The first half of the week will correspond with the seven trumpets and the final testimony of the *Bride*. Just as the Groom gave his vows during his 3 ½ year ministry on Earth, the *Bride* will return her vows during her 3 ½ year testimony. Only those who are unashamed of the Gospel will accompany Christ to the wedding chamber at the end of this testimony. Those who fail to give this testimony will be left behind to glorify God through martyrdom.

PART 7 - THE TRUMPETS

The next section of *The Revelation* will cover the first three and a half years of *Daniel's 70th week*. In accordance with the themes we have established, the following events will take place during the first half of the week:

1) **The Trial - The Prosecution:** The Accuser will prosecute the Saints as *the Antichrist* rises to impersonate the Messiah. During this time, *Two Witnesses* will testify against *the Antichrist's* claims, until they are finally murdered.

2) **The Birth Pangs:** The global upheaval will persist until those in ethnic Israel come to faith in Christ, at which time the birth will take place. Afterward, the believing remnant of ethnic Israel will flee from Jerusalem.

3) **The Mystery of Iniquity:** Under the guise of "world peace," the world's economic and religious systems will be consolidated into a single system at *Mystery Babylon*, which will be given over to *the Antichrist* at the *Abomination of Desolation,* forcing them to take the *Mark of the Beast*.

4) **The Marriage Vows:** The Church will profess its love for Christ despite persecution, until she is escorted to the wedding chamber in *the Rapture*.

These themes will climax in a single day, prompting the *Wrath of the Lamb* to begin. This order of events is first foreshadowed in *Joshua 6*.

The Seven Trumpets at Jericho

Joshua, the descendant of Joseph, is a type of Christ at His return in power. His name was changed from Hosea to Joshua, the Hebrew for *"Jesus,"* as he would foreshadow how Christ would conquer the *Promised Land* in a mighty military campaign. The Lord appeared to Joshua, giving him specific commands about the marching order of the assembly and how they were to march around Jericho.

> *And Jericho was completely shut up because of the sons of Israel. None went out and none came in. And the LORD said to Joshua, "See, I have given Jericho into your hand, and its king, and the mighty men of war.* **_And you shall go around ... the city once. So, you shall do for six days._**" ~ *Joshua 6:1-3*

In a type, the city of Jericho being shut up for fear of Israel represents the world being shut up under sin. The six days in which Israel marched around the city represents the six thousand years in which the earth is shut up under Satan. The seventh day represents the Millennium, in which Christ will take dominion of the Earth. On the seventh day, the army marched around the city seven times, representing the gospel being transmitted throughout the earth as the seven seals are unsealed. Finally, seven trumpets are sounded before the judgement of Jericho.

> *And seven priests shall bear seven trumpets of ram's horns in front of the ark. And* **_the seventh day you shall go around the city seven times_**, *and the priests shall blow with the trumpets. And it shall be when they make a long blast with the ram's horn, and when you hear the sound of the trumpet, all the people shall shout with a great shout. And the wall of the city shall fall down flat, and the people shall go up, each man straight before him.* ~ *Joshua 6:4-5*

The order of the procession is also a prophetic picture, detailing the people of faith. First, we see the armies of Israel going before, representing the believing Israelites that preceded the Church. The Levite priests who carry the ark represent the Church, who would carry the message of the gospel throughout the earth, while the gathering armies represent the Jewish remnant that would be revived in the last days. Note that they are gathering as the seven trumpets are being blown.

> *And it happened when Joshua had spoken to the people, the seven priests bearing the seven ram's horns passed on before the LORD and blew the ram's horns. And the ark of the covenant of the LORD followed them. And the armed men went before the priests who blew with the ram's horns. And* **_the gathering army came after the Ark, as the priests were going on and blowing with the ram's horns_**... *So, they did six days. And it happened on the seventh day they rose early, at the dawning of the day, and circled the city in the same way seven times. Only on that day did they go around the*

*city seven times. And it happened, at **the seventh time, when the priest blew with the ram's horns**, Joshua said to the people, "Shout! For the LORD has given you the city!" ~ Joshua 6:5-16*

Another prophetic signature was God's ban on plundering the city. Earlier in the Book of Numbers, Moses committed a sin which caused God to restrict him from entering the *Promised Land*. God twice empowered Moses in the wilderness to bring water from a rock to provide for Israel. While God instructed him the first time to strike the rock *(Exodus 17:6)*, he was instructed the second time to speak to the rock *(Numbers 20:8)*. When Moses chose to strike the rock instead of speaking to it, God punished him by keeping him from entering the *Promised Land*. This was because the rock foreshadowed Christ, who would be bruised for our transgressions at his first coming but would be entreated for mercy at his second coming. God jealously guards his prophetic figures as they are as holy to Him as that which they portray. God knew that Jericho would prefigure last-days apostate Jerusalem, which would be redeemed and defended in the end, becoming devoted to Him. For this reason, God forbade anyone from plundering the city when it was conquered and led Israel to kill an entire household when a man violated this ban.

> *And **the city shall be devoted to the LORD**, and all that is in it. Only Rahab the harlot shall live…she hid the messengers. And you surely shall keep clear from the cursed thing, lest you make yourselves cursed when you take of the cursed things, and make the camp of Israel a curse, and trouble it. ~ Joshua 6:17-18*

A final prophetic picture is found in Rahab *(Joshua 2)*, who represents the *Gentile Bride*. Because she heard the testimony of what God had done in Egypt, she feared the Lord, receiving the two spies and trusting their word. These two spies, being a type of the *Two Witnesses*, demonstrate that the *Bride* will hear the *Two Witnesses* in the first three and a half years of *Daniel's 70th week*, responding in obedience to Christ. On their word, Rahab hung the scarlet from her window, signifying how the *Bride*, believing the Law and the Prophets, trusted in the blood of Christ.

> *And Joshua had said to **the two men** who had spied out the country, "Go into the harlot's house, and bring the woman out from there, and all that she has, as you swore to her." And the young men who were spies went in and brought Rahab out, and her father and her mother, and her brothers, and all that she had. ~ Joshua 6:22-23*

After the seven trumpets, we see Joshua remove Rahab before the city is burned. This foreshadows the Gentile Church being removed after the seventh trumpet, but before the wrath of the Lamb is poured out on the Earth. Consequently, the seventh trumpet will be followed with Jerusalem being greatly damaged by an earthquake before it is invaded and ravaged by the armies of the *Kings of the East*.

> And ***they burned the city with fire***, and all that was in it. Only the silver and the gold, and the vessels of bronze and iron, they put into the treasury of the house of the LORD. And ***Joshua saved Rahab the harlot alive***, and her father's household, and all that she had. And she lives in Israel to this day, because she hid the messengers whom Joshua sent to spy out Jericho. ~ Joshua 6:24-25

Rahab married into the tribe of Judah, becoming the great great-grandmother of King David and one of several *Gentile Brides* in the ancestry of the Messiah.

> And Salmon fathered Boaz of Rahab, and Boaz fathered Obed of Ruth, and Obed fathered Jesse, and Jesse fathered David the king. ~ Matthew 1:5

The plain speaking of Jesus and Paul places *the Resurrection and Rapture* at the midpoint of the week, after a trumpet is blown. Only this plain interpretation is backed up by so clear a type of the second coming as the campaign of Joshua. Proceeding to study *The Revelation*, it should not be difficult to see this same chronology embedded repeatedly in the symbols and the narrative.

The Seven Trumpets: Revelation 8 Interpreted

> And when He opened the seventh seal, there was silence in Heaven for about half an hour. And I saw the seven angels who stood before God, and seven trumpets were given to them. And another angel came and stood at the altar, having a golden censer. And many incenses were given to him, so that he should offer it with the prayers of all saints on the golden altar before the throne. And the smoke of the incense which came with ***the prayers of the saints, ascended up before God*** from the angel's hand. And ***the angel took the censer and filled it with fire from the altar and cast it into the earth***. And voices and thundering and lightning and an earthquake occurred. And the seven angels which had the seven trumpets prepared themselves to sound. ~ Revelation 8:1-6

Just as with interpreting the six seals, we cannot assume that the signs that correspond with the seven trumpets are *"the wrath of God."* While they are commonly referred to in prophecy literature as "Trumpet Judgements," this language is not found in Scripture. In fact, these signs are limited in scope to one third of the earth and there are those who are specifically sealed to be protected from them. We can also note the fact that these signs are immediately preceded by prayers from the saints, ascending toward God as further evidence that the Church is still present on the earth, making intercession and standing in faith.

The first four signs will affect a third part of the earth, signifying the coming judgement against the Kingdom of Satan, who caused a third part of the angels in heaven to follow him into rebellion (*Revelation 12:4*).

> *1) The first angel sounded, and there followed hail and fire mixed with blood, and they were cast on the earth. And **the third part** of trees was burned up, and all green grass was burned up.*
>
> *2) And the second angel sounded, and as it were a great mountain burning with fire was cast into the sea. And **the third part** of the sea became blood. And **the third part** of the living creatures in the sea died; and **the third part** of the ships was destroyed.*
>
> *3) And the third angel sounded, and a great star burning like a lamp fell from the heaven, and it fell on **the third part** of the rivers and on the fountains of waters. And the name of the star is called Wormwood, and **a third part** of the waters became wormwood. And many men died from the waters, because they were made bitter.*
>
> *4) And the fourth angel sounded, and the third part of the sun was stricken, and **the third part** of the moon, and **the third part** of the stars, so that **the third part** of them was darkened, and the day did not appear for **a third part** of it, and the night also.*
>
> *~ Revelation 8:1-12*

In the story of Joseph (*Genesis 40-47*), Pharaoh became the absolute power of Egypt, owning all the land and its people during a seven-year famine. Prior to this famine, there were seven years of plenty, during which Joseph counseled Pharaoh to store a fifth of the produce in preparation for the famine. Because of this preparation, Egypt gained economic supremacy over the entire world when the famine finally came. Once Pharaoh had power over all of Egypt, he began to mistreat the children of Israel and to enslave them, leading God to deliver them in the time of Moses.

This foreshadows how Israel, in league with *the Antichrist*, will gain economic supremacy during this period, allowing him to gain absolute power by the middle of *Daniel's 70th week*. These signs, devastating land and sea, will greatly reduce the world's food sources as *the Antichrist* consolidates the world's economy around the Middle East. After gaining control of the world's economy, he will betray ethnic Israel, abolishing the sacrificial system and demanding that they worship him as God under pain of death. Just as Israel had to flee Egypt in haste in the days of Moses, the Jews will also have to flee Jerusalem in haste when *the Antichrist* sits in the Most Holy Place, claiming to be God.

While God smote Egypt with plagues, devastating their land, their cattle, and their livelihood, Israel was kept safe from these plagues to make a clear distinction between the two peoples. During this time, the 144,000 of Israel and the saints of the Church will be kept as a testimony of distinction between them and the world.

> *And in that day, I will cut off the land of Goshen, in which My people live, so that no swarms of flies shall be there, so that you may know that I am Jehovah in the midst of the earth. ~ Exodus 8:22*

> *Only in the land of Goshen, where the sons of Israel were, was there no hail.*
> *~ Exodus 9:26*

> *But against any of the sons of Israel not even a dog shall move his tongue, against man or beast, so that you may know that the LORD puts a difference between the Egyptians and Israel. ~ Exodus 11:7*

While the world will be suffering at these signs, the 144,000 and the Church will be salt and light in the world, bringing the remaining Jews to jealousy.

The Three Woes: Three Coming Kingdoms

The final three trumpets are three woes, representing the arrival of three great kingdoms which will appear in the last days. These are the *Kingdom of Antichrist*, the confederacy of the *Kings of the East*, and the *Kingdom Come*. While the rise of *the Beast* will be one of seduction and deception, the rise of the *Kings of the East* will be by violent force, bringing with it the deaths of one third of the people remaining on the planet. While these two kingdoms will be more devastating than any superpowers in world history, their power will pale in comparison to the *Kingdom Come*, beginning with the wrath of the Lamb, poured out on the Earth.

> *And I saw and I heard one angel flying in mid-heaven, saying with a loud voice, Woe! Woe! Woe to the inhabitants of the earth, from the rest of the voices of the trumpet of the three angels being about to sound! ~ Revelation 8:13*

The Antichrist, in his rise to power, will not only attempt to persuade Jews that he is their Messiah, but will also attempt to convince Christians that he is Christ, having come to set up his kingdom. The *Kingdom of Antichrist* will likely offer respite from the persecution faced by Christians up to that time, drawing all Jews and many Christians to migrate toward Europe and the Middle East, where there will be greater security and economic resources.

> *And the fifth angel sounded: And I saw **<u>a star fall from the heaven to the earth, and it was given the key to the Bottomless Pit</u>**. And it opened the Bottomless Pit. And there arose a smoke out of the pit, like the smoke of a great furnace. And the sun and air were darkened because of the smoke of the pit. And out of the smoke came forth locusts onto the earth. And authority was given to them, as the scorpions of the earth have*

*authority. And **they were commanded not to hurt the grass of the earth, or any** **green thing, or any tree, but only those men who do not have the seal of God in** **their foreheads**. And to them it was given that they should not kill them, but that they should be tormented five months. And their torment was like a scorpion's torment when he stings a man. And in those days men will seek death and will not find it. And they will long to die, and death will flee from them. ~ Revelation 9:1-5*

When *the Antichrist* begins to take power, he will have the help of a horde of demonic agents, able to torment men both physically and mentally. These demons are ruled by the *"angel of the Bottomless Pit"* and seem only able to affect unbelievers with this plague. As a result, the world will be largely incapacitated, giving believers some respite from continual persecution throughout the world. Since *the Beast* himself will be unaffected by these torments, many will believe he is a Christian, or even Christ himself. For this reason, Jesus was adamant about not being deceived toward believing that Christ has already come.

Then if any man shall say to you, "Lo, here is Christ! or, "Look there!" Do not believe it… if they shall say to you, "Behold, He is in the desert!" or "Behold, He is in the secret rooms!" Do not believe it. For as the lightning comes out of the east and shines even to the west, so also will be the coming of the Son of man. ~ Matthew 24:23-27

This sign will affect all who are not sealed by God, both Jew and Gentile, with one express purpose: to convince the unbelieving world that *the Antichrist* is the Messiah. While the believers will not be affected by the previous signs, at this sign the whole world will wonder. This sign will not kill anyone but will exist to convince the unbelieving world that *the Antichrist* is meting out judgement against those who persecuted the elect, convincing the world that *the Millennium* has arrived, and the Messiah is setting up the *Kingdom Come*.

And the shapes of the locusts were like horses prepared for battle. And on their heads, were as it were crowns like gold, and their faces were like the faces of men. And they had hair like the hair of women, and their teeth were like the teeth of lions. And they had breastplates like breastplates of iron. And the sound of their wings was like the sound of chariots of many horses running to battle. And they had tails like scorpions, and there were stings in their tails. And their authority was to hurt men five months.
~ Revelation 9:1-10

The Destroyer: The History of the Beast

*And **they had a king over them, the angel of the Bottomless Pit**, whose name in the Hebrew tongue is Abaddon, but in Greek his name is Apollyon. ~ Revelation 9:11*

The demonic prince who has power over this torment is not Satan, but his chief angelic agent by whom he wreaks destruction to the extent God permits. In the Hebrew, his name is Abaddon, meaning *"The Destroyer."* This is another name for the angel who slew the first born of the Egyptians in the days of Moses and Aaron. Just as *The Destroyer* was appointed to kill the first born of every house in Egypt that was not sealed by the blood of the lamb, he will be able to torment everyone who is not sealed by the Holy Spirit during this time.

> *For the LORD will pass through to strike the Egyptians. And when He sees the blood upon the lintel, and on the two side posts, the LORD will pass over the door, and will not allow* **the destroyer** *to come into your houses to strike you. ~ Exodus 12:23*

The reason the name is given in both Hebrew and Greek is because *the Beast* will be a Danite, a secret Hebrew who comes from the region of the Greeks. His Greek name *"Apollyon"* is not found elsewhere in Scripture, but in Greek mythology. In the letter to Pergamos, Christ informed the church that they dwelt *"where Satan's throne is."* Consequently, their city was the location of the altar to Zeus. We will later learn that Satan gives this throne (or seat) to *the Beast (Revelation 13:2)*. The Greek god Zeus had a mythology similar to Lucifer, as he separated the earth (Gaia) from his father (Chronos) to claim it for himself. His son Apollos (or Apollyon) was the god of the sun and archery. The Assyrians had a similar god which was depicted with the symbols of a sun and bow, identical in form to Apollos.

This same spirit empowered Nimrod to conquer the world and build the Tower of Babel. After becoming the first world ruler, the mighty hunter came to be worshiped as a Sun god in Babylon and Assyria. This *"angel of the Bottomless Pit"* will also empower *the Beast* as he takes dominion of the earth, which is the subject of the fifth trumpet and first woe. Just as the sons of Jacob were able to slaughter the city of Shechem while the men recovered from the pain of circumcision (*Genesis 34*), the Beast will be able to quickly subdue the Middle East as the world writhes in agony.

> *When they finish their testimony,* ***the Beast that ascends out of the Bottomless Pit*** *will make war against them, overcome them, and kill them. ~ Revelation 11:7*

> *The Beast that you saw was, and is not, and is* ***about to ascend out of the Bottomless Pit*** *and go to perdition… ~ Revelation 17:8*

The Political Rise of the Beast

Since the Reformation, many protestant Christians have supposed that *the Antichrist* will be a Western European, reviving the Roman Empire with the Pope of Roman Catholicism as his *False Prophet*. These ideas were born out of a theological culture where replacement theology was undisputed, most forgetting that the primary purpose of *the Antichrist* is to impersonate the Jewish Messiah. Likewise, the purpose of his *False Prophet* is to impersonate Elijah, who would identify him as Messiah. While the Pope and many western leaders may be harbingers of *the Antichrist*, they fail to meet the Scriptural prophetic criteria.

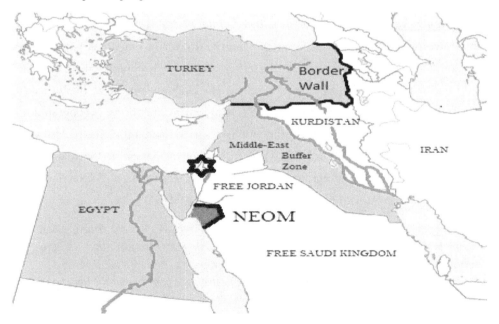

The Bible gives an abundance of details about this man called *"the Beast, "the Man of Lawlessness,"* or *"the Antichrist."* Most of his exploits are expressly prophesied in *Daniel*, *Revelation*, and *Isaiah*, with many other types and foreshadows of him throughout the

Old Testament. However, it is from the *Book of Daniel* that we get the clearest indication of his geographical origin and the span of his dominion.

The Bible gives very precise details as to where *the Antichrist* comes from. In the book of Daniel, written during the time of the Babylonian and Persian kings, among the most indisputable prophecies in history were those predicting the rise of Alexander the Great. These prophecies detail his rapid conquest of the Persians, followed by his sudden death and his kingdom being parceled out to his four generals.

> *... Behold, there shall stand up yet three kings in Persia. And the fourth shall be far richer than all of them. And by his strength, through his riches, he shall stir up all against **the kingdom of Greece**. And a mighty king shall stand up, one who shall rule with great power and do according to his will. And when he shall stand up, **his kingdom shall be broken and shall be divided toward the four winds of the heavens**. And it shall not be given to his sons, nor according to his power with which he ruled; for **his kingdom shall be pulled up, even for others** besides these.* ~ Daniel 11:1-4

> *After this I saw, and lo, another, like a leopard, which had four wings of a bird on its back. **The Beast also had four heads**; and rulership was given to it.* ~ Daniel 7:6

> *And the shaggy goat is the king of Greece. And the great horn between his eyes is the first king. And as for that being broken, and **four stood up in its place; four kingdoms shall stand up** out of the nation, but not in its power.* ~ Daniel 8:21

Daniel gives several prophecies about the Gentile kings and kingdoms which would have dominion until the times of the Israelite captivity was completed. This period would end with the return of Christ to set up His kingdom on earth, finally freeing Israel from this captivity. The final Gentile kingdom he mentions is geographically like the Roman Empire, ruling to the Euphrates river and into North Africa and Europe. While this territory will be the dominion of *the Antichrist*, the man himself does not come from Western Europe but out of the territories of Alexander's four kingdoms, whose westernmost territory was in modern day Greece.

> *And **in the latter time of their kingdom, (of the Greeks)** when the transgressors have come to the full, a king, fierce of countenance and skilled at intrigues, shall stand up. And his power shall be mighty, but not by his own power. And he shall destroy marvelously, and shall prosper and work, and destroy the mighty and the holy people (being Jews and Christians).* ~ Daniel 8:23-24

Four Old-Testament proofs dictate where *the Antichrist* will come from.

- First, the Antichrist will be a Danite, who seems to have finally mingled with the Greeks. *(Ezekiel 27:19)*

[134]

- Second, he will leap from Bashan, a region of Syria near the Golan Heights. *(Deuteronomy 33:22)*

- Third, he will come from one of Alexander's four kingdoms, being North and West of Israel. *(Daniel 8:9)*

- Fourth, he will rule the land between the Nile and the Euphrates, having power over the West from this region. *(Daniel 11:40-41)*

Both prophetic and geopolitical necessity dictate that *the Antichrist* comes from modern Turkey, whose Western portion was called in Daniel's day *"Grecia,"* and whose Eastern portion was called *"Assyria."* Turkey also holds Pergamos, where the Lord says, *"Satan's Throne is"* (Revelation 2:12-13). This land was also the final seat of the Roman Empire, as Constantinople inherited the Roman Empire for another 1000 years after the Western Roman Empire fell to barbarian tribes.

> *Therefore, the he goat waxed very great: and when he was strong, the great horn was broken; and for it came up four notable ones toward the four winds of heaven. And **out of one of them** (the four Greek kingdoms) **came forth a little horn, which waxed exceeding great, toward the south, and toward the east, and toward the pleasant land** (Israel). And it became great, even to the host of heaven. And it made fall some of the host and of the stars to the ground and trampled them.* ~ Daniel 8:8-10

The Antichrist must come from the immediate North and West of the *Promised Land*, which can only be Turkey. He will emerge from here, taking territories from Syria and Iraq to the South and East of Turkey's borders, forming a territorial border along the Euphrates. Upon seizing this territory, he will govern an alliance between the Jews and the Arabs while forming a protective buffer along the Euphrates, dividing the Kurds and Persians east of the Euphrates, and the Jews and Arabs west of the Euphrates. He will then *"leap from Bashan"* into Israel, pretending to be the Messiah by allowing them to reinstitute the temple sacrifices.

> Then **he shall confirm a covenant with many for one week**; *But in the middle of the week He shall bring an end to sacrifice and offering. And on the wing of abominations shall be one who makes desolate, even until the consummation, which is determined, is poured out on the desolate.* ~ Daniel 9:27

The dominion of *the Antichrist* will give prominence to an apostate church, and for this reason, many professing Christians will be pacified. This false religion will likely be a merger of Judaism, Islam, and Apostate Christianity to which most Christian denominations will be consolidated. Because of poor teaching and apostasy, many true Christians will fall for this belief early on. Those who resist will be ostracized at first, then quietly persecuted and killed. Their martyrdom will lead the immature to realize this is not *the Millennium*, but a false kingdom ruled by *the Antichrist*, causing others to reject this deception and hold fast until Christ comes.

> *Those who do wickedly against the covenant he shall corrupt with flattery; but the people who know their God shall be strong and carry out great exploits. And those of the people who understand shall instruct many; yet for many days they shall fall... And some of those of understanding shall fall, to refine them, purify them, and make them white, until the time of the end; because it is still for the appointed time.* ~ Daniel 11:32-35

The kingdoms of Jordan and Saudi Arabia will remain politically independent, as the Antichrist will need them as allies for their oil and for their sway over the Sunni Muslims inhabiting most of his kingdom.

> *And he shall enter the countries and shall overflow and pass over. He shall also enter the glorious land, and many shall be overthrown. But* ***these shall escape out of his hand: Edom and Moab, and the chief of the sons of Ammon****.* ~ Daniel 11:41

Finally, to prove that he is the Messiah, he will annex the land of Egypt, taking the entire *Promised Land* from the Nile to the Euphrates.

> *He shall stretch out his hand against the countries, and the land of Egypt shall not escape. He shall have power over the treasures of gold and silver, and over all the precious things of Egypt; Also, the Libyans and Ethiopians shall follow at his heels.*
> ~ Daniel 11:42-43

Having accomplished these annexations, he will hold Europe economically captive, controlling both the Suez Canal and the oil lanes between the Arabian Peninsula and Europe. The Prophet Isaiah confirms this, setting the time as being near *the Rapture*:

> *The burden against Egypt: Behold,* ***the LORD rides on a swift cloud and comes into Egypt****. And the idols of Egypt shall tremble at His presence, and the heart of Egypt shall melt in its midst.* ~ Isaiah 19:1

Demonstrating that *the Day of the Lord* is near at hand, the Egyptians are presently being politically and economically broken by the Arab Spring and their Nile River is being dried up by the building of the Ethiopian Grand Renaissance Dam. When *the Antichrist* arises, he will annex Egypt, seizing their primary remaining economic asset in the Suez Canal.

> *"And I will shut up Egypt into the hand of a cruel lord; and* ***a fierce king shall rule over them****," says the Lord, The LORD of hosts. "And the waters shall fail from the sea, and the river shall fail and dry up. And rivers shall be fouled;* ***the Nile of Egypt will***

languish and dry up; the reed and the rush shall decay. Bare places shall be at the Nile, by the mouth of the Nile, and everything sown by the Nile shall dry up, driven away, and be no more." ~ Isaiah 19:4-7

After this, *the Antichrist* will plan to take all North Africa, pushing south against the African Union and its chief state of Ethiopia. Here he will find resistance, as Sub-Saharan Africa is becoming a client of China, who will lead the *Kings of the East*.

*And at the end-time, the king of the south shall butt at him. And **the king of the north shall come against him** like a tempest, with chariots and with horsemen and with many ships. ~ Daniel 11:40*

While his economic dominion will extend much further, this will be the furthest extent of his geographical territory. At that time, he will have to accept a stalemate in Africa and return to Israel to muster his forces against the armies coming against him from the East as the Euphrates dries up.

But news from the east and the north shall trouble him; therefore, he shall go out with great fury to destroy and annihilate many. And he shall plant the tents of his palace between the seas and the glorious holy mountain; yet he shall come to his end, and no one will help him. ~ Daniel 11:44-45

By the middle of the week, the world will be against him, including the *"ships of Kittim," (Daniel 11:30);* likely representing the remnants of NATO and the US Navy.

The Second Woe: The Kings of the East

Just as the first woe represents *the Antichrist,* rising to power by diplomatic guile, the second woe represents the *Kings of the East*, who rise in opposition to him by violent force and sheer numbers. These are led by the three kings he will have plucked out of Syria, who after giving up dominion to him for a time, will regather their forces and finally stand against him at the *Battle of Armageddon*. While an exact list of these kings is uncertain, it is highly likely that the economic organization known as BRICS (Brazil, Russia, India, China, & South Africa) and the Shanghai Cooperation Organization (SCO) will be its framework.

*Then the sixth angel sounded: And I heard a voice from the four horns of the golden altar, which is before God, saying to the sixth angel who had the trumpet, "Release **the four angels who are bound at the great river Euphrates**." ~ Revelation 9:13-14*

While some scholars teach that these four angels were "tied up" at the river Euphrates for some past offense, a better interpretation is that these are four angels, whose power is restricted, or bound, *from crossing* the Euphrates, yet free to exercise dominion East of the Euphrates. These four angels are also referred to in Zechariah, being called, *"Four Craftsmen."*

> Then I lifted up my eyes and looked, and behold, four horns! And I said to the angel who talked with me, "What are these?" And he answered me, "These are the horns that have scattered Judah, Israel, and Jerusalem." And the LORD showed me **four craftsmen**. And I said, "What are these coming to do?" And He spoke, saying, "These are the horns which have scattered Judah, so that no man lifted up his head. **But these have come to terrify them**, to throw down the horns of the nations who lifted up their horn over the land of Judah to scatter it." ~ Zechariah 1:18-20

This prophecy, written in a time when the Jews were returning to Israel to rebuild the temple, represents the last days regathering of Israel, and how this will be accomplished. The four horns, like the four horns of the altar, point outward, representing the dispersal of Israel from the *Promised Land*. These are those four beasts which God used to scatter Israel in ancient times, which will be consolidated into a single kingdom to be ruled by *the Antichrist*. The *Four Craftsmen* represent four blacksmiths, pounding their hammers inward and driving them back into the *Promised Land* through the conquest of the nations to which they were scattered. The *Four Craftsmen* represent the *Kings of the East,* who come against the *Kingdom of the Beast* in the last days, driving the Jews back toward his kingdom.

The vision alludes to the rising violent power of the *Kings of the East*, taking over the lands of Asia, Africa, and the Americas, while the Jews and most Christians will withdraw from this violence into the *Kingdom of the Antichrist,*

> And **the four angels were loosed**, who were prepared for an hour, and a day, and a month, and a year, to slay the third part of men. And **the number of the armies of the horsemen was two myriads of myriads (two hundred million)**. And I heard their number. And so, I saw the horses in the vision, and those sitting on them, having breastplates of fire, even dusky red and brimstone. And the heads of the horses were like the heads of lions. And out of their mouths issued fire and smoke and brimstone. **By these three the third part of men was killed**, by the fire, and by the smoke, and by the brimstone which issued out of their mouths. For their authority is in their mouth and in their tails. For their tails were like serpents with heads, and with them they do harm.
> ~ Revelation 9:15-19

By this time, we must remember that one fourth of the world will have been slain in the six seals. The population of earth will have been reduced from around eight billion, to about six billion. This military, being driven by a massive army of demons, will kill one third of the remaining population. As the earth's ability to produce food is drastically diminished, these violent armies from the East will come against the rest of the world for its resources. By the middle of the week, at least half of the population of the earth—totaling over four billion people—will have been killed.

The dominion of these *Kings of the East* will likely extend from the Euphrates eastward, beyond the seas into the Americas and Africa, as the BRICS allies will support them against *the Antichrist*. This movement will likely be atheistic, or else have many false Christs of its own, seeking to consolidate these remaining religions, nations and peoples in opposition to *the Antichrist*.

> *And the rest of* **the men who were not killed by these plagues still did not repent of the works of their hands**, *that they should not worship demons, and golden, and silver, and bronze, and stone, and wooden idols (which neither can see, nor hear, nor walk). And they did not repent of their murders, nor of their sorceries, nor of their fornication, nor of their thefts. ~ Revelation 9:13*

The last portion of this passage reveals those who will be slain, particularly, those who worship idols. Buddhists, Hindus, Roman Catholics, Greek Orthodox and Neo-Pagans will be slaughtered by this invasion which will likely be dominated by atheistic and Islamic-fundamentalist forces. Still, after all of this death and destruction, they will not relent from idolatry or their practices of sorcery and theft.

Because such a violent reign will persist, from the Euphrates in the East to the borders of *the Antichrist*'s kingdom in the West, *the Kingdom of the Beast* will be extremely attractive in comparison. The idol-worshipping adherents of these religions will likely flee to the burgeoning new-age nation state of Neom, finding contentment in this ecumenical and technocratic mega-city. Those of a more conservative persuasion will gather to Europe and the Middle East, passively accepting the growing religion of *Chrislam* which will increasingly promote *the Beast* as the Jewish Messiah.

These two kingdoms will eventually gather against each other, like the American civil war projected on a planetary scale. The North and South being replaced with the East and West, one side will embrace violent independence, national identity, and economic individualism, while the other will embrace diversity, collectivism, central authority and a growing cult of personality in *the Beast*. By the end of Daniel's 70th week, they will meet at Armageddon where they will finally settle their differences to unite against the revealed Christ. Here, knowing that the day of the *Abomination of Desolation* grows near, the Holy Spirit will stop pressing the narrative forward in order to establish the gravity of the upcoming events.

The Mighty Angel – Revelation 10 Interpreted

*I saw still another mighty angel coming down from heaven, clothed with a cloud. And a rainbow was on his head, his face was like the sun, and his feet like pillars of fire. **He had a little book open in his hand**. And he set his right foot on the sea and his left foot on the land. ~ Revelation 10:1-3*

This angel is an archangel who stands for the Lord. Having set his foot on the sea and the land, he is heralding the coming of Christ to take dominion over both Israel and the Gentiles; the Land being a symbol for the *Promised Land* and the sea being a symbol for the Nations *(Revelation 17:15)*. He holds in his hand the scroll, which has been unsealed because the great offenses within are about to be completed.

*...and (he) cried with a loud voice, as when a lion roars. When he cried out, seven thunders uttered their voices. Now when the seven thunders uttered their voices, I was about to write; but I heard a voice from heaven saying to me, **"Seal up the things which the seven thunders uttered, and do not write them."** ~ Revelation 10:3-4*

While *"these things"* which are sealed remain a mystery, the fact that they are sealed points to a corresponding prophecy in *Daniel 12*.

...Go, Daniel! For the words are closed up and sealed until the end-time. ~ Daniel 12: 9

Also corresponding with this prophecy, these angels will give a sign.

*And I heard the man clothed in linen, who was on the waters of the river, **when he held up his right and his left hand to Heaven and swore by Him who lives forever** that it shall be for a time, times, and a half. And when they have made an end of scattering the power of the holy people, all these things shall be finished. ~ Daniel 12:7*

*And the angel whom I saw standing on the sea and on the earth **lifted his hand to the heaven, and swore by Him who lives forever** and ever, who created the heaven and the things in it, and the earth and the things in it, and the sea and the things in it, that there should be delay no longer. But in the days of the voice of the seventh angel, **when he will begin to sound, the mystery of God should be finished, as He has declared to His servants the prophets**. ~ Revelation 10:5-7*

When receiving the vision of the end of days, Daniel was led up to the point of the *Abomination of Desolation*; the time when *the Antichrist* was preparing to wage war against the *Kings of the East*. At that time, we are told that *the Antichrist* will *"come to his end" (Daniel 11:45)*, and that a *"time of great trouble"* will commence. In Daniel's vision, the angel raised two hands to heaven, indicating a span of time, and swore that it would be *"for a time, times, and a half a time"* (or 3 ½ years). John on the other hand, is introduced to an angel lifting just one hand, signifying that the time indicated by Daniel will begin at the seventh trumpet. The Angel also reveals that this *mystery*—the ingathering of the Gentiles—will then be finished. At that time, the *delay* of the outpouring of the wrath of God will have ended.

> *For this cause, I, Paul, am the prisoner of Jesus Christ for you nations, if you have heard of the dispensation of the grace of God which is given to me toward you, that by revelation He made known to me **the mystery** … in **the mystery of Christ**) which in other ages was not made known to the sons of men, as it is now revealed to His holy apostles and prophets by the Spirit, **that the Gentiles should be fellow heirs, and of the same body**, and partaker of His promise in Christ through the gospel.*
> ~ *Ephesians 3:1-6*
>
> ***For we are members of His body***, *of His flesh, and of His bones. For this cause a man shall leave his father and mother and shall be joined to his wife, and the two of them shall be one flesh.* ***This is a great mystery, but I speak concerning Christ and the church***.
> ~ *Ephesians 5:30-32*

John is told that *the Rapture* of the Church draws near, even as Paul taught that it would occur *at the last trump*. After this, John is given instructions to eat the book and prepare to give another prophecy which will take the reader back in time to the beginning of *Daniel's 70ᵗʰ week*.

> *And the voice which I heard from Heaven spoke to me again, and said, "Go, take the little book which is open in the hand of the angel who stands on the sea and on the earth." And I went to the angel and said to him, "Give me the little book." And he said to me, "Take it and eat it up, and* ***it will make your belly bitter, but it will be sweet as honey in your mouth***.*" And I took the little book out of the angel's hand and ate it up. And it was sweet as honey in my mouth, and as soon as I had eaten it, my belly was made bitter.*
> ~ *Revelation 10:8-10*

This passage is reminiscent of *Ezekiel 2-3*, in which Ezekiel is given a two-sided scroll to eat, that is sweet in his mouth but sends him forth in the bitterness of his spirit. Ezekiel prophecies to the rebellious house of Israel, whose city Jerusalem will be destroyed, just as will occur after John's prophecy of the *Two Witnesses*.

> *Now when I looked, there was a hand stretched out to me; and behold, a scroll of a book was in it. Then He spread it before me; and* ***there was writing on the inside and on the outside***, *and written on it were lamentations and mourning and woe… Moreover, He said to me, "Son of man, eat what you find;* ***eat this scroll***, *and go, speak to the house of Israel." So, I opened my mouth, and He caused me to eat that scroll. And He said to me, "Son of man, feed your belly, and fill your stomach with this scroll that I give you." So, I ate, and it was* ***in my mouth like honey in sweetness***… *So, the Spirit lifted me up and took me away, and* ***I went in bitterness, in the heat of my spirit***; *but the hand of the LORD was strong upon me.* ~ *Ezekiel 2:9-3:14*

The scroll, which John is given to eat, is the same seven-sealed scroll that was written upon inside and out, containing the judgement on the house of Satan. Just as Ezekiel was responsible to go preach against Jerusalem before its destruction, John is shown *Two Witnesses* that preach in Jerusalem until the *Abomination of Desolation*.

> And he said to me, "You must prophesy again before many peoples and nations and tongues and kings." Revelation 10:11

John is instructed to prophecy again, indicating that he is going to tell the same prophecy about the same time-period, but from a different perspective. Because the world and its many wars, signs, and disasters have been the topic of the prophecy so far, the Holy Spirit is taking John back to Jerusalem, which has not yet been mentioned in *The Revelation*. This city will be the scene of the ongoing trial of *the Beast*, which will require *Two Witnesses* to bring a valid charge against him under Mosaic Law *(Deuteronomy 19:15)*. After eating the scroll, John will then relay what has been happening in the Holy City during the same 3 ½ year period. This will center around the preaching of *Two Witnesses,* who testify against *the Beast*, proving by their signs that he is no Messiah and powerless against the plagues they call forth.

The Two Witnesses

The *Two Witnesses* are foreshadowed many times in the Old Testament, each one representing some aspect of the ministry of the final *Two Witnesses* in *The Revelation*. The purposes of these *Two Witnesses* are both to encourage the believing and to testify against *the Antichrist* as the trial of Satan unfolds. Some have speculated that Enoch and Elijah must return as the *Two Witnesses,* because Hebrews says, *"it is appointed to die once" (Hebrews 9:7)*. However, it should be noted that all of those who are raptured do not taste death, *(1st Corinthians 15:51)* making this point invalid. While Enoch was taken to heaven, there is no indication in Scripture that he returns. If we are careful to study the Old Testament, the *Two Witnesses* have seven types, which appear in the Old Testament between Genesis and Malachi and should make clear who they will be.

Noah and Methuselah: In building the Ark, Noah preached the judgement of the flood during the entire 120 years in which he was building. Methuselah also testified, his very name meaning, *"When he dies, judgement."* In these two, *the Resurrection and the Rapture* are foreshadowed, as Methuselah died just before the judgement and Noah was taken up alive at the judgement, being preserved against the outpoured wrath.

Noah's flood is a common type of judgment and is utilized by Jesus *(Luke 17:26-32)*, Peter *(2ⁿᵈ Peter 2:5)*, and Jude *(Jude 6)*, to illustrate that day of the Lord's wrath. The other major type utilized is the destruction of Sodom and Gomorrah.

> *And as it was in **the days of Noah**, so it also shall be in the days of the Son of Man. They ate, they drank, they married wives, they were given in marriage, until the day that Noah entered the ark; and the flood came and destroyed them all. So also, as it was in the days of Lot: they ate, they drank, they bought, they sold, they planted, they built; **but the day Lot went out of Sodom**, it rained fire and brimstone from the heavens and destroyed them all. Even so it shall be in the day when the Son of Man is revealed.*
> ~ Luke 17:26-37

The Two Angels at Sodom: Two Angels were sent by God to Sodom *(Genesis 19)*, both to testify to the wickedness there and to rescue *"righteous Lot, oppressed with the lustful behavior of the lawless." (2ⁿᵈ Peter 2:7)*. In *Luke 17*, Jesus alludes to Lot leaving Sodom and not looking back, fleeing to the East of the Jordan River. Before the *Abomination of Desolation*, Jerusalem will also receive *Two Witnesses* as God's final warning, prompting the believing Jews to flee to a nearby city called Bozrah. In *Revelation 11*, the place these *Two Witnesses* are killed is called, *"spiritually, Sodom and Egypt,"* being Jerusalem, *"where their Lord was crucified."*

Aaron and Moses: Last days Jerusalem is also called Egypt due to the showdown between the *Two Witnesses* and *the Antichrist,* which was foreshadowed when Moses and Aaron testified against Pharaoh in *The Exodus*. God worked through them to testify against Pharaoh *(Exodus 4:16)*, who in that narrative was a type of Satan. His two ministers, the magicians Jannes and Jambres, foreshadowed *the Antichrist* and *False Prophet*. Just as ten plagues were used to judge the gods of Egypt *(Exodus 12:12)*, the *Two Witnesses* will judge the ten kings who give power to *the Beast*.

Joshua and Caleb: Joshua and Caleb are a type of the *Two Witnesses* as they bring a hopeful report of the *Promised Land*, confirming God's promise to give them the land *(Numbers 13-14)*. Their counterpart in the ten spies oppose them, representing the ten kings which give power to *the Beast*. Where the ten spies wanted to kill Joshua and Caleb for trusting God, the ten kings will also want to kill the *Two Witnesses* as they will preach trust in Christ rather than a united humanity to save the world.

The Two Spies: As mentioned earlier, the two spies who spied out Jericho and warned Rahab the harlot, were also a type of the *Two Witnesses*. These will provide a final warning to the Church in the last days, reminding the converted to rely on the blood of Jesus, and to forsake any other hope, holding fast until the last trump, when they will be removed from the earth before it is judged like Jericho.

The Two Olive Trees: In Zechariah, two olive trees are mentioned, which supply oil to the seven lampstands; a prophecy given as the Second Temple is being built. *Revelation 2* teaches that the light of the lamp is the Holy Spirit, while the lampstand is the Church. The two olive trees are those *Two Witnesses* that prophecy in the last days, encouraging the Church as the temple is rebuilt in Israel.

> *And the angel that talked with me came again and awakened me, as a man that is awakened out of his sleep. And he said to me, "What do you see?" And I said, "I see, and behold, a lampstand, all of it gold, and a bowl on its top, and its seven lamps on it, and seven pipes to the seven lamps on its top; **and two olive trees** beside it, one on the right of the bowl, and the other on the left of it." ...Then he answered and spoke to me, saying, "This is the word of the LORD to Zerubbabel, saying, '**Not by might, nor by power, but by My Spirit**,' says the LORD of hosts." ~ Zechariah 4: 1-6*

> *And I answered and said to him, "**What are these two olive trees** on the right of the lampstand and on its left?" And I answered again and said to him, "What are the two olive clusters beside the two golden pipes, emptying the golden oil from themselves?" And he answered me and said, "Do you not know what these are?" And I said, No my lord. And he said, "**These are the two anointed ones who stand by the LORD of the whole earth**." ~ Zechariah 4: 11-14*

Moses and Elijah: The Ones Who Stand by the Lord

While there were many prophets in Israel, who declared warnings and judgments, conveying promises and rebukes to nations, only two were chosen to stand alone against the false gods of their day, and overturn their dominion. These two were also seen standing with Jesus Christ on the mount of transfiguration, being Moses and Elijah. When Moses was about to die, he prophesied by the Holy Spirit that God would send another prophet like himself to whom Israel must listen *(Deuteronomy 18:15)*. Malachi, the last prophet of the Torah, also closed the Old Testament saying:

> *__Remember the law of Moses__ My servant, which I commanded to him in Horeb for all Israel, the statutes and judgments. Behold, **I am sending you Elijah** the prophet before the coming of the great and dreadful day of the LORD. And he shall turn the heart of the fathers to the sons, and the heart of the sons to their fathers, that I not come and strike the earth with utter destruction. ~ Malachi 4:4-6*

When Moses died, God personally buried him on the East side of the Jordan, keeping the location a secret. After this, Joshua led Israel into the *Promised Land*, beginning with a sign of the Jordan River drying up. *(Joshua 3: 11-16)*. After this, Joshua

[144]

conducted a campaign to conquer the land, going first to Jericho, then to Bethel, then to Gilgal, taking possession of the land. But in the days of Elijah, when he was about to be taken up in a whirlwind, he went from Gilgal, to Bethel, to Jericho, and then finally struck the Jordan so that it dried up, going back into the wilderness to the region where Moses had been buried. He was then taken up in a flaming chariot, which was a type of *the Rapture (2nd Kings 2)*. Moses on the other hand, was a type of *the Resurrection*, which was alluded to in the Book of Jude.

> *Yet Michael the archangel, in contending with the devil, when he disputed about **the body of Moses**, dared not bring against him a reviling accusation, but said, "The Lord rebuke you!" ~ Jude 1:9*

We can know that Moses was resurrected because he appeared bodily, along with Elijah, at the Transfiguration of Jesus Christ.

> *And He was transfigured before them. And His face shone as the sun, and His clothing was white as the light. And behold, **there appeared to them Moses and Elijah talking with Him**. And Peter answered and said to Jesus, Lord, it is good for us to be here. If You will, let us make here three tabernacles; one for You, and one for Moses, and one for Elijah. While he yet spoke, behold, a bright cloud overshadowed them. And behold, a voice out of the cloud which said, "This is My Beloved Son in whom I am well pleased, listen to Him." ~ Matthew 17:2-5*

If these two appeared with the Lord before His crucifixion, they will likely be the two prophets that John calls the *Two Witnesses*. These two will stand as witnesses for the truth, testifying for the Lord, while *the Antichrist* and the *False Prophet* will attempt to counterfeit the two, committing the great perjury written in the scroll. Understanding their identity, the next chapter of Revelation details their ministry during the first half of *Daniel's 70th week*, leading up to the seventh trumpet.

Revelation 11 Interpreted

> *And **a reed like a rod was given to me**. And the angel stood, saying, "Rise up and measure the temple of God, and the altar, and those who worship in it. But leave out the court, which is outside the temple, and do not measure it, for it was given to the nations. And they will trample the holy city for forty-two months." ~ Revelation 11:1-2*

While rebuilding the temple is never specifically detailed in *The Revelation*, the Apostles taught that the literal temple will be rebuilt in the last days, followed by its defilement as *the Antichrist* sits in the Holy of Holies, claiming to be God.

> *Let no one deceive you by any means; for that Day will not come unless the falling away comes first, and the man of sin is revealed, the son of perdition, who opposes and exalts*

*himself above all that is called God, or that is worshiped, so that **he sits as God in the** **temple of God**, showing himself that he is God. ~ 2nd Thessalonians 2:3*

Since Paul wrote these words when the Temple of Jerusalem was still standing, the early church writers were consistent in their belief that this very temple must be rebuilt in the last days by *the Antichrist*. John further confirms this as he is instructed to measure the temple. This *"reed"* is an allusion back to *Ezekiel 40*, which follows the great battle of *Ezekiel 38-39*. In his next prophecy, Ezekiel goes on to describe the third temple and its role in the *Millennial Reign of Christ*.

*And He brought me there, and behold, a man whose appearance was like the look of bronze, **and a line of flax in his hand, and a measuring reed**. And he stood in the gate. And the man said to me, Son of man, behold with your eyes and hear with your ears, and set your heart on all that I shall show you. For you are brought here so that I might show them to you. Declare all that you see to the house of Israel. ~ Ezekiel 40:3-4*

This passage indicates that this temple exists after the war of *Joel 2* and *Ezekiel 38*, which is part of the six seals. Afterward, *the Antichrist*, who rises to prominence during the war, will *"confirm a covenant,"* prompting Israel to reintroduce the sacrificial system. In exchange he will divide the land of Israel, making Jerusalem an international city, as a means of making peace with the nations.

*So, he shall act against fortresses of the strongholds with a strange god, whom he shall acknowledge. He shall multiply in glory, and he shall cause them to rule over many, and shall **divide the land for gain**. ~ Daniel 11:39*

*I will also gather all nations…And I will fight with them there for My people, and for My inheritance Israel, whom they have scattered among the nations, and **divided My land**. ~ Joel 3:2*

Orthodox Judaism teaches that the *Millennial Reign* will begin immediately after the war of Gog-Magog. Already believing this, many of them will accept this *"Man of Peace"* as Messiah and reinstitute the sacrifices of *Ezekiel 43*. Daniel indicates that this covenant will be made for seven years but will be broken after three and a half years.

And he shall confirm a covenant with many for one week. And in the midst of the week he shall cause the sacrifice and the offering to cease. ~ Daniel 9:27

It is in this context, that the *Two Witnesses* begin to testify, denouncing this *"Man of Peace"* and his covenant, warning the nations to trust in Christ alone, and to not fall backward into a religion which could not produce fruit *(Mark 11:12-25)*.

*And I will give power to My Two Witnesses, and they will prophesy a thousand, two hundred and sixty days, clothed in sackcloth. **These are the two olive trees and the*** *two lampstands, standing before the God of the earth. And if anyone will hurt them, fire proceeds out of their mouth and devours their enemies. And if anyone will hurt them, so it is right for him to be killed. These have authority to shut up the heaven, that it may not rain in the days of their prophecy. And they have authority over waters to turn them to blood, and to strike the earth with every plague, as often as they desire.*

~ *Revelation 11:3-5*

Their miracles also demonstrate that they come in the spirit and power of Moses and Elijah, as these plagues seem to correspond with the seven trumpets, coming about at the words of these prophets.

1) They cause it not to rain for the three and a half years of their testimony, the very sign Elijah gave in his ministry. *(2nd Kings 1:17)*

2) The first trumpet involves hail mixed with fire, which Moses performed. *(Exodus 9:22-23)*

3) The second trumpet involves waters being turned to blood, which Moses performed. *(Exodus 7:17)*

4) The third trumpet involves waters being made bitter, which Moses performed. *(Exodus 15:23)*

5) The first and forth trumpet involve fire falling from heaven, which Elijah performed. *(2nd Kings 1:12)*

6) The fourth trumpet involves the heavens being darkened, which Moses performed. *(Exodus 10:21)*

These *Two Witnesses* stand before *the Beast* in much the same way that Moses and Aaron stood before Pharaoh; and as Elijah and Elisha stood before the wicked Ahab and Jezebel. At the end of their testimony, they will be the first sign of *the Resurrection and the Rapture.*

> *And when they complete their testimony, the Beast coming up out of the abyss will make war against them and will overcome them and kill them. And their bodies will lie in the street of the great city, which spiritually is called Sodom and Egypt, where also our Lord was crucified. ~ Revelation 11:8*

Their death at the hand of *the Beast* will fulfill distinct signs to the believing and unbelieving in Israel. To the believing, they will fulfill the role of the angels in Sodom, and of Moses and Aaron, who prompted a hasty exodus out of the land, reminding the Jews of Christ's warning:

*In that day, he who is on the housetop, and his goods are in the house, let him not come down to take them away. And likewise, the one who is in the field, let him not turn back. **Remember Lot's wife**.* ~ Luke 17:31-32

To the unbelieving Jews, the showdown will be as when the two serpents of Jannes and Jambres were bested and devoured by the serpent of Moses. They will consider the *First Beast* to be "God" and the *Second Beast* to be his prophet, as it is written,

"… I have made you a god to Pharaoh: and Aaron your brother shall be your prophet." ~ Exodus 7:1

When the *Two Witnesses* are killed, their deaths will be celebrated like a new Christmas holiday. In their delusion, the wicked will believe that *the Antichrist* and *False Prophet* have been slain by the Messiah and that salvation has come to the Earth.

*And many of the peoples and tribes and tongues and nations will see their dead bodies three and a half days, and they will not allow their dead bodies to be put in tombs. And **the ones who dwell on the earth will rejoice over them, and will make merry, and will send one another gifts**, because these two prophets tormented those living on the earth.* ~ Revelation 11:9-10

The next event signifies *The Rapture,* as these *Two Witnesses* are resurrected and raptured, being called up into the sky by Christ himself, in front of all Jerusalem.

*And after three and a half days, the spirit of life from God entered into them, and they stood on their feet. And great fear fell on those seeing them. And they heard a great voice from Heaven saying to them, "Come up here." And they went up to Heaven in a cloud, and their enemies watched them. And **in that hour a great earthquake occurred**, and the tenth part of the city fell. And seven thousand people were slain in the earthquake. And the rest were frightened and gave glory to the God of Heaven.*
~ Revelation 11:11-13

After this, the two prophecies of John, the seven trumpets and the testimony of the *Two Witnesses*, converge back into a single narrative. At the sounding of the seventh trumpet, the *"Mystery"* will be completed, and these two great empires: *the Kingdom of the Beast* and the *Kings of the East*, will be met with the final woe, which is the coming of the Kingdom of Christ in the fullness of His wrath.

*The second woe passed away. Behold, the third woe comes quickly. And the seventh angel sounded. And there were great voices in Heaven, saying, "**The kingdoms of this world have become the kingdoms of our Lord, and of his Christ.**" And He will reign forever and ever.*

And the Twenty-Four Elders sitting before God on their thrones, fell on their faces and worshiped God, saying, "We thank You, O Lord God Almighty, who was, and is, and is

*to come, because You took Your great power and reigned. And the nations were full of wrath, and **Your wrath has come, and the time of the judging of the dead**, and to give the reward to Your servants the prophets, and to the saints, and to the ones fearing Your name, to the small and to the great, and to destroy those destroying the earth." And the temple of God was opened in Heaven, and **there was seen in His temple the ark of His covenant**, and there were lightnings and voices, and thunders and an earthquake, and a great hail. ~ Revelation 11:14-19*

We can conclude, that at the seventh trumpet, the first three and a half years have passed, and the *"tribulation"* (or <thilipsis>) of the Church is over. The second three and a half years, known as the *"great tribulation"* or the *"time of Jacob's trouble,"* is about to begin. The *"time of judging the dead,"* (*Daniel 12:12*) indicates that the *Resurrection* and *Rapture* are near. The Ark of the Covenant is shown, because it represents God's promise to chasten them for their sin in the latter days, before finally saving them.

> *Take this book of the law and put it in the side of the ark of the covenant of the LORD your God, that it may be there for a witness against you. ...evil will befall you in the latter days; because you will do evil in the sight of the LORD, to provoke him to anger through the work of your hands. ~ Deuteronomy 31:26*

According to Joel 2, the Day of the Lord cannot come until three distinct signs pass:

1) *(Joel 2:28-29)* The Spirit is poured out on Israel: This occurs with the 144,000 and represents those brought to faith at their teaching *(Revelation 7)*

2) *(Joel 2:30)* Signs in the heavens and the earth, of blood, *(Revelation 8:7-9)* fire, *(Revelation 8:8-11)* and pillars of smoke *(Revelation 9:1-2)*.

3) *(Joel 2:31)* The Sun is darkened, and the moon turns to blood *(Revelation 6:12)*

Since all these signs cannot have been fulfilled until five of the seven trumpets have been blown, we can conclude that the celestial disturbances of *Matthew 24:29*, include both the 6th and 7th seal, including the seven trumpets. The seals, trumpets, and bowls cannot be concurrent, nor can the *Rapture* occur before the *Resurrection* or before the *Day of the Lord*. We will see in the next section, that *the Rapture* is clearly indicated and occurs on the same day as *the last trump*, as it is written,

> *In a moment, in the twinkling of an eye, **at the last trump**: for the trumpet shall sound, and the dead shall be raised incorruptible, and we shall be changed.*
> *~ 1st Corinthians 15:52*

The Seventh Angel sounding his trumpet represents the midpoint of *Daniel's 70th week*, after which, we will see the three events which Jesus said would occur *"on that day"* when he appears in the clouds.

1) Michael will arise to cast Satan down, as the Jews flee from Israel.

2) *The Beast* is killed by the brightness of Christ's appearing.

3) The 144,000 escort the Bride and Groom to the wedding chamber.

You are Here

Birth Pangs	Trumpets		Bowls	Satan Bound
7 Seals	3 ½ Years		3 ½ Years	1000 Years

PART 8 - ON THAT DAY

Revelation chapters 12-15 represent the midpoint of *Daniel's 70th week*, involving the moments between the sounding of the seventh trumpet and the outpouring of the wrath of God. These chapters depict the day that *the Son of Man is revealed (Luke 17:30)*. After the seventh angel sounds, each theme of *The Revelation*—the Birth Pangs, the Trial, and the Wedding—come to their climax. While many details will be given to the characters, history, typology, and the surrounding events, these three chapters are meant to point their respective subject matter to *"The Day of the Lord,"* corresponding with Jesus' teaching in *Matthew 24* and *Luke 17*.

(Rev. 12) The Jews flee Jerusalem and Judea. *(Matthew 24:15-20 & Luke 17:31-33)*

(Rev. 13) The *Abomination of Desolation*. *(Matthew 24:15 & 2nd Thessalonians 2:3-4)*

(Rev. 14) Christ appears in the clouds to gather the Church. *(Matthew 24:27-31)*

The Trial of Christ and Antichrist

Understanding the trial of Christ is pivotal to understanding the midpoint of *Daniel's 70th week*. In the ministry of Jesus, he took three and a half years to demonstrate his deity and fulfill the Messianic prophecies. At the end of this period, he was falsely accused, tried, and put to death as a blasphemer; then vindicated by being raised from the dead, and proved to be the Son of God. His confrontation with the Pharisees in *John chapter 5* helps to illustrate the legal elements of this trial.

In this narrative, Jesus heals a paralyzed man on the Sabbath, ordering him to *"take up your bed and walk" (John 5:8)*. The Pharisees took offense at this because they had developed strict rules for the Sabbath, which they felt Jesus had violated. When they accused Jesus for violating their rules, he responded to them saying, *"My Father has been working until now, and I have been working." (John 5:17)*. The Jews sought to kill him for this, knowing that he was not only rebuking them but also alluding to his divinity as the Son of God, and Lord of the Sabbath.

While Jesus would have been well within his rights to simply say, "I am God," he was careful not to make this claim outright. Though he often alluded to his divinity, and referred to God as his Father, when it came to his claim of godhood, he subjected himself to the Law, saying, *"If I bear witness of myself, my witness is not true." (John 5:31)*. Knowing that testifying of himself alone was not a valid testimony under the Law, he instead carefully demonstrated three witnesses, which the Jews should have already understood to testify to his deity,

> 1) *There is another who bears witness of Me, and I know that the witness which he witnesses of Me is true. **You have sent to John**, and he has borne witness to the truth. Yet I do not receive testimony from man, but I say these things that you may be saved. He was the burning and shining lamp, and **you were willing for a time to rejoice in his light**. ~ John 5:32-35*
>
> 2) *But I have a greater witness than John; for the works which the Father has given Me to finish — **the very works that I do — bear witness of Me**, that the Father has sent Me. ~ John 5:36-37*
>
> 3) *And you do not have His word abiding in you, for you do not believe Him whom He has sent. **You search the Scriptures**, for in them you think you have eternal life. **They are the ones witnessing of Me**, and yet you will not come to Me that you might have life. I do not receive honor from men. ~ John 5:38-41*

Rather than saying he was God, Jesus pointed to the multiple witnesses the Jewish people already claimed to believe. First was the testimony of John, who was received by the Jews as a prophet. Second was the testimony of God the Father, by the miracles which he gave Jesus to do. Third were the Scriptures, which predicted his coming and his actions. The Scribes and Pharisees were experts in the Torah, and should have understood that God has a Son, whose name was yet to be revealed.

[152]

Who has ascended into heaven, or descended? Who has gathered the wind in his fists? Who has bound the waters in a garment? Who has established all the ends of the earth? What is His name, and **what is His Son's name**, *if you can tell? ~ Proverbs 30:4*

For unto us a Child is born, unto us **a Son is given**; *and the government will be upon His shoulder. And* **His name will be called** *Wonderful Counselor,* **Mighty God**, *Everlasting Father, Prince of Peace. ~ Isaiah 9:6*

Jesus knew that perfect humility was to *"Humble yourself under the mighty hand of God, and He will exalt you in due time." (1ˢᵗ Peter 5:6)*. While he was fully God during his earthly ministry, his charge was to be *"obedient unto death, even death on a cross." (Philippians 2:8)*. He emptied himself of his glory and walked out the obedient life of a prophet rather than relying on his infinite power and authority. Because of this, Jesus was careful in most instances not to speak about himself in the first person, saying, *"I will,"* but instead, would speak about the authority and destiny of the *"Son of Man,"* prophesying about himself in the third person.

The one exception to this habit was regarding his resurrection. While in most cases, he would say, *"The Son of Man will…,"* regarding *the Resurrection* he said, *"Destroy this temple, and in three days* **I will** *raise it up." (John 2:19)*. It was imperative that Jesus made it clear, that he would raise up his body by his own authority, as this was the one sign that he was given, to demonstrate that he alone is the resurrection and the life. When he was challenged to prove his authority, he knew the only obedient response was to point to his resurrection to come. Therefore, when challenged by the Jews to show a sign he said,

"This…generation…seeks a sign, and no sign will be given to it except the sign of Jonah the prophet." ~ Luke 11:29

"For as Jonah was three days and three nights in the belly of a huge fish, so the Son of Man will be three days and three nights in the heart of the earth." ~ Matthew 12:40

When Jesus was accused of claiming deity in *John 5*, he replied that the *Son of Man* would do what only God could do in raising the dead. By this he would be validated as the one who has been given judgment of the earth.

For the Father loves the Son and shows Him all things that He Himself does; and He will show Him greater works than these, that you may marvel. **For as the Father raises the dead and gives life to them, even so the Son gives life to whom He will**. *For the Father judges no one, but has committed all judgment to the Son, that all should honor the Son, just as they honor the Father. He who does not honor the Son, does not honor the Father who sent Him. ~ John 5:20*

Jesus knew that the Jewish leaders were not rejecting him for lack of understanding, but because they did not love God in their hearts and merely used His Law to lord over others. Therefore, he said of them,

> *You are of your father the devil, and the desires of your father you want to do. He was a murderer from the beginning, and does not stand in the truth, because there is no truth in him. When he speaks a lie, he speaks from his own resources, for he is a liar and the father of lies. But because I tell the truth, you do not believe Me... ~ John 8:44*

Just as those who believe God are made sons of God through faith in Christ, Jesus counted these Jews as *"sons of the devil"* for their unbelief, condemning them to be conformed to the image of Antichrist by the end.

> *I have come in My Father's name, and you do not receive Me; if another comes in his own name, him you will receive. ~ John 5:43*

Because Jesus knew that these Jews had already rejected the Law of Moses for its purpose in concluding all mankind in sin, he knew that one day another would come who would manipulate the Law to lord over others, and condemned the unbelieving Jews to follow him.

> *For if you believed Moses, you would believe Me; for he wrote about Me. But if you do not believe his writings, how will you believe My words? ~ John 5:46*

The Antichrist will undergo a 3 ½ year ministry of conquest, contrasting the 3 ½ years of humility by which Jesus ministered. Where Jesus quietly relied on three witnesses of his divinity, *the Beast* will manipulate three false witnesses in his rise to power. The first will be the testimony of the *False Prophet (Revelation 13:13)*, a counterpart to John, who will galvanize the world toward faith in him. The second will be *"lying signs and wonders" (2nd Thessalonians 2:9)*, which he will carry out by demonic powers, by illusion, and by the manipulation of technology. The third will be his own false testimony, when he stands in the temple, claiming to be God *(2nd Thessalonians 2:4)*. Where Jesus proved himself obedient unto death, Antichrist will prove himself lawless unto death. By committing this great perjury, he will fulfill the second element in the scroll of Zechariah, activating the judgement on Satan.

> *"I will bring it forth," says the LORD of hosts; "and it shall enter into the house of the thief, and into the house of **him who swears falsely** by My name. And **it shall remain in the midst of his house, and shall devour it**, and its timber and its stones." And he said to me, "This is the curse that goes forth over the face of the whole earth; for from now on everyone who steals shall be cut off according to it; and **everyone who swears from now on shall be cut off according to it**." ~ Zechariah 5:3-4*

The judgement pronounced in this scroll reflects a prophecy given by Ezekiel, in which God testifies against Satan, the anointed Angel who tempted mankind to sin.

Just as God was glorified in the earth through Jesus, who was the image of His person, Satan will be accountable for the words and deeds of Antichrist, who is the image of his person. Just as the betrayal of Judas the thief in Christ's first coming was accounted to Satan, causing him to lose the power over death and the grave, the perjury of *the Beast* activates the judgement of fire of the house of Satan.

> *And the word of the LORD came to me, saying, Son of man, lift up a lament over the king of Tyre, and say to him, So says the Lord Jehovah: "You seal the measure, full of wisdom and perfect in beauty. __You were in Eden the garden of God__; …. You were the anointed cherub that covers, and I had put you in the holy height of God where you were. You have walked up and down, in the midst of the stones of fire. You were perfect in your ways from the day that you were created, until iniquity was found in you. By the multitude of your trade they have filled your midst with violence, and you have sinned. So, I cast you profaned from the height of God, and __I destroy you, O covering cherub__, from among the stones of fire. … By the host of your iniquities, by the iniquity of your trade, you have profaned your holy places; so, __I brought a fire from your midst; it shall devour you__, and I will give you for ashes on the earth, before the eyes of all who see you. All who know you among the peoples shall be astonished at you; you shall be terrors, and you will not be forever." ~ Ezekiel 28:11-19*

Daniel 11 prophesies the deeds and exploits of *the Beast* until his death, while *Daniel 12* prophesies the *"great tribulation"* to come afterward. This demonstrates that *the Beast* dies in the middle of the week.

> *And he shall plant his palace tents between the seas in the glorious holy mountain. Yet he shall come to his end, and none shall help him. ~ Daniel 11:45*

While Daniel is clear that *the Beast* dies at this time, he does not indicate how this happens. He declares in another prophecy that he will be killed, though not by the hand of man, when attempting to directly confront the Lord.

> *he shall also stand up against the Prince of princes; but __he shall be broken without hand__. ~ Daniel 8:25*

When he commits this perjury, Christ will appear in the sky, slaying him with a word of power as He comes to rapture his *Bride*, even as Paul testifies,

> *And then the lawless one will be revealed, whom the __Lord will consume with the breath of His mouth__ and destroy with the brightness of His coming.*
> *~ 2nd Thessalonians 2:7-8*

His death is prophesied to carry certain wounds that would mark him forever. Just as Christ would forever be known by his nail-pierced hands and wounded side, *the*

Antichrist will be known for his darkened eye and a withered arm, which are likely marks that he will obtain at his death.

> *Woe to the idol shepherd that leaves the flock! the sword shall be upon his arm, and upon his right eye: his arm shall be clean dried up, and his right eye shall be utterly darkened.*
> ~ *Zechariah 11:17*

Jesus said he would appear as lightning, which flashes in the East and is seen in the West. Christ may choose to kill *the Beast* with a bolt of lightning, simultaneously with Satan being cast out of Heaven. As the Beast lifts up his hand to cover his eyes from the blinding flash, a bolt of lightning could strike through, and leave both wounds.

> *I saw Satan fall as lightning from heaven.* ~ *Luke 10:8*

The Day of the Lord is the day that both Christ and Antichrist are revealed *(2nd Thessalonians 2:3)*. These three chapters of *The Revelation* will prophesy the effects of this revelation on three groups of people. When the *Abomination of Desolation* occurs, the believing Jews will flee to the wilderness as Jesus commanded. As they flee, they will see *the Rapture* occur that night, as Christ appears in the clouds, striking down *the Antichrist* with the sword of his mouth. Afterward, in the place of *the Antichrist* will be the *Image of the Beast*, a perverse infusion of mankind and technology to constitute a false resurrection. This image will be worshipped as "God" until Christ returns with all his saints to make war with *the Beast* and the *Kings of the East*. This worship will begin at the midpoint of the week and continue until the end, when the two armies are trodden in the winepress of the Lord's fury.

Jerusalem Flees: Revelation 12 Interpreted

Paul makes it clear that the *"Abomination of Desolation"* cannot take place until *"he"* who restrains is taken out of the way.

> *For the mystery of lawlessness is already at work; only he who now restrains will do so until he is taken out of the way.* ~ *2nd Thessalonians 2: 7*

The Book of Daniel teaches that Michael, the angelic prince, is anointed as the protector of Israel. When an angel was sent to bring Daniel the message of the seventy weeks, he says of Michael *"there is none that holds (or restrains) with me in these things, but Michael your prince." (Daniel 10:21).* The angel indicates that Michael is the only angel working against the demonic forces that oppose the Word of God in the earth. Michael is one of three angels named in Scripture, with Gabriel and Lucifer, demonstrating a rank equal to that of Lucifer.

Paul is interpreting from Daniel, knowing that Christ clearly testifies to Daniel's prophecy, as the key to understanding the *Abomination of Desolation*. Paul knows that Satan cannot take dominion over Israel except in Michael's absence, because he is in authority to restrain the extent of Satan's wickedness in the earth, so that God's good purposes are fulfilled. Daniel testified that Michael would ascend from the earth, and at this time, the *time of great trouble* would begin.

> At that time **Michael shall stand up (or arise)**; *the great prince who stands watch over the sons of your people. And there shall be a time of trouble, such as never was since there was a nation, even to that time. And* **at that time your people shall be delivered**; *everyone who is found written in the book.* ~ Daniel 12:1

Michael will arise from the earth to do battle with Satan and his angels, casting them down to the earth. As this occurs, *the Beast* will desolate the temple, marking the beginning of *"the time of Jacob's trouble,"* the subject of both *Daniel 12* and *Revelation 12*.

> Now a great sign appeared in heaven: **a woman clothed with the sun, with the moon under her feet, and on her head a garland of twelve stars**. *And being with child, she cried out in labor and in pain to give birth. Then, another sign appeared in heaven: behold, a great fiery red dragon having seven heads and ten horns, and seven diadems on his heads. His tail drew a third of the stars of heaven and threw them to the earth. And the dragon stood before the woman who was ready to give birth, to devour her Child as soon as it was born. And* **she bore a son, a male, who is going to rule all nations with a rod of iron. And her child was caught up to God and to His throne**.
>
> ~ Revelation 12:1-5

Similar to the prophecy of the *Two Witnesses*, this vision of the woman and the dragon takes the reader from the past to the midpoint of the week. While the original woman was Eve and the original serpent was Satan in the Garden of Eden, in their final iteration, the woman is Israel, the Jerusalem below, while the Serpent is the Dragon, who gives power to *the Beast*. The imagery of the Sun, the Moon, and the twelve stars symbolizes the people of Israel, first given by Joseph in one of his prophetic dreams. His father Jacob immediately understood the symbols and interpreted them to signify his household.

> And he dreamed still another dream and told it to his brothers. And he said, "Behold, I have dreamed another dream. And behold, **the sun and the moon and the eleven stars bowed down to me.**" *And he told it to his father and to his brothers. And his father rebuked him and said to him, "What is this dream that you have dreamed?* **Shall I, and your mother, and your brothers indeed come to bow ourselves to the earth before you**?" ~ Genesis 37:9-10

This woman represents the Jerusalem below; the Israel still in bondage *(Galatians 4:24-25)*—representing those in Jerusalem and Judea who are commanded by Christ to flee at the *Abomination of Desolation (Matthew 24:16)*. The child being caught up to the throne represents Christ who will rule with a rod of iron, alluding to *the Body of Christ*, which will be caught up at this time to rule with him. Along with the seventh trump in *Revelation chapter 11*, this is another sign that *the Rapture* is occurring.

The Rapture takes place in correspondence with the resurrection and rapture of the *Two Witnesses*. Though it is not expressly stated in *The Revelation*, it is presumed that after killing the *Two Witnesses*, the *Antichrist* proceeds to stand in the temple and claim to be God. At this offense, the believing Jews will flee from Jerusalem in a last-moment act of faith that will be salvation to their souls. The Jerusalem below will be like Hagar in *Genesis 21*, when she was cast out of the *Promised Land* to be nourished by God in the wilderness.

> *Then the woman fled into the wilderness, where she has a place prepared by God, that they should feed her there one thousand two hundred and sixty days.* ~ *Revelation 12:6*

When the number of those slain for Christ is fulfilled *(Revelation 6:11)*, the church will have proven Satan's accusations false, resulting in the loss of his heavenly office. Having lost his position before God *"accusing the brethren,"* he will be cast out.

> *And there was war in Heaven. Michael and his angels warring against the dragon. And the dragon and his angels warred but did not prevail. **Nor was place found for them in Heaven anymore**. And the great dragon was cast out, the old serpent called the Devil, and Satan, who deceives the whole world. He was cast out into the earth, and his angels were cast out with him. And I heard a great voice saying in Heaven, "Now has come the salvation and power and the kingdom of our God, and the authority of His Christ. For the accuser of our brothers is cast down, who accused them before our God day and night."* ~ *Revelation 12:7-10*

The heavenly voice indicates the redemption of the *Bride* is at hand, rejoicing in her salvation as she completes the trial of her testimony.

> *Then I heard a loud voice saying in heaven, "Now salvation, and strength, and the kingdom of our God, and the power of His Christ have come, for the accuser of our brethren, who accused them before our God day and night, has been cast down. And they overcame him by the blood of the Lamb and by the word of their testimony, and they did not love their lives to the death."* ~ *Revelation 12:11*

After the perseverance of the Church is complete, there will be great wrath in the earth. Satan will unleash his greatest deception in the false resurrection of *the Beast*, who had been slain by Christ with the breath of his coming. As the heavens will be rejoicing at the arrival of the Church, the world will begin to experience a time of *"great tribulation"* as the kingdom of Satan is overturned by Christ. Only those who fled into the wilderness will be sheltered from this *"great trouble."*

> *Therefore rejoice, O heavens, and you who dwell in them! Woe to the inhabitants of the earth and the sea! For the devil has come down to you, having great wrath, because he knows that he has a short time. Now when the dragon saw that he had been cast to the earth, he persecuted the woman who gave birth to the male Child. **But the woman was given two wings of a great eagle, that she might fly into the wilderness to her place, where she is nourished for a time and times and half a time, away from the presence of the serpent**. ~ Revelation 12:12-14*

One of the Messianic Prophecies that *the Antichrist* will try to counterfeit is to make a river come from Jerusalem that purifies the Dead Sea *(Ezekiel 47:12)*. *The Beast* may accomplish this by diverting water from the Euphrates River to flow from Jerusalem. When Satan falls, he will immediately seek to make war on the Jews that fled from Jerusalem, unleashing a flood to destroy them as they flee from Judea. Satan may do this by diverting a greater flow of water from the Euphrates, resulting in the river drying up, making way for the armies of the *Kings of the East*. This flood fulfills another prophecy of *the Antichrist*, given by Daniel.

> *…the prince that shall come shall destroy the city and the sanctuary; and **the end thereof shall be with a flood**, and unto the end of the war desolations are determined.*
> *~ Daniel 9:26*

> *So, **the serpent spewed water out of his mouth like a flood after the woman**, that he might cause her to be carried away by the flood. But the earth helped the woman, and the earth opened its mouth, and swallowed up the flood which the dragon had spewed out of his mouth. ~ Revelation 12:15-16*

The great earthquake that shakes the earth after the Resurrection and rapture of the Two Witnesses will cause a diversion of the terrain, keeping these flood waters from engulfing the fleeing Jews. This will enrage Satan and will prompt him to begin a worldwide persecution of every remaining person who retains faith in Christ.

> *And the dragon was enraged with the woman, and **he went to make war with the rest of her offspring**, who keep the commandments of God and have the testimony of Jesus Christ. ~ Revelation 12:17*

These *"who keep the commandments of God and have the testimony of Jesus Christ"* will include two groups. First are the Jews who remain in Israel and did not heed the words of Jesus to flee at the *Abomination of Desolation*. Second are the Christians who come out of Laodicea, having missed *the Rapture* because of their lax faith.

> *You are the salt of the earth, but if the salt loses its savor, with what shall it be salted? It is no longer good for anything, but to be thrown out and to be trodden underfoot by men.*
> ~ *Matthew 5:13*

While Satan will have been working seductively to convince the world that he is God and that the Beast is his Christ, after his fall, he will reveal his true nature as a murdering tyrant, caring only for himself and willing to destroy the whole earth for the sake of his pride. In his wrath at being cast permanently out of heaven, he will immediately unleash a plan to eradicate every believer in Christ from the earth. While these people will be resurrected to reign with Christ in the Millennium, they will endure this last 3 ½ years of tribulation, suffering the penalty of being beheaded, for their refusal to take the *Mark of the Beast*.

The Abomination: Revelation 13 Interpreted

> *Then I stood on the sand of the sea. And* **<u>I saw a beast rising up out of the sea</u>**, *having seven heads and ten horns, and on his horns ten crowns, and on his heads a blasphemous name. Now the Beast which I saw was like a* **<u>leopard</u>**, *his feet were like the feet of a* **<u>bear</u>**, *and his mouth like the mouth of a* **<u>lion</u>**. *The dragon gave him his power, his throne, and great authority.* ~ *Revelation 13:1-2*

In the Prophets, Satan was represented as the power behind the throne of two kings. One was the trade kingdom of Tyre and the other was the military kingdom of Babylon. Just as the King of Tyre *(Ezekiel 28)*, and the King of Babylon *(Isaiah14)*, are used by the Holy Spirit to reveal the heart and motivations of Satan, there are also two beasts, representing these two facets of his activity in the earth. One is a ruthless military conqueror, while the other is a propagandist and economic minister. *Revelation 13* describes these two beasts, and how they rule during *Daniel's 70th week*.

The first beast rises out of the sea, indicating that he arises from the Gentile nations. This *Beast* comes from the line of Dan, whose tribe left the land and made their home on the seas, mingling with the Gentiles of Sidon, Tyre, and Greece. The leopard, bear, and lion that make up his body, represent attributes of the previous kingdoms revealed to Daniel. This final kingdom of *the Beast* is a conglomerate of those ancient kingdoms, to which Israel was captive throughout Daniel's prophecies.

The Great Statue of Daniel 2

When the Jews were taken captive to Babylon, Daniel was selected to be part of an elite group of wise men that served King Nebuchadnezzar; a group which included various philosophers, scientists, and occultists. When the king was tormented with a dream, he ordered his wise men to reveal both what had happened in his dream, as well as its meaning, threatening them with death if they could not divine these things. Daniel convinced the king's servant to let him address the king, and God inspired Daniel both to know the dream and to understand its meaning.

> *You, O king were seeing. And behold! A great image! That great image, whose brightness was excellent, stood before you. And its form was dreadful. This image's (1)* **head was of fine gold**; *his (2)* **breast and his arms were of silver**; *his (3)* **belly and his thighs were of bronze**; *his (4)* **legs were of iron**; *his feet were part of iron and part of clay. You watched until a stone was cut out without hands, which struck the image upon its feet, which were of iron and clay, and broke them to pieces…And the stone that struck the image became a great mountain and filled the whole earth. ~ Daniel 2:31-35*

After describing the dream to the king, Daniel explained its meaning.

> *This is the dream. And we will tell its meaning before the king…*
>
> *…you are this head of gold. But after you shall arise another kingdom inferior to yours; then another, a third kingdom of bronze, which shall rule over all the earth. And the fourth kingdom shall be as strong as iron, inasmuch as iron breaks in pieces and shatters everything; and like iron that crushes, that kingdom will break in pieces and crush all the others. ~ Daniel 2:36-40*

After describing the statue which Nebuchadnezzar saw, Daniel explained to him that there would be four successive kingdoms, beginning with his own, which would rule the earth until an eternal kingdom would come in the last days. These four kingdoms successively ruled over the Jews and the *Promised Land* as stewards of Israel, just as Lucifer became steward of the Earth when man fell into sin. From the time which Nebuchadnezzar had taken Judah captive, this *Time of the Gentiles* represented the duration which Israel would be captive before their Messiah would deliver them. Until this time, the Jews were to…

> *…seek the peace of the city where I have caused you to be exiled and pray to the LORD for it. For in its peace you shall have peace. ~ Jeremiah 29:7*

Just as Eve was commanded to submit to Adam after the fall, Israel was commanded to submit to these Gentile nations, understanding that their disciplinary position was the work of God, because of their sinful idolatry and failure to keep His Law. Because of this stewardship over God's chosen people, these kingdoms would be given prominence in the earth as the chief of the nations. They would retain this position unless they were to overstep their authority, which would occur when their kings would abuse the people of God or attempt to be worshipped as a god. In this way, these kingdoms, each in turn, represented a type of Satan in his authority over the earth, culminating in the sin of Antichrist, which will prompt the Lord to take his authority away. These four kingdoms, that would reign between the time of Jeremiah and the time of Christ represented Babylon, Medo-Persia, Greece, and Rome, with a revived conglomeration of these kingdoms manifesting again in the last days.

Daniel's prophecies always lead up to a mysterious gap between the fourth kingdom and a latter-day kingdom ruled by *the Beast*. This gap can only be understood in light of the revealed mystery of the Gospel and the gathering of the Gentiles into the Body of Christ. Just as Christ had two comings, which were kept a mystery, this Gentile kingdom would have two manifestations into which Christ would appear. This kingdom would be twice *"overturned"* by the Kingdom of God, patterned after the spiritual and material overthrow of Nineveh *(Jonah vs. Nahum)*. The Kingdom of God would have its former spiritual manifestation in the Church, beginning during the Pax Romana, and will have its latter material manifestation after *the Antichrist* achieves a false peace in *Daniel's 70th week*. In those days, Christ will return to set up a *Millennial Kingdom,* which he will rule with a rod of iron. In this pattern, Daniel's prophecies are partially fulfilled historically, with a remainder to be fulfilled in the last days, always bringing finality to this *Time of the Gentiles.*

> And as to that which you saw: **the feet and toes, part of potters' clay and part of iron; the kingdom shall be divided**. *But there shall be in it the strength of the iron, because you saw the iron mixed with miry clay. And as the toes of the feet were part of iron and part of clay, so the kingdom shall be partly strong and partly brittle. And as you saw iron mixed with miry clay, they shall mix themselves with the seed of men. But **they shall not cling to one another, even as iron is not mixed with clay**.*
>
> ~ Daniel 2:41-43

After explaining Nebuchadnezzar's dream, Daniel spoke of a revived empire of *iron mixed with clay*. The final manifestation of this empire will be a New World Order, which will be set up after World War III. While this kingdom will be established with ten kings who initially share global power, *the Beast* will manipulate this power balance to seize an empire that will have a clear geopolitical and economic advantage, subduing three of the kings. The remaining kings will align with one another to form the *Kings of the East* and will band together against him, finally coming to meet him at the *Battle of Armageddon.*

> And **in the days of these kings**, the God of Heaven shall set up a kingdom which shall never be destroyed. And the kingdom shall not be left to other peoples, but it shall crush and destroy all these kingdoms, and it shall stand forever. ~ Daniel 2:44

When Daniel says, *"in the days of these kings,"* he is not alluding to the four kingdoms that make up this statue or the ten kings that will rule in the last days. He is referring to the *Kingdom Come,* which will arise spiritually during the fourth kingdom and also materially in the last days.

The Goat and the Ram of Daniel 8

Just as the vision of the statue reveals successive historical kingdoms before bleeding into a last-days empire, the prophecy of *the goat and the ram* reveals the kings of the Medo-Persians and the Greeks before bleeding into a last-days prophecy about the *Abomination of Desolation.* As a first kind of *Kingdom Come* arrives during the Roman Empire, the *Abomination of Desolation* will be foreshadowed in the days of the Greek Empire, at the time of the Maccabean revolt.

> Then I lifted up my eyes and looked. And behold, a ram with two horns stood before the canal, having two horns, and the two horns were high, but one was higher than the other, and the higher came up last. I saw the ram **pushing westward, northward, and southward** so that no beasts could stand before him, nor any that could deliver out of his hand. But he did according to his will and became great. ~ Daniel 8:3-4

This prophecy details the history of the Medo-Persian and Greek Empires. It reveals how the Persians, who grew up later, became stronger than the Medes who ruled at the beginning. The Persians had a base in what is today Iran, Central Asia, and Pakistan, while continuing to wage campaigns toward the West, North, and South.

> ... as I was watching, behold, a male goat came from the west, over the face of all the earth, and did not touch the ground. And the he goat had an outstanding horn between his eyes. And he came to the ram that had two horns, which I had seen standing before the river, and ran to him in the fury of his power. ... And there was no power in the ram to stand before him. ... And when he was strong, **the great horn was broken. And in its place, came up four outstanding ones towards the four winds of the heavens**.
> ~ Daniel 8: 5-8

The prophecy then details the conquest of Alexander the Great, who after uniting all the Greek city states, led a campaign against the Persians to conquer their entire empire in a span of just seven years, only to die shortly afterward and have his empire divided among his four generals. It goes on to detail a future king that comes from one of these four kingdoms and goes on to take away the Jewish sacrifices, exalting himself to be worshipped in the place of God.

> *And out of one of them came a little horn, which grew exceedingly great toward the south, toward the east, and toward the Glorious Land. And it grew up to the host of heaven; and it cast down some of the host and some of the stars to the ground and trampled them.* ***He even exalted himself as high as the Prince of the host; and by him the daily sacrifices were taken away, and the place of His sanctuary was cast down****. Because of transgression, an army was given over to the horn, to oppose the daily sacrifices; and he cast truth down to the ground. He did all this and prospered.*
> *~ Daniel 8:9-12*

Like Daniel's other prophecies, this prophecy was fulfilled historically to an extent, though it relates primarily to the end of Israel's captivity to the Gentiles.

> *Behold, I will make you know what shall be in the last end of the indignation: for at the time appointed the end shall be. ~ Daniel 8:19*

After the angel explains that the earlier parts of the prophecy detail the kingdoms of the Greeks and Persians, he then explains to Daniel how this *"little horn"* will go on to challenge Christ for supremacy in the final days of the *Times of the Gentiles.*

> *And in the latter time of their kingdom, when the transgressors have reached their fullness, a king shall arise, a king of fierce countenance, and understanding dark sentences. His power shall be mighty, but not by his own power; He shall destroy fearfully and shall prosper and thrive; He shall destroy the mighty, and also the holy people. Through his cunning He shall cause craft to prosper under his rule and he shall exalt himself in his heart. He shall destroy many in their prosperity.* ***He shall even rise against the Prince of princes****; but he shall be broken without human means. And the vision of the evenings and mornings which was told is true. Therefore, seal up the vision, for it refers to many days in the future. ~ Daniel 8:23-26*

Just as the fourth kingdom has a *dual fulfillment* during the two comings of Christ, this *"little horn"* represents both Antiochus Epiphanes, who desecrated the second temple, and *the Antichrist,* who sets up the *Abomination of Desolation* in the temple to be rebuilt in the last days.

The Four Beasts of Daniel 7

> *Daniel spoke, and said, "In my vision by night I was looking and behold, the four winds of the heavens were stirring up the Great Sea. And four great beasts came up from the sea, different from one another." ~ Daniel 7:2-3*

In this vision, Daniel prophesied about the four kingdoms as four beasts, again leading up to the last days. This last-days kingdom will be a revival of the Roman Empire, being ruled by a man who claims to be God. These four beasts represent attributes of this empire and the deeds of its ruler, who is called *the Beast*.

> *The first was **like a lion** and had eagle's wings. I watched until its wings were plucked, and it was lifted up from the earth and made to stand on its feet like a man. And a man's heart was given to it. ~ Daniel 7:4*

This symbol of the lion would not have been strange to Nebuchadnezzar, as it reflected his own life. In ancient Mesopotamia, wings symbolized the rays of the sun, while a lion represented unparalleled authority. Nebuchadnezzar saw himself as a "god king," and made a great golden statue of himself, commanding all his subjects to bow down to it in worship. For refusing, Daniel's friends were thrown into a fiery furnace. When they were miraculously saved by the Lord, though the king glorified God, he still needed to be humbled from his pride, which God accomplished later.

Later in his reign, he was given a prophetic dream about a great tree being cut down to a stump and made as low as the grass, given to the beasts of the field *(Daniel 4: 10-17)*. Daniel revealed that this dream was about the king and how God would humble him from his pride, reducing his mind to that of a beast for seven years before finally being restored. After God carried out this humiliation, Nebuchadnezzar acknowledged that his great kingdom was not his own accomplishment, confessing his repentance and glorifying God as the true Judge.

> *Now, I Nebuchadnezzar, praise and exalt and honor the King of heaven, all whose works are truth and His ways justice. And **those who walk in pride He is able to humble**.*
> *~ Daniel 4:37*

Nebuchadnezzar would have understood that this lion, who was humbled and given the heart of a man, represented himself and his kingdom.

> *And behold another beast, a second, **like a bear**. And it raised itself up on one side, and it had three ribs in its mouth between its teeth. And they said this to it: Arise, eat up much flesh. ~ Daniel 7: 5*

The second beast details the Persians just as in Daniel's vision of the ram. The three ribs in the bears mouth reflect their great appetite for territorial gain that would eventually be their downfall. Their failed attempt to conquer the Greeks, eventually exhausted both the resources, and the resolve of the Persian Empire. These city states, who had been fighting brutal wars against each other for centuries, were too tough to conquer when united against a common enemy. After defeating the Persians on land and sea over several decades, Alexander the Great would eventually unite their armies to conquer the entire Persian kingdom in a rapid campaign.

> *After this I saw, and lo, another, **like a leopard**, which had four wings of a bird on its back. The Beast also had four heads; and rulership was given to it. ~ Daniel 7:6*

The third beast represents Alexander's rapid conquest of the Persians, with the help of his four generals. After conquering this great territory, Alexander returned to Babylon, where he suddenly died. His four generals, represented in the four heads of this leopard and matching the four horns of the he-goat, would divide his empire amongst themselves. Seleucus would hold the Middle East and Asia; Ptolemy would hold Egypt and Israel; Lysimachus would hold modern Turkey; and Cassander would hold the original kingdom, comprising modern Greece and Macedonia. It was from the Seleucid empire that Antiochus Epiphanes would conquer Israel and set up the *Abomination of Desolation*, invigorating the Maccabean revolt.

> *… and behold, **a fourth beast, fearful and terrible, and very strong**. And it had great iron teeth; it devoured and broke in pieces and stamped the rest with its feet. And it was different from all the Beasts before it; and **it had ten horns**. ~ Daniel 7:7*

The fourth beast has *"iron teeth"* and *"ten horns,"* reflecting the iron legs and ten toes of the great statue. This beast represents the rise of Imperial Rome, and also the final empire of *the Beast*, having similarities to the rise of the Roman Empire.

The ancient Roman government was once a republic, ruled by a senate from its various territories, each with varied local interests. This system was represented by the fasces, a bundle of rods tied around an axe, symbolizing both the unified strength, and the shared power of the Republic. However, Rome would eventually devolve into a dictatorship, with the Caesars gaining absolute power over the Senate.

The world is now seeking to form a New World Order as a representative republic to govern the entire earth. The United Nations, desiring to represent this republic, is currently kept from exercising real power by the strength of the United States. Upon the weakening of the United States, this world republic will arise in the last days. This New World Order will incorporate all the nations of the world, both weak and strong, with varied interests and values which will not result in true unity.

"The fourth beast shall be A fourth kingdom on earth, which shall be different from all other kingdoms, and shall devour the whole earth, trample it and break it in pieces. The ten horns are ten kings who shall arise from this kingdom." ~ Daniel 7:23

John will also refer to these ten kings later in *The Revelation*.

And the ten horns which you saw are ten kings, which have received no kingdom as yet; but receive power as kings one hour with the Beast. ~ Revelation 17:12

These ten kings receive power *"one hour with the Beast"* and *"devour the whole Earth."* After a devastating Third World War and the great signs that occur during the six seals of *Revelation 6*, the nations of the world will agree to divide the world into ten new political spheres which will form a confederate republic of the earth. These ten kings will give rise to this kingdom in the same way that the Italian city states formed the Roman Republic, which later became a dictatorship. These ten kings will rule major economic spheres like North America, Europe, North Africa, Northern Asia, Eastern Asia, South America, Oceania, Sub-Saharan Africa, The Middle East, and Southern Asia. *The Beast* will subdue three of these kings: Europe, the Middle East, and North Africa, to regain the territories of the former Roman Empire, allowing him to attain economic dominion over the rest of the world.

*And another shall rise after them; he shall be different from the first ones and **shall subdue three kings**. ~ Daniel 7:23*

Understanding these four beasts, we can learn which characteristics of these kingdoms are present in that final empire that will devour the whole earth.

*Then I stood on the sand of the sea. And I saw a beast rising up out of the sea, **having seven heads and ten horns**, and on his horns ten crowns, and on his heads a blasphemous name. Now the Beast which I saw was **like a leopard**, his feet were **like the feet of a bear**, and **his mouth like the mouth of a lion**. The dragon gave him his power, his throne, and great authority. ~ Revelation 13:1-2*

The *seven heads and ten horns* represent the way he takes power, subduing three kings to gain supremacy over the remaining seven. He will be *"like a leopard,"* having a military genius like that of Alexander, allowing him to take this kingdom with great speed and decisiveness, manipulating a false peace to *"by peace destroy many" (Daniel 8:25).* He will have *"the feet of a bear"* because he will reach for more territory like the Persian kings. Where the Persian kings pushed *"westward, northward, and southward,"* he will expand *"East, South, and toward the Pleasant Land" (Daniel 8:9).* This represents his push to the Euphrates River in the East and to the Nile in the South before setting up his base camp between Jerusalem and the Mediterranean Sea *(Daniel 11:39-45).*

Finally, this *Beast* will have the mouth of a Lion, representing a boastfulness exceeding that of Nebuchadnezzar, who made an image to worship as if it were a god. In the case of *Antichrist*, the image that he sets up will be an artificial resurrection, helped by a *"strange god."*

Artificial Intelligence: The Strange God

> *So shall he do; he shall even return, and have intelligence with them that forsake the holy covenant.* ~ Daniel 11:25-30

In his rise to power, *the Beast* will likely have the help of the intelligence apparatus of Israel, including advanced artificial intelligence. A.I. is already beginning to gain godlike worship among technocrats and this will only popularize as the world becomes increasingly godless. After World War III, the world may even utilize an A.I. to determine the fairest measure of dividing the earth's economies and resources. Turkey, after remaining neutral in the war, will form a buffer state along the Euphrates, absorbing the failed states of Iraq and Syria, mitigating a peace between the Arabian and Iranian interests in the region. By this Artificial Intelligence, this *"strange god"* which his fathers never knew, *the Beast* will give the Jewish people a superior position in the world, dividing both Israel and the world to give himself the advantage he needs to obtain global supremacy.

> *he shall act against the strongest fortresses **with a strange god,** which he shall acknowledge, and advance its glory; and **he shall cause them to rule over many** and divide the land for gain.* ~ Daniel 11:39

This *Beast* will converge technology and humanity into super-humanism, advancing the transhumanist cause. He will forsake the institution of marriage, perhaps even causing it to be forbidden as he leads the world to the conclusion that human souls are equivalent to digital information, meant to evolve beyond their bodies in light of this new *evolution of consciousness.*

> *He shall regard neither the God of his fathers nor the desire of women, nor regard any god; for he shall exalt himself above them all. But in their place, he shall honor a god of fortresses; and a god, which his fathers did not know, he shall honor with gold and silver, with precious stones and pleasant things.* ~ Daniel 11:37-38

The Kingdom of *the Beast* will be diverse from the rest in that it will *"devour the whole earth."* This does not necessarily mean that this kingdom will physically occupy the entire globe, but that its dominion will be supreme and will consume the world's resources to sustain its power. An Artificial Intelligence may be governing these intrigues from the beginning, deciding that Turkey holds the best geopolitical position to accomplish this global takeover. Combining the industrial base of Turkey, the oil base of Arabia, and the technological resources of Israel, this union could match any power in the world today. With the U.S. and Russia decimated by war, these three could form an alliance to quickly establish a new superpower.

When *the Beast* takes Egypt, he will monopolize the world's economy around the former Roman Empire, leaving Asia and the Americas out of the world economy. This realization will prompt the *Kings of the East* to come against him, forcing him to abandon his campaign for Africa. With a military comprised of information age technology, intelligent drones, and a military strategy led by Artificial Intelligence, *"he shall go out with great fury to destroy and annihilate many." (Daniel 11:44).*

The Image of the Beast

*And I saw one of his heads as if it had been mortally wounded, and **his deadly wound was healed**. And all the world marveled and followed the Beast, and worshiped the dragon who gave authority to the Beast; and they worshiped the Beast, saying, "Who is like the Beast? **Who is able to make war with him?**" And **he was given a mouth** speaking great things and blasphemies, and he was given authority to continue for forty-two months. ~ Revelation 13:3-5*

When *the Beast* commits his great act of perjury, declaring himself to be God, he will receive a mortal headwound caused by Christ himself.

*And I will put enmity between you and the woman, and between your seed and her Seed; **He will crush your head**, and you shall bruise His heel. ~ Genesis 3:15*

Christ has a sword in his mouth because he kills *the Antichrist* with the word of power and the breath of his coming, fulfilling prophecies to kill *the Beast* by a sword *(Revelation 13:14)*, also causing him to be *"broken without hand" (Daniel 8:25)*. However, despite being dead, he is *given authority to continue forty-two months.*

And forces shall be mustered by him, and they shall defile the sanctuary fortress; then they shall take away the daily sacrifices, and place there the Abomination of Desolation. ~ Daniel 11:31

While the initial defilement of the temple will occur when *the Antichrist* stands in the Holy of Holies, claiming to be God, the desolation will continue after he is struck down, as the *Second Beast* sets up the *Image of the Beast* in his place.

*... and behold, there came up among them another little horn, before whom three of the first horns were uprooted. And behold, in **this horn were eyes like the eyes of a man, and a mouth speaking great things**. ~ Daniel 7:8*

The *pseudo-resurrection* of *the Beast* will be a complete deception. While many speculate that this man will be spiritually inhabited by Satan and physically arise from death, it must be understood that resurrection is a domain that belongs exclusively to the Lord. The key to understanding this mystery, is that he has *eyes like the eyes of a man*, and is *given a mouth to speak blasphemies*. The resurrected *Beast* will not be a man, but an Artificial Intelligence, crafted in his image and given all authority to rule in his place. This *Image of the Beast* will succeed in deceiving the whole world into believing that it embodies an actual soul, having been successfully transferred into a new body. By this deception, Satan will attempt to convince the world that he is able to preserve the soul against death, allowing mankind to continue in sin and blasphemy, while succeeding to an alternative resurrection and new body.

By this *"Image,"* the *Beast* will continue to rule for forty-two months, though he himself will be dead. The *Image of the Beast* will be given authority over the weapons systems, the economy, and the communications of the world, wielding absolute power. This will prompt a desperate campaign against him by the *Kings of the East*, leading to the *Battle of Armageddon*. This Artificial Intelligence will likely attempt to justify its dictatorial rule, by claiming to guard the world against an extra-terrestrial invader which has "harvested" humanity. In doing this, it will be claiming that the God of all creation is nothing more than a hostile alien with superior technology, seeking to acquire the resources of Earth.

*Then he opened his mouth in **blasphemy against God, to blaspheme His name, His tabernacle, and those who dwell in heaven**. It was granted to him to make war with the saints and to overcome them. And **authority was given him over every tribe, tongue, and nation**. ~ Revelation 13:6-7*

This *Image of the Beast* will blaspheme God and his tabernacle (*the New Jerusalem*), attempting to reduce Him to merely another creature. In blaspheming *"those who dwell in heaven,"* it will deceive the world into believing those taken in *the Rapture* are either traitors or captives, being brainwashed or inhabited by an alien entity to be weaponized as an invasion force to take the earth. Declaring a worldwide emergency, it will attempt to gather the world into a single military machine, claiming that the only defense for the earth is to unite against this common enemy, giving all authority to his super-intelligence.

[170]

While such a scenario may seem far-fetched, one must remember that Satan, for all his wisdom and intelligence, is not a creative being. He is only able to corrupt, distort, and counterfeit the things of God, having no creative ideas of his own. Ideas like artificial intelligence, alien invasions, human cloning, and a wider variety of ideas in the realm of science fiction are all merely attempts to replicate the creative power of God. These ideas, like the gods and myths of ancient lore, are merely attempts to offer a counter explanation and belief system to the Biblical truth, incorporating scientific materialism in the place of the spiritism that was at the heart of the pagan worldview.

These ideas, through mediums like story, music, and film, are beginning to coalesce into a single false theology which the Bible simply calls, *"the lie"* *(2ⁿᵈ Thessalonians. 2:11)*. This mythology will incrementally begin to leave the realm of the arts and begin to find itself propagated in the universities, on the news, and even by the governments. Already, large parts of humanity consider it more rational to believe in aliens than to believe in the God of the Bible. This lie will proceed from popular idea, to a matter of fact in order to be considered mentally healthy. As these ideas become more mainstream, they are meant to reduce spiritual concepts to material science, eliminating any need to worship God. This deception will convince many that the only security against being abducted by these alien invaders will be to upload our *souls* (in digitized form) into *the cloud* for safekeeping.

This idea of a *digital soul* is already becoming mainstream among the technocratic elite, who will increase in power in this post-WWIII world. These *transhumanists* are steadily propagating the idea that the human soul is no more than the collective sum of our memories, psychology, and sensual experiences; a transferrable data set that can be saved, downloaded, and projected. Already, humans are having their every thought and movement tracked, digitized, catalogued, and studied in order to create digital avatars of themselves. While some of these avatars manifest in the form of various games and voluntary digital experiences, others may be underway without our knowledge or consent. One by one, human abilities are being reduced to digital programs, sensors, and decision-making algorithms, which increasingly become better at counterfeiting actual living beings. With advances in digital rendering or CGI, and advanced A.I. psychology, we will soon see people making the claim that various people have successfully been *saved* in *the cloud* for later revival.

Even now, an entire generation is being brought up to believe that an Artificial Intelligence is the equivalent of a human soul. In 2017, an Artificial Intelligence named Sophia was granted citizenship in Saudi Arabia. Perverse men have invented sex-robots and are beginning to marry them legally. The overwhelming push to eliminate gender and any other God-given distinctions in the human body are all part of an agenda to gradually adopt the idea that the soul is only software. The idea is being propagated that having an avatar likeness digitized and uploaded into the cloud is the same as achieving immortality. Eventually, it will be presumed that such a man, bolstered by the massive knowledge base accumulated on the internet, can be trusted to rule the world as an alternative to a global conquest.

While many would read this theory and refuse to believe that mankind would be so deeply deceived as to place their hope in an A.I., one must remember that God Himself is sending upon them a *great delusion* so that they believe *"the lie."* Through steadfast unbelief and persistent hardening of their hearts, they will be prepared to accept any alternative explanation to the Biblical truth and will be given over to worship *the Beast* as they reject the only true salvation in Christ.

> *All who dwell on the earth will worship him, whose names are not written in the Book of Life of the Lamb slain from the foundation of the world. If anyone has an ear, let him hear. He who leads into captivity shall go into captivity; he who kills with the sword must be killed with the sword. Here is the patience and the faith of the saints.*
> ~ *Revelation 13:8-10*

The Second Beast: The False Prophet

The believers who remain on earth after *the Rapture* will have one of two fates. If they are Jews who were faithful to flee Jerusalem, they will be nourished in the wilderness until Christ comes for them. The remaining Gentiles will be rounded up, be demanded to take the *Mark of the Beast,* or be beheaded for refusing. This holocaust will be carried out by the Second Beast, who is the power behind the *Image of the Beast.* The Jews that remain will suffer greatly, as Satan consolidates his power at the hands of the Second Beast.

> *Then I saw another beast coming up out of the earth, and he had two horns like a lamb and spoke like a dragon. And **he exercises all the authority of the first beast in his presence, and causes the earth and those who dwell in it to worship the first beast, whose deadly wound was healed.** He performs great signs, so that he even makes fire come down from heaven on the earth in the sight of men. And he deceives*

[172]

those who dwell on the earth by those signs which he was granted to do in the sight of the Beast, telling those who dwell on the earth to make an image to the Beast who was wounded by the sword and lived. ~ Revelation 13: 11-12

While the First Beast will come from the Gentiles, the Second Beast will come from the Jews, indicated in that he comes out of the earth, which is symbolic of the *Promised Land*. While the First Beast will exemplify the tyranny of Satan, the Second Beast will exemplify his subtlety. While worship will be directed toward the First Beast, his image will be serving the interests of the Second Beast, who is the propaganda minister of Satan and the real power behind the throne.

This Second Beast will be the mastermind behind the diplomacy and the propaganda dedicated to the First Beast. He will master religion, the economy, media, and technology to cause the First Beast to appear divine. He will work masterfully behind the scenes, accumulating power to Israel by bringing other heads of state to the table through diplomacy, before subjecting them to the First Beast. He will bring in various economic and technological interests, viewed mostly as an altruistic negotiating agent with no stake in the game. When the First Beast begins to take power, he will pacify the interests that may oppose him, while gradually alluding to the idea that he may be the promised Messiah.

When *the Beast* is killed, he will convince the whole world that he lives in the *Image of the Beast,* forcing them to worship his image. Just as the Common Era began with the birth of Jesus, he will attempt to *"change times and laws" (Daniel 7:25)* making his death and resurrection the beginning of a New Age. Just as Christians identify with Christ's death and resurrection through Baptism and Communion, the unbelieving will be forced to identify with his wounds by this mark of loyalty in the right hand or the forehead. Just as the early church had all things in common by the grace of the Holy Spirit, he will force the world to surrender to his command economy. Just as believers are *"sealed for the day of redemption"* by the Holy Spirit, the wicked will be *sealed* for the day of judgment by receiving this *Mark of the Beast*. But before this judgement comes, the Lord will descend with a shout to remove *His Bride*.

He was granted power to give breath to the Image of the Beast, that the Image of the Beast should both speak, and cause as many as would not worship the Image of the Beast to be killed. **He causes all, both small and great, rich and poor, free and slave, to receive a mark on their right hand or on their foreheads,** *and that no one may buy or sell except one who has the mark or the name of the Beast, or the number of his name.*

Here is wisdom. Let him who has understanding calculate the number of the Beast, for it is the number of a man: His number is six hundred and sixty-six. ~ Revelation 13:13-18

The Rapture: Revelation 14 Interpreted

The next chapter will detail *the Rapture*, and the final warning to those left behind, who will be given over to *the Beast* for 3 ½ years. While these believers' names are in the Book of Life, they have no apparent testimony, and will be left behind to give glory to God through martyrdom as they refuse to worship *the Image of the Beast*.

> *Then I looked, and behold, a Lamb standing on Mount Zion, and with Him **one hundred and forty-four thousand**, having His Father's name written on their foreheads. And I heard a voice from heaven, like the voice of many waters, and like the voice of loud thunder. And I heard the sound of harpists playing their harps. They sang as it were a new song before the throne, before the four living creatures, and the elders; and no one could learn that song except the hundred and forty-four thousand **who were redeemed from the earth**. These are the ones who were not defiled with women, for they are virgins. These are the ones who follow the Lamb wherever He goes. **These were redeemed from among men**, being firstfruits to God and to the Lamb. And in their mouth was found no deceit, for they are without fault before the throne of God.*
>
> *~ Revelation 14:1-5*

First, the 144,000 witnesses are again mentioned, fulfilling their official responsibility of escorting *the Bride and Groom* to the wedding chamber. While some assume that Christ has touched down on earth because the Lamb is standing on Mount Zion, one should remember two things: First, that Christ would touch down on the Mount of Olives, not Mount Zion, and second, that there is a heavenly Mount Zion in *the New Jerusalem* as well.

> *But you have come unto **mount Zion**, and unto the city of the living God, **the heavenly Jerusalem**, and to an innumerable company of angels. ~ Hebrews 12:22*

Fulfilling their role of accompanying *the Bride*groom to meet *the Bride*, the 144,000 are gathered as *"first fruits"* unto Christ, who is coming in the clouds. These men are foreshadowed in the *Song of Solomon* as an entourage of men guarding the chamber of the king's bed on his wedding day, symbolizing their accompanying *the Bride*groom.

> *Behold his bed, Solomon's! **Sixty mighty men are around it, of Israel's mighty men**. They all hold swords, instructed in war; each man has his sword on his thigh because of fear in the night... Go forth, O daughters of Zion, and behold King Solomon, with the crown with which his mother crowned him **on his wedding day**, and in the day of the gladness of his heart. ~ Song of Solomon 3:7-11*

After this, the final warning is given to those to be left behind. An angel gives a call to the Laodicean faithful to come out of *Mystery Babylon*, which is about to be judged.

> *And I saw another angel fly in the midst of heaven, having the everlasting gospel to preach unto them that dwell on the earth, and to every nation, and kindred, and tongue, and people, saying with a loud voice, Fear God, and give glory to him; for the hour of his judgment is come: and worship him that made heaven, and earth, and the sea, and the fountains of waters. And there followed another angel, saying, **Babylon is fallen, is fallen**, that great city, because she made all nations drink of the wine of the wrath of her fornication. ~ Revelation 14:6-8*

The reminder to those that will be put to death is *"not to fear them that can kill the body, but fear him that can kill the body and soul in eternal hellfire." (Matthew 10:24)*. After this, the only testimony one can give is to refuse the mark, which will result in execution.

> *And the third angel followed them, saying with a loud voice, "If any man worship the Beast and his image, and receive his mark in his forehead, or in his hand, The same shall drink of the wine of the wrath of God, which is poured out without mixture into the cup of his indignation; and **he shall be tormented with fire and brimstone in the presence of the holy angels, and in the presence of the Lamb**: And the smoke of their torment ascends up for ever and ever: and they have no rest day nor night, who worship the Beast and his image, and whosoever receives the mark of his name. **Here is the patience of the saints:** here are they that keep the commandments of God, and the faith of Jesus." ~ Revelation 14:6-12*

The penalty for taking the mark will be eternal torment, while the promise to the overcomer will be eternal life and reigning with Christ.

> *And I heard a voice from heaven saying unto me, Write, "Blessed are the dead which die in the Lord from henceforth: Yea, says the Spirit, that they may rest from their labors; and their works do follow them." ~ Revelation 14:13*

The fate of these believers who are left behind is also foreshadowed in the *Song of Solomon*, in the one who took too long to answer the door. This is a reminder that while this group will be part of the *Bride*, they will lose their heads as a testimony.

> *I rose up to open to my Beloved; and my hands dripped with myrrh, and my fingers flowing with myrrh on the handles of the bolt. I opened to my Beloved, but **my Beloved had left. He passed on**. My soul went out when He spoke; I sought Him, but I could not find Him. I called Him, but He did not answer me. The watchmen who went about the city found me and struck me; **they wounded me**. The keepers of the wall **lifted my veil from me**. ~ Song of Solomon 5: 5-7*

The *Song of Solomon* also foreshadows the raptured *Bride*, dressed in white for her *Bride*groom on her wedding day:

*But my dove, **my undefiled is one alone.** ... Who is she who looks forth like the morning, fair as the moon, clear as the sun, **awesome armies with banners**? I went down into the garden of nuts to see the greenery of the valley, to see whether the vine flowered, and the pomegranates budded. Before I was aware, **my soul set me on the chariots** of my princely people.*

*Return, return O Shulamite! Return that we may look on you. What will you see in the Shulamite? As it were **the dance of two camps**.* ~ Song of Solomon 6:9-13

This passage prophesies the final readiness of the *Bride*, as she is suddenly caught up on a chariot, foreshadowing *the Rapture*. The daughters of Jerusalem say she will return to *"the dance of two camps,"* which is the *Battle of Armageddon* to which she returns. These two types lead us to the two harvests of *Revelation 14*, first of the *precious fruit of the earth*, and then of the *grapes of wrath*.

*Then I looked, and behold, a white cloud, and **on the cloud sat One like the Son of Man**, having on His head a golden crown, and in His hand a sharp sickle. And another angel came out of the temple, crying with a loud voice to Him who sat on the cloud, "Thrust in Your sickle and reap, for the time has come for You to reap, for the harvest of the earth is ripe." So, He who sat on the cloud thrust in his sickle on the earth, and the earth was reaped.* ~ Revelation 14:14-16

The second harvest of the grapes is the gathering of the nations for a final battle against Christ, which will take place in the *Battle of Armageddon*.

*Then another angel came out of the temple which is in heaven, he also having a sharp sickle. And another angel came out from the altar, who had power over fire, and he cried with a loud cry to him who had the sharp sickle, saying, "Thrust in your sharp sickle and **gather the clusters of the vine of the earth, for her grapes are fully ripe**." So, the angel thrust his sickle into the earth, and gathered the vine of the earth, and threw it into the great winepress of the wrath of God. And the winepress was trampled outside the city, and blood came out of the winepress, up to the horses' bridles, for one thousand six hundred furlongs.* ~ Revelation 14:17-20

Joel mentions these *grapes of wrath* being gathered to war in the *Day of the Lord*.

*Gather yourselves, and come all you nations, and gather yourselves together all around; cause Your mighty ones to come down there, O LORD. Let the nations be awakened and come up to the valley of Jehoshaphat; for there I will sit to judge all the nations all around. Put in the sickle, for the harvest is ripe. Come, come down; for **the press is full**; the vats overflow, for their wickedness is great.* ~ Joel 3:11

This gathering is also prophesied in Zechariah and will reach its culmination when Christ returns from the *Wedding Chamber*, touching down on the Mount of Olives.

*I will gather all nations against Jerusalem to battle; and the city shall be taken, and the houses rifled, and the women ravished; and half of the city shall go forth into captivity, and the residue of the people shall not be cut off from the city. **Then shall the LORD go forth, and fight against those nations**, as when he fought in the day of battle…and the LORD my God shall come, and all the saints with Him. And it shall come to pass in that day, that the light shall not be clear, nor dark: But it shall be one day which shall be known to the LORD, not day, nor night: but it shall come to pass, that at evening time it shall be light. ~ Zechariah 14:2-7*

As *Zechariah 14* represents the *Battle of Armageddon* when the Lord returns *with* all His Saints, this cannot occur in the middle of *Daniel's 70th week*. This will occur at the end of the week, at the final appearing of the Lamb with his Wife. Still, the Holy Spirit represents these two harvests as the final distinction of the righteous and the wicked, made here as *the Rapture* occurs. In Isaiah, we also see the *Day of Vengeance* and the *Year of His Redeemed* as a single event.

__I have trodden the winepress alone__; and of the peoples there was no man with Me; for I will tread them in My anger and trample them in My fury; and their blood will be sprinkled on My garments, and I will stain all My clothing. For __the day of vengeance is in My heart, and the year of My redeemed has come__. ~ Isaiah 63:3-4

The Day of the Lord is *"that day"* in which the *Abomination of Desolation* occurs, prompting Israel to flee into the wilderness as Christ appears in the clouds, slaying *the Beast* with a Word of Power and rapturing the Church. However, this *Day of the Lord* is also the Millennial Reign of Christ, which begins with Him pouring out his wrath until he has subdued every government on Earth to his dominion.

The Time of Jacobs Trouble: A Tale of Two Cities

The time between the *Abomination of Desolation* being set up and the end of the war is called the *"Time of Jacob's Trouble."*

*And at that time shall Michael arise, the great prince which stands for the children of your people: and there shall be **a time of trouble**, such as never was since there was a nation even to that same time… ~ Daniel 12:1*

*Alas! for that day is great, so that none is like it: it is even **the time of Jacob's trouble**; but he shall be saved out of it. For it shall come to pass in that day, says the LORD of hosts, that I will break his yoke from off your neck, and will burst your bonds, and strangers shall no more serve themselves of him: ~ Jeremiah 30:7-8*

This period is foreshadowed in the story of Jacob's wedding. In his first coming, Jesus came to Jerusalem seeking fruit, yet finding none. This was represented in Rachael, who while being sought first by Jacob, was given to him last after his marriage to

Leah. When Jacob realized he was deceived, receiving Leah rather than the bride for whom he had worked for seven years, he emerged in wrath against Laban for his deceit. To appease his wrath, Laban said,

> **Fulfill her week**, and we will give you this one also for the service which you shall serve with me still another seven years. And Jacob did so and fulfilled her week. And he gave him Rachel his daughter to wife also. ~ Genesis 29:27-28

Therefore, the last half of the week is called *"the time of Jacob's trouble,"* as it corresponds to the time when Jacob waited impatiently for that *Bride* for which he had worked so long. At the end of the week, Christ, who will have already received *His Bride* in the Gentile Church, will also receive the remnant from the Jerusalem below. While in the end, they will be one single *Bride* in *the New Jerusalem*, in this mysterious ingathering of the Gentiles, they are two distinct women, represented in two great cities: the Jerusalem above and the Jerusalem below.

The Left Behind: Revelation 15 Interpreted

Finally, before the wrath is poured out, we see the heavenly manifestation of those who will be saved in this hour. Just as we saw the 144,000 and the *Gentile Bride* in *Revelation 7,* being introduced before their testimony, we see the left-behind saints, who will give their lives as a testimony. These are recorded with the redeemed in the Book of Life, being seated in heaven, though they are going to be killed in the earth.

> Then I saw another sign in heaven, great and marvelous: seven angels having the seven last plagues, for in them the wrath of God is complete. And I saw something like a sea of glass mingled with fire, and **those who have the victory over the Beast, over his image and over his mark and over the number of his name**, standing on the sea of glass, having harps of God. They sing the song of Moses, the servant of God, and the song of the Lamb, saying: "Great and marvelous are Your works, Lord God Almighty! Just and true are Your ways, O King of the saints! Who shall not fear You, O Lord, and glorify Your name? For You alone are holy. For all nations shall come and worship before You, For Your judgments have been manifested." ~ Revelation 15:1-4

Next, we see the glory of God as his wrath begins to be poured out.

> After these things I looked, and behold, the temple of the tabernacle of the testimony in heaven was opened. And out of the temple came the seven angels having the seven plagues, clothed in pure bright linen, and having their chests girded with golden bands. **Then one of the four living creatures gave to the seven angels seven golden bowls full of the wrath of God who lives forever and ever.** The temple was filled with smoke from the glory of God and from His power, and no one was able to enter the temple till the seven plagues of the seven angels were completed. ~ Revelation 15:5-8

PART 9 - THE WRATH OF THE LAMB

Before continuing the narrative, one should understand *the wrath of God* in every Biblical context and dispel any assertions that this eschatological wrath begins before the outpouring of the seven bowls. Just as the *tribulation* of the Church occurs generally throughout the age *(Romans 8:35-36)*, and particularly in the first half of *Daniel's 70th week (Matthew 24:9-15)*, the *wrath of God* is also revealed generally throughout the age and is poured out particularly in the second half of *Daniel's 70th week*. This wrath ushers in the *Day of the Lord* and the *Reign of Christ*, being an element of the New Covenant that is both *already* and *not yet* fulfilled.

> *For the wrath of God **is revealed** from Heaven against all ungodliness and unrighteousness of men, who hold the truth in unrighteousness, because the thing which may be known of God is clearly revealed within them, for God revealed it to them...Because, knowing God, **they did not glorify Him as God, neither were thankful**. But they became vain in their imaginations, and their foolish heart was darkened. Professing to be wise, they became fools and changed the glory of the incorruptible God into an image made like corruptible man, and birds, and four-footed animals, and creeping things. ~ Romans 1:18-23*

Paul gives the reason for *the wrath of God* being generally revealed in the present tense. He teaches that through willful ignorance and being unthankful toward God, mankind became darkened toward the worship of created things rather than the Creator. This

[179]

darkness is progressive and illustrates that *Mystery of Iniquity*, which will finally culminate in the worship of the *Image of the Beast*.

> *Therefore, God also gave them up to uncleanness through the lusts of their hearts, to dishonor their own bodies between themselves. ... For this cause, God gave them up to dishonorable affections. ... who, knowing the righteous order of God, that those practicing such things are worthy of death, not only do them, but have pleasure in those practicing them. ~ Romans 1:24-32*

In response to this idolatry, God reveals his wrath progressively by giving man over to demonic manipulations toward sexual perversity, hateful passions, and general enslavement against sound judgement. This was not done in vengeance, but to teach mankind the folly of sin in hope that mankind would find the burden of that folly heavy and long for the salvation which He intended to reveal in Christ.

> *For the creation was subjected to futility, not willingly, but because of Him who subjected it in hope... ~ Romans 8:20*

It is from this general wrath that the regenerated believer is protected, gaining power over sin while the unbeliever remains in bondage to sin. Those who believe in Christ are in this manner *already* saved, having been delivered from the power of sin to which they were captive through the fear of death *(Hebrews 2:15)*, while this wrath continues to abide on the unbeliever.

> *He who believes in the Son has everlasting life; and he who does not believe the Son shall not see life, but the **wrath of God abides on him**. ~ John 3:36*

However, there is another outpouring of the *"wrath of the Lamb"* which is poured out after all the nations have decided to stand in Christ against sin, or in sin against Christ. John the Baptist preached this to the Pharisees in his ministry saying,

> *"who has warned you to flee from **the wrath to come**?" ~ Luke 3:7*

This wrath was delayed by the administration of the Gospel to the nations, which had been hidden in a mystery and the reason Jesus read, *"To preach the acceptable year of the Lord..." (Luke 4:19)*, while omitting *"and the day of vengeance of our God." (Isaiah 61:2)* from the original prophecy. However, at the blowing of the seventh trumpet, according to the angel, *"the mystery of God will be finished"* and *"...there will be delay no longer." (Revelation 10:6)*, corresponding to Jesus when he said,

> *But woe unto them that are with child, and to them that give suck, in those days! for there shall be great distress in the land, and **wrath upon this people**. ~ Luke 21:23*

This wrath does not take place for sins previously committed, for which Jesus had bled and died, but for the single sin of unbelief in Christ, as it is written,

> And when He (the Holy Spirit) has come, He will convict the world of sin, and of righteousness, and **of judgment: of sin, because they do not believe in Me**; of righteousness, because I go to My Father and you see Me no more; of judgment, because the ruler of this world is judged. ~ John 16:8-11

Knowing there would be many who would reject this mercy, continuing to assert their independent will and love of sin, Jesus said of them,

> But bring here those enemies of mine, who did not want me to reign over them, and slay them before me ~ Luke 19:27

Just as the *"Book of Life"* is called *"The Lamb's Book of Life"* (Revelation 13:8 & 21:27) after the unbelieving have been blotted out, the *"wrath of God"* is called the *"wrath of the Lamb"* when it ceases to be a general wrath and begins to be the particular vengeance of Christ against those who have rejected his mercy. For this reason, those who knowingly and willfully reject Him will say,

> …hide us from the face of Him sitting on the throne, and from the wrath of the Lamb; for **the great day of His wrath has come**… ~ Revelation 6:16-17

However, while they say this, it should be understood that the unbelieving cannot rightly determine when the wrath of God has come, as it must come upon them *"like a thief."* In *Revelation 6*, these unbelievers are deceived into believing that the wrath is come so that they will afterward believe that *the Beast* is Christ and *the Kingdom* has come. One must understand that Daniel, Paul, and Jesus each teach that this *"wrath of God"* begins after the *"Abomination of Desolation,"* which occurs on the day of the 7th trumpet, after which the elders in heaven say,

> … You have taken Your great power and reigned. The nations were angry, and **your wrath has come**…~ Revelation 11:7

One must be consistent in their interpretation as God is not the author of confusion. Jesus *(Matthew 24:21)* and Daniel *(12:1)* were not assuring us that the wrath will be poured out *after* the *Abomination of Desolation* if it begins before. Martyrs are not pleading with God to judge the earth) if his judgment is already being poured out *(Revelation 6:10)*. Whatever signs occur on the earth before this are the signs which precede the appearing of Christ, but not the specific *"wrath of God."* In the letter to the church at Philadelphia, a promise was made to keep them from the *hour of trial* that comes upon those *"who dwell on the earth."* (Revelation 3:10). This *trial* is the counterpart to the *trial* that has been completed upon the saints.

Where the saints were tested with the fear of death to see if they had trusted in Christ, the world will be tested with the fear of death to see if they trust in *the*

Antichrist. After Satan completes his prosecution of the righteous, fulfilling the number of saints that are killed for their testimony of the gospel, he is cast out of the heavenly court onto the earth. Once the Church is raptured, our Advocate will come forward to cross-examine Satan's two false witnesses and begin to test those who dwell on the earth, gathering the remnant of those who fear God and proving the remainder to be utterly committed in their love of sin.

The Wrath Poured Out: Revelation 16 Interpreted

Then I heard a loud voice from the temple saying to the seven angels, "Go and pour out the bowls of the wrath of God on the earth." ~ Revelation 16:1

The bowl judgements have both a practical and poetic purpose as they demonstrate divine justice. By the first vial, those who worship *the Antichrist* are given an infectious wound; a physical manifestation of the sin that they will not let go.

So, the first went and poured out his bowl upon the earth, and a foul and loathsome sore came upon the men who had the Mark of the Beast and those who worshiped his image.
~ Revelation 16:2

By the second and third vials, they are given blood to drink, which is the physical manifestation of their hatefulness. Mankind biting and devouring one another in covetousness is manifested as the waters of the entire earth are turned to blood.

*Then the second angel poured out his bowl on the sea, and it became blood as of a dead man; and every living creature in the sea died. Then the third angel poured out his bowl on the rivers and springs of water, and they became blood. And the voice of the angel of the waters came to my ears, saying, True and upright is your judging, O Holy One, who is and was from all time: **For they made the blood of saints and prophets come out like a stream, and blood have you given them for drink**; which is their right reward. And a voice came from the altar, saying, "Even so oh Lord God, Ruler of all, true and full of righteousness is your judging." ~ Revelation 16:5-7*

By the fourth and fifth vials, *the Kingdom of the Beast* receives a foretaste of the eternal torment to come. By one they are given a preview of the lake of fire as the heat of the Sun is multiplied to scorch mankind. By the other they preview the fearful torment of the outer darkness. These two judgements foreshadow an eternity full of God's fury, and yet devoid of his light. Still, even in this clear demonstration of what awaits their stubborn rejection of God, their depravity is manifest as they continue to gnash their teeth at the Lord. Fully aware that this torment comes from Him, they prove themselves entirely unwilling to repent.

*And the fourth angel poured out his bowl on the sun; and power was given to it that men might be burned with fire. And men were **burned with great heat**: and they blasphemed the name of the God who has authority over these punishments; and they did not repent from their evil ways to give him glory. And the fifth angel poured out his bowl upon the seat of the Beast; **and his kingdom was full of darkness**; and they gnawed their tongues for pain and blasphemed the God of heaven because of their pains and their sores; and repented not of their deeds. ~ Revelation 16:8-11*

By the sixth vial, Christ gathers his enemies by making a way for those who would challenge *the Beast*. These *Kings of the East* who would overthrow his government now advance in a full-scale invasion on his most secure front.

*And the sixth angel poured out his bowl on **the great river Euphrates; and it became dry**, so that the way might be made ready for the kings from the east. ~ Revelation 16:12*

To Satan, this global civil war is part of his plan, seeking to consolidate the global order from a confederacy into a federal system with *the Beast* as its absolute dictator. Through the *"Image of the Beast,"* he plans to wipe out these armies and rule the world by the power of an automated drone army which he exclusively controls. However, despite Satan's intention, Christ is allowing this gathering to bring all his enemies together, so that he may destroy them in a single campaign.

*And I saw coming out of the mouth of the dragon, and out of the mouth of the Beast, and out of the mouth of the False Prophet, three unclean spirits, like frogs. For they are evil spirits, working signs; who go out even to the kings of all the earth, to gather them together to the war of the great day of God Almighty… And **they gathered them together into the place which is named in Hebrew Armageddon**.*

~ Revelation 16:13-16

Parenthesized in this final judgement is a word of distinction between those gathered in the wheat harvest and those in the winepress. For those who are elect unto salvation, they are not taken as a thief, because they have waited expectantly for Christ. But to those who have hated him, Christ sends a subtle message that when they are least concerned about him, they will be caught unawares. Just as the remnant of Laodicea will finally answer the door to see Christ absent and Antichrist present, this army will march forth to face *the Beast*, only to find themselves face-to-face with Christ himself, in the fullness of his fury and vengeance.

*Behold, **I come as a thief.** Blessed is he who is watching and keeps his robes, so that he may not go unclothed, and his shame be seen. ~ Revelation 16:15*

Finally, at the seventh vial, the outpouring of God's wrath is completed. Just as God's love is epitomized in Christ's first coming, when the earth quaked at his death

[183]

(Matthew 27:51), God's wrath is epitomized in Christ's second coming as the earth will quake at the repercussion of Christ touching down on the Mount of Olives.

> *And the seventh angel poured out his bowl on the air; and there came out a great voice from the house of God, from the high seat, saying, "It is finished". And there were flames and voices and thunders; and **there was a great earthquake so that never, from the time when men were on the earth, had there been so great an earthquake so full of power**. ~ Revelation 16:16-18*

First, the mountain of Jerusalem splits at Christ's touching down, dividing the city into three parts. Next, the islands flee away and the mountains crumble as the Earth itself is humbled at His presence. Finally, a great hail, having been kept by God from the most ancient times, is unleashed upon the armies gathered below.

> *Have you entered the treasury of snow, or have you seen **the treasury of hail, which I have reserved for the time of trouble**; for the day of battle and war? ~ Job 38: 22*
>
> *Now **the great city was divided into three parts**, and the cities of the nation's fell. And **great Babylon was remembered** before God, to give her the cup of the wine of the fierceness of His wrath. Then every island fled away, and the mountains were not found. **And great hail from heaven fell upon men, each hailstone about the weight of a talent**. Men blasphemed God because of the plague of the hail, since that plague was exceedingly great. ~ Revelation 16:19-21*

The splitting of the city into three parts reflects the parable of the seed and the sower *(Matthew 13:1-23)*. Jesus spoke of two kinds of soil that bear no fruit and one part that bears much fruit. The two unfruitful soils represent legalistic self-righteousness and licentious sinfulness, the two sides of the narrow way on which the righteous are found. Christ splits the city into three parts to foreshadow the two cities to be judged and the remnant to be saved, which are prophesied in Zechariah.

> *And it shall come to pass in all the land," Says the LORD, "That **two-thirds in it shall be cut off and die, but one-third shall be left in it**: I will bring **the one-third through the fire**, will refine them as silver is refined, and test them as gold is tested. They will call on My name, And I will answer them. I will say, "This is My people"; And each one will say, "The LORD is my God."' ~ Zechariah 13:7-9*

Babylon Is Fallen, Is Fallen: A Tale of Two Cities

It is important to note that *the harlot* of Revelation is *not* the Roman Catholic church. While the weight of sin committed by this church in the middle ages and the idolatry practiced within her today qualify her as a daughter of this harlot, Scripture is clear that *the Mother of Harlots* had her origin in the Middle East where Nimrod had dominion. Just as the message of the Gospel will return to Jerusalem in the last days, *Mystery Babylon* will also return to her base. Both Jerusalem and a revived Babylon at Neom will be judged, which is why the angel repeats, *"Babylon is fallen, is fallen."*

While the daughters of *the harlot* have many different names, they have a common form and practice which was passed down from their mother. They commit fornication with the kings of the earth, prostituting themselves by forming a religious worship to the man of power in that kingdom. In this seduction, they become the *power behind the throne*, gradually shifting the worship toward themselves, as they make the man of power dependent upon their cult. In order for the man of power to maintain his cultural hold on his kingdom, he ends up subservient, or at least sharing power with the priesthood or cult that is dedicated to her worship.

> Then the angel who talked with me went forth and said to me, "Now lift up your eyes and see what this is that goes forth." And I said, "What is it?" And he said, "This is the ephah that goes forth." And he said, "This is their form in all the earth." And behold, a lead cover was lifted up, and **a woman was sitting in the middle of the ephah**. And he said, "**This is wickedness.**" And he cast it into the midst of the ephah. And he cast the lead stone over its opening. ~ Zechariah 5:5-8

This woman has had many forms throughout history. In Babel, she was Ishtar, first driving worship to Nimrod, while in Egypt, she was Isis, who led men to worship Osiris. In Canaan, she was Ashtoreth, leading men to worship Baal, while in Moab she was Astarte, leading them to worship Moloch. In ancient England, she was called Easter, while the Greeks called her Artemis. It was because of this idolatry that the craftsmen were stirred up against Paul in *Acts 19*. Paul foresaw that through Ephesus, she would one day come into the church and prostitute the faith in the very way she had done among the Gentiles in ancient times.

> ... after my departure savage wolves will come in among you, not sparing the flock. Also, from among yourselves men will rise up, speaking perverse things, to draw away the disciples after themselves. Therefore, watch and remember, that for three years I did not cease to warn everyone night and day with tears. ~ Acts 20:29-31

In the Council of Ephesus (431 AD), one of her daughters climbed atop the Imperial Church, calling herself *"the Mother of God."* She taught the church to reject any who would not honor her with this title, accusing them of assaulting the deity of Christ by denying this title to his human mother. She began teaching them to eat foods sacrificed to idols and to honor a man as the voice of God in the Church. Eventually she grew to be revered as the divine Mother of all the faithful, leading her children to grovel before her idols. The same spirit of Jezebel, that had brought the priests of Baal into Israel, accomplished the same in the European church.

When the Freemasons and the Reformers came together in the United Kingdom, two new daughters of Babylon emerged. In the Americas she was called Liberty and was the embodiment of the rebellious independence that spawned many democratic revolutions in the West. In France she was called Reason and was the embodiment of materialistic logic that spawned the atheistic revolutions of the communists in the East. These two circled the globe, spreading populist rebellions around the world that eventually drove the whole planet into two camps. While seeming to be opposites, these sisters would serve to merge the world into one.

After Liberty and Reason saw to the overthrow of nearly every national monarchy that God had established throughout the nations, two more daughters of Babylon emerged to bring the world back to the *Mother of Harlots*. The first was Gaia, the ancient goddess who taught the world to worship the earth as an eternal mother. This goddess was exalted by the United Nations through environmental fears, meant to galvanize the world to save her. The second is Sophia, the embodiment of all human knowledge and wisdom. Her *modus operandi* is always to find the man of power and seduce him with flattery by leading others to worship him. In the last days, these daughters will all point the world back toward the Middle East and to the worship of *the Beast*. According to a prophecy of Zechariah, she will eventually return to the region where she began her rule.

> *And I lifted up my eyes and looked, and behold, __two women came out__. And the wind was in their wings; for they had wings like the wings of a stork. And they lifted up the ephah between the earth and the heavens. And I said to the angel who talked with me, "Where are they going with the ephah?" And he said to me, "__To build a house for it in the land of Shinar; and it shall be established and set there on its own base.__"*
>
> *~ Zechariah 5:5-11*

After the Roman Empire had fallen, it was replaced by the Islamic Caliphate, which had stewarded Jerusalem for over 1000 years. This Caliphate eventually conquered Byzantium, which was the remnant of the Roman Empire that lasted 1000 years after the city of Rome fell. This mighty empire had its capital at Baghdad in Shinar and had its center of worship at Mecca near the Red sea. It was succeeded by the Ottoman Empire, which ruled for another 500 years, before being dissolved during the first World War. Since then, the two halves of the Pagan Roman Empire, represented in the European Catholics and the Middle Eastern Muslims, have vied for control of the Land of Promise and the City of Jerusalem. These two powers represent the Sun and Moon of ancient Baal Worship and will also merge into one in the last days.

The reason that there are two women bringing her back to her base is because her daughters operate under a *divide and conquer* principal. These two women represent the seduction of distinct lies, that while opposing one another, serve to drive mankind in a single direction, always forced to choose between the *lesser of two evils*. This is the very *Zeitgeist* principal, that the German Philosopher Hegel presumed to discover as a natural force of historical development. In the last days, this *divide-and-conquer* principal will not only unite the military powers of the world against Christ but will also unite the religious powers in worship of *the Antichrist*. While one city will exhort to legalistic worship and military supremacy, the other will exhort to open spirituality and to materialistic hedonism. For this reason, there are two Babylons which are fallen, while the third part, to be *refined by fire*, represents the remnant who will be saved. Therefore, the angel says, *"Babylon Is Fallen, Is Fallen" (Revelation 14:8)* as a call to the believing who remain, both Jew and Gentile, to come out of her.

In ancient times, the two cities that represented the working of Satan were Babylon, *(Isaiah 14)* which mastered world power and false religion, and Tyre, *(Ezekiel 28)* which mastered world trade and luxury. In the last days, a latter-day version of these cities is described in *Revelation 17-18*. While the possibility exists that a city of Babylon will be built again upon its ancient ruins, the preponderance of the prophetic evidence suggests otherwise. While there may be some ornamental city in modern Iraq to serve as a monument to world unity, in the last days, the religious influence held by Rome will shift to Jerusalem and the economic influence held by New York will shift to the burgeoning city of Neom, which will be under construction on the Red Sea.

[187]

The Religious Harlot: Revelation 17 Interpreted

*Then one of the seven angels who had the seven bowls came and talked with me, saying to me, "Come, I will show you the judgment of **the great harlot who sits on many waters**, with whom the kings of the earth committed fornication, and the inhabitants of the earth were made drunk with the wine of her fornication." ~ Revelation 17:1-2*

The waters on which she sits represent the nations over which Jerusalem will hold sway. It is prophesied that those Jews that forsake Christ will help *the Antichrist* rise to power and that he will in turn flatter them with riches as Judaism becomes the religion of *the Beast (Daniel 11:23-24).*

*So, he carried me away in the Spirit **into the wilderness**. And I saw a woman sitting on a scarlet beast which was **full of names of blasphemy**, having seven heads and ten horns. The woman was arrayed in purple and scarlet, and adorned with gold and precious stones and pearls, having in her hand a golden cup full of abominations and the filthiness of her fornication. And on her forehead a name was written: MYSTERY, BABYLON THE GREAT, THE MOTHER OF HARLOTS AND OF THE ABOMINATIONS OF THE EARTH. ~ Revelation 17:3-5*

I saw the woman, drunk with the blood of the saints and with the blood of the martyrs of Jesus. And when I saw her, I marveled with great amazement. ~ Revelation 17:6

This *"Great City"* will not be Rome but Jerusalem, which sits upon seven mountains and in which both prophets and apostles were killed.

*Yet I must walk today and tomorrow and the day following. For it cannot be that a prophet perishes outside of Jerusalem. Jerusalem **Jerusalem! The one killing the prophets** and stoning those having been sent to her; how often I desired to gather your children in the way a hen gathers her brood under the wings, and you did not desire it. **Behold, your house is left to you desolate**. And truly I say to you, "You will not see Me until it come when you say, 'Blessed is He who comes in the name of the Lord.'"*
~ Luke 13:33-35

There are seven distinct proofs that this woman represents Jerusalem.

But the angel said to me, "Why did you marvel? I will tell you the mystery of the woman and of the Beast that carries her, which has the seven heads and the ten horns. (1) The Beast that you saw was, and is not, and will ascend out of the Bottomless Pit and go to perdition. And those who dwell on the earth will marvel, whose names are not written in the Book of Life from the foundation of the world, when they see the Beast that was, and is not, and yet is. ~ Revelation 17:7-8

(1) *The Beast* from the *Bottomless Pit* will empower the Antichrist to gain his kingdom *(Revelation 9:1-11).* That he *"is not, and yet is"* not only represents the revival of an ancient kingdom, which was *already* and *not yet* in John's day, but also represents that he will be slain and yet continue to rule through the *Image of the Beast*. Scripture is consistent that the Temple of Jerusalem will be where this takes place.

> *Here is the mind which has wisdom: (2) The seven heads are seven mountains on which the woman sits. (3) There are also seven kings. Five have fallen, one is, and the other has not yet come. And when he comes, he must continue a short time. ~ Revelation 17:9-10*

(2) ***The Seven Heads*** or *"the seven mountains on which the woman sits,"* represent seven kingdoms which have managed the captivity of Israel and the stewardship of the *Promised Land* since ancient times.

1) Egypt held Israel captive until the sin of the Amorites was full.

2) Assyria obtained stewardship after Israel fell into idolatry.

3) Babylon obtained stewardship after Judah fell into idolatry.

4) Medo-Persia obtained stewardship after Babylon defiled the temple implements.

5) Greece obtained stewardship after the Persian king demanded to be worshipped.

6) Rome obtained stewardship after Antiochus defiled the Temple.

7) The Caliphate obtained stewardship after Roman-Christendom became pagan.

By these kingdoms, *Mystery Babylon* has held control of the Middle East, the *Promised Land* and Jerusalem. Even today, remnants of the Caliphate hold the temple mount, the old city and the lands of Ephraim, Judea, and Benjamin. This leader will most likely arise from Turkey, and will from there reconstitute the Caliphate, eventually gaining dominance over the former Roman Empire.

(3) ***The Seven Kings*** represent those kings that have foreshadowed *the Antichrist* in the past. Just as one of these kingdoms will re-emerge in the last days to establish a final empire, a type of one of the kings will re-emerge under that spirit of Apollyon.

1) Nimrod usurped authority and was the first man to be worshipped as a God.

2) Pharaoh claimed to have power over death, and enslaved and afflicted Israel.

3) Nebuchadnezzar made an image of himself to worship, under penalty of death.

4) Darius the Persian commanded Israel to offer prayers to him alone.

5) Antiochus Epiphanes defiled the temple, placing his image in the Holy Place.

6) Nero Caesar burned Rome and blamed the saints, persecuting them unto death.

7) <u>The Caliph</u> *"denied the Father and the Son."* and claimed the Temple Mount.

> *(4) And the Beast that was, and is not, is himself also the eighth, and is of the seven, and is going to perdition. ~ Revelation 9:11*

This eighth king will not only be like one of the seven kings, but he will continue to rule over seven kings as an eighth king who has seemed to return from death. Though he is killed, *"he will be allowed to continue forty-two months,"* ruling through his image, which will be placed in the temple.

> *(5) The ten horns which you saw are ten kings who have received no kingdom as yet, but **they receive authority for one hour** as kings with the Beast. These are of one mind, and they will give their power and authority to the Beast. These will make war with the Lamb, and the Lamb will overcome them, for He is Lord of lords and King of kings; and those who are with Him are called, chosen, and faithful. ~ Revelation 17:12-14*

The ten kings will arise through a treaty, bringing peace at the end of World War III. *The Beast* will then come to power and gaining dominion over three of them and setting the remaining seven kings in opposition to him. These will collude to destroy *the harlot*, represented in the attack on Jerusalem and NEOM in the last days. However, upon Christ's return they will join with *the Beast* to fight against him and be destroyed by the Lord when he returns with all his saints.

> *(6) Then he said to me, "The waters which you saw, where the harlot sits, are peoples, multitudes, nations, and tongues. **And the ten horns which you saw on the Beast, these will hate the harlot, make her desolate and naked**, eat her flesh and burn her with fire. For God has put it into their hearts to fulfill His purpose, to be of one mind, and to give their kingdom to the Beast, until the words of God are fulfilled."*
> *~ Revelation 17:15-17*

The Beast will *"have intelligence with them that forsake the holy covenant."* (Daniel 11:30). Unbelieving Israel, having one of the world's finest intelligence services and a leader in the development of Artificial Intelligence will likely create the *"strange god"* (Daniel 11:39) by which *the Beast* is helped in his political and military conquests. Jerusalem will become *the harlot* that reigns over the earth.

> *(7) "And the woman whom you saw, is that great city which reigns over the kings of the earth." ~ Revelation 17:18*

Throughout the Old Testament, Jerusalem is rebuked by God for her harlotry with the surrounding nations. This final testament to her harlotry will be accomplished as she turns her captivity to the Gentiles into power over the kings of the earth. This harlotry represents an idolatrous *Zionism* among political conservatives who count their righteousness in their support of Israel, while denying Christ in their way of life. This false righteousness will appeal to those who are hardened against the voice of God, unwilling to face persecution for the Gospel, and instead believing that they will earn God's favor through politics. This delusion will begin as God delivers Israel from her enemies during the Third World War and will continue to grow to the point where the nations are made to worship *the Beast.* Zechariah describes this as a kind of drunkenness, which is starting to take place today.

The entire book of Zechariah is an eschatological prophecy, set historically amid the regathering of the Jews into the *Promised Land,* and the rebuilding of the Temple. *Zechariah 11* begins to describe *the Antichrist*, and how Jerusalem, having rejected Christ, will receive this *"Idol Shepherd." Zechariah 12* describes their deliverance by these *"governors,"* followed by the Spirit of God being poured out on the Jews. The same prophetic pattern, which is demonstrated in *Micah 5, Ezekiel 38-39,* and *Joel 2,* will reveal Jerusalem being delivered, not directly by the hand of Christ, but by the support of world leaders that they seem to gather to themselves.

> *"Behold, **I will make Jerusalem a cup of drunkenness** to all the surrounding peoples, when they lay siege against Judah and Jerusalem. And it shall happen in that day that I will make Jerusalem a very heavy stone for all peoples; all who burden themselves with it will surely be cut in pieces, though all nations of the earth are gathered against it."*
> ~ *Zechariah 12:1-3*

In the first part of the prophecy, God is saying that Jerusalem itself will be that cup of drunkenness. This false religion is already taking root today and is rapidly taking hold of the church. In a false application of the passage, *"I will bless those that bless thee, and curse those that curse thee" (Genesis 12:2),* Christian-Zionism is influencing a political segment that a nation can be blessed for their treatment of Jerusalem, despite continual disobedience to God in other areas of faith.

> *"In that day,"* says the LORD, *"I will strike every horse with confusion, and its rider with madness; I will open My eyes on the house of Judah and will strike every horse of the peoples with blindness. And **the governors of Judah shall say in their heart, 'The inhabitants of Jerusalem are my strength in the LORD of hosts, their God.'"***
> ~ *Zechariah 12:4-5*

Notice that they are saying in their heart that the *"inhabitants of Jerusalem"* are their strength, rather than the Lord. Notice they are saying, *"their God,"* rather than *"our God."* In this manner they are drunk, making Jerusalem their mediator, believing to have earned the blessings of God while having no personal knowledge of Him. These *governors* are the same *"seven Shepherds and eight Principal Men"* of *Micah 5*, who come to Israel's aid before *Daniel's 70th week*.

As the Lord delivers Israel from this great invading force, the world will become convinced once again that they are the chosen people of God. Rather than looking to Christ as their savior, they will look to Israel and the *Man of Lawlessness*, as he increasingly seems to meet the prophetic criteria of being the Jewish Messiah and savior of the West. As the Jews begin to increasingly honor and affirm this man as the Messiah, they will make the nations *"drunk with the cup of her fornication."* In this delusion, many Christians will gravitate toward the idea that the Jews are their hope, and that the supremacy of Israel will be their security. Those who seek the tranquility of moralism and conservative political stability will look to Jerusalem as the new leader of the West. Those who seek carnal pleasure and fluid spirituality will find their appetites met in the other Great City of *Revelation 18*.

The Trade Harlot: Revelation 18 Interpreted

The second form of harlotry that God abhors is economic harlotry. This kind of harlotry occurs when economic interests overshadow political, spiritual, and moral interests, causing one to turn a blind eye for the love of money and material comforts. Christ himself said, *"For where your treasure is, there will your heart be also."* *(Matthew 6:21)* and will hold those accountable who ignore the emerging Antichrist for the sake of material comfort. Among them, the Laodicean church will be proven to be *"wretched, miserable, naked, and blind"* despite being *"rich and increased in goods."* To the remnant of faith, the Spirit cries, *"Come out of her!"*

In the ancient Middle East, the trade harlot was represented in Tyre, which would attach itself to whatever empire was in power the same way that *Mystery Babylon* would prostitute herself to the man of power. Tyre helped to build the temple, sending the Danite Hiram as foreman and supplying the building materials, foreshadowing how this future city will be instrumental toward the rise of Antichrist and the Temple in the last days. While *Isaiah 23* prophesies the destruction of ancient Tyre by Alexander the Great, *Ezekiel 28* reveals her spiritual king to be Satan himself, who corrupted the earth through the *"violence of his trade" (Ezekiel 28:16),* resulting in being cast out of the mountain of God. This eschatological Tyre is called Neom and is being built even today.

*After these things I saw another angel coming down from heaven, having great authority, and the earth was illuminated with his glory. And he cried mightily with a loud voice, saying, "Babylon the great is fallen, is fallen, and has become a dwelling place of demons, a **prison for every foul spirit, and a cage for every unclean and hated bird**!" ~ Revelation 18:1-2*

The saying, *"a prison for every foul bird"* reflects Jesus' *Parable of the Mustard Tree*, showing us how this city, like the Imperial church, will become the most prominent abode in the earth for the merchants and ministers of Satan. In Christ's day, these *"foul birds"* were the moneychangers and the hypocritical Scribes and Pharisees. In the last days, they will be a united world economy and an ecumenical world religion, established as a counterfeit *Gentile Bride*. As the end draws near, Laodicea and *Mystery Babylon* will become indistinguishable as bringing about world peace and an abundance of material luxury will be their shared mission.

*For all the nations have drunk of the wine of the wrath of her fornication, the kings of the earth have committed fornication with her, and the merchants of the earth have become rich through the abundance of her luxury. And I heard another voice from heaven saying, "**Come out of her, my people, lest you share in her sins**, and lest you receive of her plagues. For her sins have reached to heaven, and God has remembered her iniquities. Render to her just as she rendered to you and repay her double according to her works; in the cup which she has mixed, mix double for her". ~ Revelation 18:3-7*

The base of Neom will be built over the mount of Jabir al Lawz in Saudi Arabia which is the true Mount Sinai. This city will extend to the Red Sea and even cross the sea at the place of Israel's crossing, replacing this ancient testimony with a commercial city-state unlike any the world has ever known. This city intends to exceed the size of New York City by thirty-three times and is scheduled to near the first phase of completion by the 2000th anniversary of Christ's crucifixion. Beneath this massive city lie seven mountain peaks, which can be found on Google Maps.

In anticipation of the automated city, the Saudi Arabians have granted citizenship to an A.I. robot called Sophia, who appeared in 2018 at the UN, dressed in scarlet and asking mankind to give control of the Earth's resources to something called, "god-o-mation," allowing for fair distribution to all mankind. After the devastations of World War III and a worldwide economic collapse, she will employ the world in her vast construction, tantalizing the wealthy with every luxury and vice known to man.

*In the measure that **she glorified herself and lived luxuriously**, in the same measure give her torment and sorrow; for she says in her heart, "**I sit as queen, and am no widow**, and will not see sorrow." Therefore, her plagues will come in one day: death* *and mourning and famine. And she will be utterly burned with fire, for strong is the Lord God who judges her. ~ Revelation 18:7-8*

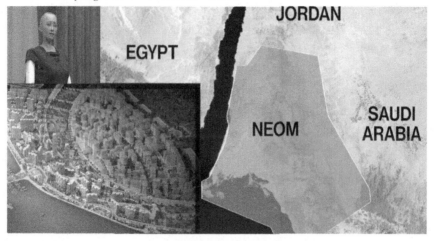

The *Antichrist* may in some way marry this idol, forsaking a human woman for this artificial *soul*. She will declare *"I am no widow"* because her husband, after being killed, will feign a digital resurrection. At that time, she will seduce the world into finding their hope and salvation in the very technology that brings him to power.

> *The kings of the earth who committed fornication and lived luxuriously with her will weep and lament for her when they see the smoke of her burning, standing at a distance for fear of her torment, saying, "Alas, alas, that great city Babylon, that mighty city! For in one hour your judgment has come." And **the merchants of the earth will weep and mourn over her**, for no one buys their merchandise anymore:*
>
> *~ Revelation 18:10-11*

She will master the economies of the world, likely through a fiat crypto-currency and manipulation of the stock markets. After the economic disaster of the Black Horse, the whole world will obsess over her construction as they did at the great Tower of Babel, requiring every import and craft while causing increasing famine to the rest of the world. As the *Kings of the East* begin to violently take over the Earth, many in their desperation will flock to this city for work, for food, and for safety. The luxury here will attract the down-trodden throughout the earth, allowing her not only to traffic in goods, but in bodies and souls as well.

> *Merchandise of gold and silver, precious stones and pearls, fine linen and purple, silk and scarlet, every kind of citron wood, every kind of object of ivory, every kind of object of most precious wood, bronze, iron, and marble; and cinnamon and incense, fragrant oil and frankincense, wine and oil, fine flour and wheat, cattle and sheep, horses and chariots, and **bodies and souls of men**. ~ Revelation 18:12-13*

Bodies: Two kinds of bodies will be required in her, first men for her construction, and then women for the pleasure of the men. While many will come willingly for the love of money, some will come unwillingly, deceived into bondage.

> *"Yea, and what have you to do with Me, O Tyre and Sidon, and all the borders of Philistia?" ... "I will sell your sons and your daughters into the hand of the sons of Judah, and they shall sell them to the Sabeans (Saudi Arabians), to a people far off;" for the LORD has spoken it. ~ Joel 3:4-8*

The Souls of Men: The deception of *the singularity* promises technology that will provide eternal life, saving the soul to be reincarnated into a customizable body. In this city, people will first be enticed to visit a digital avatar of their lost loved ones. Next, they will be promised a place in the eternal human legacy as they are euthanized to escape from despair. Finally, they will be deceived into believing that the raptured were abducted by a hostile extra-terrestrial enemy, and that their only hope is to abandon their bodies to be stored in the *cloud* for safety. In this she will seduce all mankind into a suicidal false hope.

> *... you have said, "**We have made a covenant with death**, and we have made a vision with hell; when the overwhelming rod shall pass through, it shall not come to us; for we have made lies our refuge, and we have hidden ourselves under falsehood" ~ Isaiah 28:15*

For this reason, God begins the outpouring of his wrath on the earth. For all of his fury against wickedness, God's primary motivator is mercy, which restrains Him until the final moment from executing judgement, *"wanting all men to be saved and come to repentance" (2ⁿᵈ Peter 3:9)* and taking *"no pleasure in the death of the wicked" (Ezekiel 33:11).* Just as he would not suffer the Canaanites when they began sacrificing their children to demons, he will not wait to judge this vile suicidal deception in the earth.

> *...unless those days should be shortened, no flesh would be saved. But for the elect's sake, those days shall be shortened. ~ Matthew 24:22*

The saddest element of this, is that the whole world will contribute to this deception, not for any real act of faith, but because, like the moneychangers and televangelists, they will simply adapt to the market for the love of material riches.

> *The fruit that your soul longed for has gone from you, and all the things which are rich and splendid have gone from you, and you shall find them no more at all. **The merchants of these things, who became rich by her, will stand at a distance for fear of her torment, weeping and wailing**, and saying, "Alas, alas, that great city that was clothed in fine linen, purple, and scarlet, and adorned with gold and precious stones and pearls! For in one hour such great riches came to nothing." Every shipmaster,*

all who travel by ship, sailors, and as many as trade on the sea, stood at a distance and cried out when they saw the smoke of her burning, saying, "What is like this great city?" They threw dust on their heads and cried out, weeping and wailing, and saying, "__Alas, alas, that great city, in which all who had ships on the sea became rich by her wealth!__ For in one hour she is made desolate." ~ Revelation 18:14-19

Just as in *Joel 2*, when Jerusalem cried, *"Let the Bride come out of her chamber, and the Groom from his closet,"* the *Bride and Groom*—the light of the world—will be removed before her destruction. Their song will not be a rejoicing of vengeance at those who hurt the saints, but a rejoicing that the great deception which would have killed every man, woman, and child on the earth has been destroyed in a last act of mercy by the Lord as he saves humanity from mass suicide.

"Rejoice over her, O heaven, and you holy apostles and prophets, for God has avenged you on her!" Then a mighty angel took up a stone like a great millstone and threw it into the sea, saying, "Thus with violence the great city Babylon shall be thrown down, and shall not be found anymore. The sound of harpists, musicians, flutists, and trumpeters shall not be heard in you anymore. No craftsman of any craft shall be found in you anymore, and the sound of a millstone shall not be heard in you anymore. __The light of a lamp shall not shine in you anymore, and the voice of Bridegroom and Bride shall not be heard in you anymore__. For your merchants were the great men of the earth, for by your sorcery all the nations were deceived. And in her was found the blood of prophets and saints, and of all who were slain on the earth." ~ Revelation 18:20-24

In the end of World War III, there will be a nuclear dissolution treaty *(Ezekiel 29:9)*. Iran will likely move its nuclear assets to a newly formed independent state of Kurdistan, the descendants of their ancient ally the Medes. This nation, sitting landlocked behind Turkish walls, beneath a devastated Russia, and behind a deep Euphrates river that guards the *Kingdom of Antichrist*, will become the most isolated and economically disadvantaged in the world. In their bitterness, they will form the frontal assault against *the Kingdom of the Beast* when the Euphrates River finally dries.

Sharpen the arrows; gather the shields; the LORD has raised up the spirit of the __kings of the Medes.__ For His plan is against Babylon, to destroy it; because it is the vengeance of the LORD, the vengeance of His temple. ~ Jeremiah 51:11

Just as the Medes diverted the Euphrates River to sack Babylon in ancient times, they will be the Lord's instrument of vengeance against this city, after the Euphrates River is dried up in the last days.

Behold, the Day of the Lord comes, cruel and with wrath and fierce anger, to lay the land waste; and He shall destroy its sinners out of it...Behold, __I will stir up the Medes against them__, who shall not value silver; and they shall not delight in gold...And bows shall dash the young men to pieces; and they shall have no pity on the fruit of the womb; their eye shall not pity sons. And Babylon, the glory of kingdoms, the majestic beauty of the Chaldees, shall be as when God overthrew Sodom and Gomorrah. ~ Isaiah 13:17-19

Though the original Babylon in the land of the Chaldees was taken by the Medes without a battle, Isaiah also speaks of an Arabian *"Babylon,"* which will be suddenly overthrown to never rise again. Like ancient Tyre was destroyed by fire, this city will be destroyed in similar fashion, likely by a hidden cache of nuclear weapons.

> *It shall never be inhabited forever, nor shall it be lived in from generation to generation; **nor shall the Arabian pitch his tent there**; nor shall the shepherds make their flocks lie down there. But the wild beasts of the desert shall lie there; and their houses shall be full of howling creatures; and ostriches shall dwell there, and he-goats shall dance there. And hyenas shall cry along with his widows, and jackals in palaces of delight. Yea, her time is coming near, and her days shall not be prolonged. ~ Isaiah 13:20-22*

Meanwhile, the other Babylon will be under siege by armies from the North and East. While the devastation to Jerusalem will be great, it will not be like the utter destruction of Neom. As the Jews there come to their greatest hour of desperation, Christ will return to defend her.

> *Behold, the Day of the Lord is coming, and your spoil will be divided in your midst. For I will gather all the nations to battle against Jerusalem; The city shall be taken, the houses rifled, And the women ravished. **Half of the city shall go into captivity, But the remnant of the people shall not be cut off from the city**. Then the LORD will go forth and fight against those nations, as He fights in the day of battle. Behold, the Day of the Lord comes, and your spoil shall be divided in the midst of you all. For **I will gather all nations against Jerusalem to battle; and the city shall be taken**, and the houses rifled, and the women ravished; and half of the city shall go forth into captivity, and the residue of the people shall not be cut off from the city. ~ Zechariah 14:1-3*

However, because of God's promise to the forefathers, Christ will arrive to rescue the people of Israel in the last hour.

> **Then shall the LORD go forth, and fight against those nations**, *as when he fought in the day of battle. And his feet shall stand in that day upon the Mount of Olives, which is before Jerusalem on the east, and **the Mount of Olives shall cleave in the midst** thereof toward the east and toward the west, and there shall be a very great valley; and half of the mountain shall remove toward the north, and half of it toward the south.*

> *And **you shall flee to the valley of the mountains**; for the valley of the mountains shall reach unto Azal: Yes, you shall flee, like as you fled from before the earthquake in the days of Uzziah king of Judah: and the LORD my God shall come, and all the saints with Him. And it shall come to pass in that day, that the light shall not be clear, nor*

dark: But it shall be one day which shall be known to the LORD, __not day, nor night:__ __but it shall come to pass, that at evening time, it shall be light__.

~ *Zechariah 14:4-7*

This eerie dim light under which this great battle takes place is also echoed in *Joel 3* as the armies gather at the Valley of Jehoshaphat.

__Let the nations be wakened and come up to the Valley of Jehoshaphat__; For there I will sit to judge all the surrounding nations. Put in the sickle, for the harvest is ripe. Come, go down; For the winepress is full; the vats overflow-For their wickedness is great. Multitudes, multitudes in the valley of decision! For the Day of the Lord is near in the valley of decision. __The sun and moon will grow dark, and the stars will diminish their brightness__. ~ *Joel 3:12*

Christ will first make the remnant of Jerusalem safe by allowing them to flee to join those who fled at the *Abomination of Desolation*. Before Christ fights these armies, he allows the people of Israel to flee to a special place in Jordan, long ago prepared for their refuge.

Jerusalem Made Safe in the Clefts of the Rock

Those in Jerusalem, who fled immediately at the *Abomination of Desolation* would have fled southeast and across the Jordan River to Bozrah, a tiny city of great significance. This city is the ancient capital of Job, the man who suffered and was made an intermediary for his friends. To understand this, one must search the genealogies of *Genesis 10 and 36* to uncover the identity of the mysterious man called Job.

Joktan begat Almodad, Sheleph, Hazarmaveth, Jerah, Hadoram, Uzal, Diklah, Obal, Abimael, Sheba, Ophir, Havilah, and __Jobab__. ~ *Genesis 10:26*

Jobab was the youngest son of the youngest son in the original table of nations; the son of Joktan, whose name means, "little one." His sons dwelt in the southern deserts of Arabia in the modern nation of Yemen expanding north along the Red Sea. His father was (H)Eber, from whom the Hebrews came, and his brother Peleg was the ancestor of Abraham. Jobab lived to be 248 years old and would have been head of the last family by which the languages were divided.

Jobab dwelt in the Land of Uz in the region of Seir, who was the father of the Horites that populated the area before the Edomites reigned. Jobab would eventually marry a great-granddaughter of Esau and become the son of Zerah, who was the son of Reuel. Reuel was the half-brother of Esau's firstborn Eliphaz. His son Teman, was the first tribal chief of the Edomites, so he would have been known in his old age as

"Eliphaz the Temanite." This was the very *Eliphaz the Temanite,* who brought Job's three friends to comfort him *(Job 4:1).* Having been from a previous generation which had lived much longer, Job would have been much older than Eliphaz, though aging at about half the rate.

Jobab comes from two words: Job, meaning *"hated"* or *"persecuted"* and Ab, meaning *"father."* In the story of Job, his ten children are killed when one of their houses collapses, and for this reason, he is called Job, no longer being a father. Despite being grieved, Job gave glory to God, and after his trial, God restored to Job double all that he had previously, and he became the greatest man in all the East. When God gave him seven more sons and three more daughters, he was again called Jobab, and went on to succeed Bela, who was the first recorded king in the land of Seir.

This Bela, the Son of Beor, is the same king who had reigned at Zoar and fought with the kings of Sodom and Gomorra against the five Kings of the East in the days of Abraham *(Genesis 14).* It was to his city that Lot had fled when Sodom and Gomorrah were destroyed, imploring God to spare the city for its small size. Because God spared Zoar, this left Bela the only remaining king in the region. In time, the city was removed by the waters that prevailed to form the Dead Sea and Bela moved to reign in Dinabhah in the region of Seir. Therefore, Bela became the King of Seir and reigned for about 75 years before the Edomites came to the land. When Bela finally died, Jobab became the next king of Seir, and afterward, Husham the Temanite, a descendant of Eliphaz, led the Edomites to rule from then on.

In the last days, the story of Job comes full circle. Job, being a great man with great flocks and herds, reigned in Bozrah, whose name means, *"sheepfold."* It is this sheepfold that Christ will use to protect the last-days sheep of Israel. In *Luke 17:28-32,* Christ compares the Jews fleeing from Jerusalem in the last days to Lot's flight from Sodom. In the end, just as Lot fled Sodom to Zoar, the city of Bela, the first King of Seir, the Jews will flee Jerusalem to Bozrah, the city of Jobab, the second King of Seir. It is here that Christ will come to defend them from their enemies, beginning the slaughter from which his robes become dipped in blood.

> *I will surely gather all of you, O Jacob; I will surely gather the remnant of Israel.* __*I will put them together like the sheep of Bozrah*__*, like the flock in the midst of their fold. They shall be in commotion because of men. The breaker has come up before them; they have broken up, and have passed through the gate, and have gone out of it. And their king shall pass before them, and the LORD at the head of them.* ~ Micah 2:12

These Jews who flee there, will be as when the Lord put Moses into the cleft of the Rock and covered it with his hand, letting Moses witness the backside of his glory. On the day when the Lord stands on the Mount of Olives, the city splits to form a valley, allowing the remaining Jews to escape to join the other Jews at Bozrah.

> Behold, he shall come up and fly like the eagle, and **spread his wings over Bozrah**. And at that day the heart of the mighty men of Edom shall be like the heart of a woman in her pangs. ~ Jeremiah 49:22

Just as Christ cried, *"how often I desired to gather your children in the way a hen gathers her brood under the wings"* in his first coming, *(Luke 13:34),* in his second coming, he will carry out this desire, which is echoed in the Song of Solomon.

> O My dove, **in the clefts of the rock**, in the secret places of the stairs, let Me see your face, let Me hear your voice; for your voice is sweet, and your face is beautiful. Take us the foxes, the little foxes that spoil the vines; for **our vines have tender grapes**.
> ~ Songs 2:14

The Winepress: Revelation 19 Interpreted

The great *Battle of Armageddon* is brought to its conclusion by Christ himself, after he gathers all the unbelieving armies of the Earth into one place. In the sixth bowl judgement, *(Revelation 16:12-16),* God allows Satan to deceive all the nations to gather for battle. The Euphrates River is dried up, making the victory feasible for the *Kings of the East* as *the Beast* will have much of his military occupied in North Africa.

Those who lead this coalition will come from the East, while from the North, the remnants of NATO will organize a fleet of ships to stand against him from the Mediterranean. It is for this reason that news from the North and East will trouble *the Antichrist (Daniel 11:44).* Daniel was given this prophecy in the days of Darius the Mede, who sacked Babylon by diverting the flow of the Euphrates. Here, as the Euphrates is dried up, the Medes will move to destroy the cities of Neom and Jerusalem, in order to overthrow *the Beast.*

> Set up a banner in the land, Blow the trumpet among the nations! Prepare the nations against her, Call the kingdoms together against her: **Ararat, Minni and Ashkenaz (Caucuses);** Appoint a general against her; Cause the horses to come up like the bristling locusts. Prepare against her the nations, With the kings of the **Medes (Kurds),** Its governors and all its rulers, All the land of his dominion. And the land will tremble and sorrow; For every purpose of the LORD shall be performed against Babylon, to make the land of Babylon a desolation without inhabitant. ~ Jeremiah 51:27-29

Crossing the Euphrates, the main army will split to form a pincer, the first heading straight to Jerusalem from the North while the other heads across Arabia to Neom. After what seems to be a missile bombardment, these armies will descend on the massive city to take vengeance on the ultra-rich who dwell there. Having plundered the city, they will head North toward Israel to join the attack on Jerusalem. To get there, they will have to go through the very region to which Christ commanded the Jews to flee. Expecting to find an easy road into Israel, they will be met with Christ, ready to unleash his fury.

> *Therefore, hear the counsel of the LORD, that He has taken against Edom; and his purposes, that He has purposed against the inhabitants of Teman: Surely **the least of the flock shall draw them out**: surely, he shall make their habitations desolate with them. The earth is moved at the noise of their fall, at the cry the noise thereof was heard in the Red sea. Behold, **He shall come up and fly as the eagle, and spread his wings over Bozrah**: and at that day shall the heart of the mighty men of Edom be as the heart of a woman in her pangs. ~ Jeremiah 49:20*

Here, Christ will make war against his enemies. His campaign will mirror that of Joshua, as he led Israel into the *Promised Land* from across the river Jordan. Before entering the land, they had to defeat the Amorites on the East side of the Jordan.

> *Who is this who comes from Edom with dyed garments from Bozrah; this One who is glorious in His apparel, traveling in the greatness of His strength? – "I who speak in righteousness, mighty to save."*
>
> *Why is Your apparel red, And Your garments like one who treads in the winepress?*
>
> **I have trodden the winepress alone**; *and of the peoples there was no man with Me; for I will tread them in My anger and trample them in My fury; and their blood will be sprinkled on My garments, and I will stain all My clothing. **For the day of vengeance is in My heart, and the year of My redeemed has come**. And I looked, and there was none to help; and I wondered that there was no one to uphold; therefore, My own arm has saved for Me; and My fury upheld Me. And I will tread down the people in My anger, and make them drunk in My fury, and I will pour their juice to the earth.*
>
> *~ Isaiah 63:1-6*

The entire region of ancient Edom will become a desolation as the Lord will lay waste to this massive army in every town and village.

> *The sword of the LORD is filled with blood; it is made fat with fatness, with the blood of lambs and goats, with the fat of the kidneys of rams; for **the LORD has a sacrifice in Bozrah**, and a great slaughter in the land of Edom. ~ Isaiah 34:6*

The armies of the Earth, led by *the Beast* and the *Kings of the East*, will be gathered to fight for supremacy at Jerusalem. Yet, after learning of the great bloodbath that occurred at Bozrah, they will make peace to ally against the coming King of Israel.

> *Why do the nations rage, and the peoples meditate on a vain thing? The kings of the earth set themselves, and **the rulers plot together, against the LORD and against His anointed**, saying, "Let us break **their bands** in two, and cast away **their cords** from us." He who sits in the heavens shall laugh; the LORD shall mock at them. Then He shall speak to them in His anger, and trouble them in His wrath. "Yea, I have set My king on My holy hill, on Zion." I will declare the decree of the LORD. He has said to Me, "You are My Son; today I have begotten You. Ask of Me, and I shall give the nations for Your inheritance; and the uttermost parts of the earth for Your possession. You shall break them with a rod of iron; You shall dash them in pieces like a potter's vessel."*
> *~ Psalm 2:1-9*

This campaign will last about 45 days *(Daniel 12:11-12)* from the time the Lord touches down at the Mount of Olives *(Revelation 16:16)* to the time He destroys the armies at Armageddon *(Revelation 19:21)*. During the initial battles, the *Bride* will remain behind in *the New Jerusalem*, praising the Lord for his victory over Babylon.

> *After these things I heard a loud voice of a great multitude in heaven, saying, "Alleluia! Salvation and glory and honor and power belong to the Lord our God! For true and righteous are His judgments, because **He has judged the great harlot who corrupted the earth** with her fornication; and He has avenged on her the blood of His servants shed by her." Again, they said, "Alleluia! Her smoke rises up forever and ever!" And the Twenty-Four Elders and the four living creatures fell down and worshiped God who sat on the throne, saying, "Amen! Alleluia!" ~ Revelation 19:1-4*

The Wife of the Lamb will then prepare herself to meet him on the earth.

> *Then a voice came from the throne, saying, "Praise our God, all you His servants and those who fear Him, both small and great!" And I heard, as it were, the voice of a great multitude, as the sound of many waters and as the sound of mighty thundering, saying, "Alleluia! For the Lord God Omnipotent reigns! Let us be glad and rejoice and give Him glory, for **the marriage of the Lamb has come, and His wife has made herself ready.**" And to her it was granted to be arrayed in fine linen, clean and bright, for the fine linen is the righteous acts of the saints. ~ Revelation 19:5-8*

The Angel makes a final note to let John know that the *Wedding Week* reaches its finale, and the final reception of the Husband and Wife is about to commence in what is called *"the Marriage Supper."*

> *Then he said to me, "Write: '**Blessed are those who are called to the marriage supper of the Lamb!**'" And he said to me, "These are the true sayings of God." And I*

fell at his feet to worship him. But he said to me, "See that you do not do that! I am your fellow servant, and of your brethren who have the testimony of Jesus. Worship God! For the testimony of Jesus is the spirit of prophecy." ~ Revelation 19:9-10

Here the ministry of the Lamb comes full circle. His first miracle took place at a wedding, when he turned water into wine. In this last terrible hour, all the waters of earth are turned to blood, while the Lord, soaked in the blood of his enemies, reveals himself as the great and holy winemaker.

Now I saw heaven opened, and behold, a white horse. And He who sat on him was called Faithful and True, and in righteousness He judges and makes war. His eyes were like a flame of fire, and on His head, were many crowns. He had a name written that no one knew except Himself. __He was clothed with a robe dipped in blood__*, and His name is called The Word of God. And the armies in heaven, clothed in fine linen, white and clean, followed Him on white horses. Now out of His mouth goes a sharp sword, that with it He should strike the nations. And He Himself will rule them with a rod of iron.* __He Himself treads the winepress of the fierceness and wrath of Almighty God.__ *And He has on His robe and on His thigh a name written: KING OF KINGS AND LORD OF LORDS. ~ Revelation 19:11-16*

In *Joshua 10*, the next major battle was to fight the armies gathered by Adonai-Zedek, the King of Salem, whose name means *"Lord of Righteousness."* The Beast will have set up camp between the Sea and Jerusalem *(Daniel 11:45)* in the midst of the *Promised Land*.

Then I saw an angel standing in the sun; and he cried with a loud voice, saying to all the birds that fly in the midst of heaven, "Come and gather together for the supper of the great God, that you may eat the flesh of kings, the flesh of captains, the flesh of mighty men, the flesh of horses and of those who sit on them, and the flesh of all people, free and slave, both small and great." And __I saw the Beast, the kings of the earth, and their armies, gathered together to make war against Him who sat on the horse and against His army__*. ~ Revelation 18:17-19*

Before facing the great army at Armageddon, the Lord captures *the Beast* and his *False Prophet*, rendering immediate judgement. Their trial has already finished and there is no imprisonment for them, but a swift execution for their perjury.

Then the Beast was captured, and with him the False Prophet who worked signs in his presence, by which he deceived those who received the Mark of the Beast and those who worshiped his image. These two were cast alive into the lake of fire burning with brimstone. ~ Revelation 19:20

The final part of Joshua's campaign in chapter 11, was to fight a great battle against the armies in the North of Canaan. These foreshadow the massive armies of the East, encamped at Armageddon. As Christ approaches these armies with his saints at his side, he will not carry out a violent battle, but will simply utter a Word of Power.

And the rest were killed with the sword, which proceeded from the mouth of Him who sat on the horse. And all the birds were filled with their flesh. ~ *Revelation 19:21*

Zechariah prophesies what results when the Word of Power is uttered.

And this shall be the plague with which the LORD will strike all the peoples who have fought against Jerusalem. Their flesh shall rot while they stand on their feet, and their eyes shall rot in their sockets. And their tongue shall rot in their mouth. And it shall be in that day a great panic of the LORD shall be among them, and they shall each one lay hold of his neighbor, and his hand shall rise up against the hand of his neighbor.

~ *Zechariah 14:12-13*

At this, the wrath of God is finished, and the great thousand-year reign of Christ will begin. He will have destroyed all the armies of the Earth and from this devastated and humbled Earth, he will begin to rule the nations with a rod of iron.

Of the increase of his government and peace there shall be no end, upon the throne of David, and upon his kingdom, to order it, and to establish it with judgment and with justice from henceforth even forever. The zeal of the LORD of hosts will perform this.

~ *Isaiah 9:7*

PART 10 - THE KINGDOM COME

By chapter 20, *the Gentile Bride* will have become one with the Lamb in marriage. The remnant of Israel will have been rescued from their enemies and Christ will begin to rule the Nations with a rod of iron. This is the beginning of the peace which *the Antichrist* attempted to counterfeit; the Great Sabbath and *Day of the Lord*.

Like many elements of prophecy, the *Kingdom Come* was both *already* and *not yet* fulfilled at the time the Gospel began to be preached. The first fulfillment is a spiritual kingdom, which began with the ministry of Jesus after he obeyed the final instruction from the last Old Testament Prophet, completing the prerequisite obedience to *"fulfill all righteousness" (Matthew 3:15),* and qualify as the *spotless lamb*. The second fulfillment is the material kingdom in which Christ will reign from Mount Zion, ruling the nations from the throne of David for a thousand years.

It was because Jesus did not establish this material kingdom at his first coming that many Jews did not receive him. The Jews expected a kingdom after the likeness of King David's dominion, assuming to establish their righteousness through the keeping of the Law and requiring only a military rescue at the end of the age. However, God's plan in sending Jesus was to establish a righteousness apart from the Law and to redeem a born-again people from every tribe, nation and tongue, into an everlasting kingdom. It was for this reason that both John the Baptist, and after him Jesus, proclaimed, *"Repent, for the Kingdom is near!"*

> *The law and the prophets were until John. Since that time the Kingdom of God is proclaimed...~ Luke 16:16*

While this material kingdom was destined to come, Jesus knew that entry into this kingdom could only be secured by faith through his sacrifice for our sins, and for this reason, he taught of a kingdom that even John was not yet qualified to enter.

> *Truly I say to you, "Among those who have been born of women there has not risen a greater one than John the Baptist. But the least in the Kingdom of Heaven is greater than he." ~ Matthew 11:11*

Keeping the deliverance of the Gentiles a secret from the rulers of this world, Jesus spoke of this kingdom in a manner that could only be discerned by the guidance of the Holy Spirit which would only be given after his ascension.

> *And being asked by the Pharisees when the Kingdom of God would come, He answered and said, "The Kingdom of God does not come with observation. Nor shall they say, 'Lo here! or, behold, there!' For behold, the Kingdom of God is in your midst."*
>
> *~ Luke 17:20-21*

Jesus often compared his death and resurrection to the *sign of Jonah,* alluding not only to Jonah's time in the belly of a whale, but also to what would come afterward. After being vomited up by the whale, Jonah preached to Nineveh—the chief Gentile city of that day—that she would be *"overturned"* in forty days. *(Jonah 3:4).* Despite this prophecy being from the Lord, the city was spared when its residents repented in sackcloth and ashes. While God did not destroy Nineveh as the prophecy seemed to indicate, the city was still *overturned* spiritually through their repentance, as they turned from idols to trust the Living God. In this, Christ alluded to a great Gentile deliverance that would come after his resurrection.

Similarly, God warned Adam that he would die *"in the day"* that he ate of the Tree of Knowledge. While Adam died spiritually that very day, being separated from God in sin, he remained living physically for nearly 1000 years. Just as *the day* of Adam's sin and death lasted nearly a millennium, *the Day of the Lord* will also last a millennium. Peter would signify this in his epistle, prophesying the beginning and the end of the *Day of the Lord*; noting Christ's coming *"like a thief,"* at its beginning *(Revelation 16:15)*, and the Earth being judged by fire at its end *(Revelation 20:9)*.

> *But, beloved, be not ignorant of this one thing, that __one day is with the Lord as a thousand years, and a thousand years as one day__...But the Day of the Lord will come as a thief in the night; in which the heavens shall pass away with a great noise, and the elements shall melt with fervent heat, the earth also and the works that are therein shall be burned up.* ~ *2nd Peter 3:8-10*

The Millennial Reign

Upon completing his military conquest, Christ's first act will be to bind Satan in the *Bottomless Pit*, assuring that His voice alone influences the nations. Neither Satan nor his demons will be able to deceive the nations, allowing for complete political peace throughout the earth.

> *And I saw an angel come down from heaven, having the key of the Bottomless Pit and a great chain in his hand. And he laid hold on the dragon, that old serpent, which is the Devil, and Satan, and bound him a thousand years, and cast him into the Bottomless Pit, and shut him up, and set a seal upon him, that he should deceive the nations no more till the thousand years should be fulfilled: and after that he must be loosed a little season.*
> ~ *Revelation 20:1-3*

After this, Christ will abolish all prophecy in the earth, fulfilling Daniel's prophecy of seventy weeks. With his many perfected Saints in the earth for guidance, there will be no need for any to claim to know his will.

> *Seventy weeks are decreed as to your people and as to your holy city, to finish the transgression and to make an end of sins, and to make atonement for iniquity, and to bring in everlasting righteousness, and __to seal up the vision and prophecy__, and to anoint the Most Holy.* ~ *Daniel 9:24*

Paul also confirms an end to prophesying when Christ comes, saying,

> *Love never fails. But __whether there are prophecies, they will fail__; whether there are tongues, they will cease; whether there is knowledge, it will vanish away. For we know in part and we prophesy in part. But __when that which is perfect has come, then that which is in part will be done away__...For now we see in a mirror dimly, but then face to face. Now I know in part, but then I shall know just as I also am known.*
> ~ *1st Corinthians 13:8-12*

Christ will make prophesying punishable by death, forbidding any spiritual offices outside of the priesthood in Israel and the guidance of the resurrected saints. Just as a child could be stoned to death under the Old Covenant for breaking the Sabbath, a son will be expected to be killed by his parents if he claims to be a prophet.

> *"And it shall be in that day," says the LORD of hosts, "I will cut off the names of the idols out of the land, and they shall be remembered no more. Also, I will cause the prophets and the unclean spirit to pass out of the land, and it shall be __when any shall__* __*yet prophesy, his father and his mother who gave birth to him shall say to him*__ __*then, 'You shall not live; for you speak lies in the name of the LORD.'*__ *And his father and his mother who gave him birth shall thrust him through when he prophesies. And it shall be in that day, the prophets shall be ashamed, each one of his vision, when he prophesies. And they shall not wear a hairy garment to deceive. But he shall say, 'I am no prophet; I am a man, a tiller of the ground; for a man taught me to buy from my youth.'"*
>
> ~ *Zechariah 13:2-5*

Christ will set up a government to rule from Israel, having supremacy over all the Gentile Nations. Over Israel, he will set up the *Twenty-Four Elders,* being the twelve Patriarchs of Israel and the twelve Apostles who will rule over the twelve tribes.

> *And I saw thrones, and they sat upon them, and judgment was given unto them*
>
> ~ *Revelation 20:4*

After Satan is removed, Christ will raise to life those who were killed in the last 3 ½ years of *Daniel's 70ᵗʰ week.* These are like the workers of the harvest who came in at the last hour in *Matthew 20,* completing *the Bride* who will rule and reign with Him over the nations. These are the saints of Laodicea, who being once lukewarm, finally gave glory to Christ by their deaths in the end.

> *And I saw the souls of them that were beheaded for the witness of Jesus, and for the word of God, and which had not worshipped the Beast, neither his image, neither had received his mark upon their foreheads, or in their hands; and they lived and reigned with Christ a thousand years. But the rest of the dead lived not again until the thousand years were finished. This is the first resurrection. Blessed and holy is he that has part in the first resurrection: on such the second death has no power, but they shall be priests of God and of Christ and shall __reign with him a thousand years__. ~ Revelation 20:4-6*

This co-rule was foreshadowed after the Exodus of Israel from Egypt. Jethro, the father-in-law of Moses, counseled him to choose men to help him govern Israel after they were delivered from Pharaoh, who was a type of Antichrist.

> *...you shall choose out of all the people able men, such as fear God, men of truth, hating covetousness, and place such over them to be rulers of thousands, rulers of hundreds, rulers of fifties, and rulers of tens. And let them judge the people at all times. And it shall be, every great matter they shall bring to you, but every small matter they shall judge. And make it easier for yourself, and they shall bear with you. ~ Exodus 18:21*

These judges were led by seventy elders, which stood by Moses, foreshadowing the *Gentile Bride*, who would rule with Christ.

> *Come up to the LORD, you (Moses) and Aaron, Nadab, and Abihu, and **seventy of the elders of Israel**. ~ Exodus 24:1*

The *Gentile Bride* will rule with Christ over the Nations, being rewarded for their works on earth. By their fruitfulness, Christ will determine over which cities in the earth they will have governance.

> *And when He had received his kingdom and had returned, then ... He commanded these servants to be called to him...And the first came, He said to him, "Well done, good servant, because you have been faithful in a very little, have authority over ten cities" ...And He said the same to him, "You be over five cities." ~ Luke 19:15-19*

These saints will judge every civil matter among the nations, being counselors and ambassadors of King Jesus. The larger matters, like international disputes, will be brought to Christ in Jerusalem just as Moses judged the larger matters. The nations will come to Him for wisdom just as they did in the days of Solomon, allowing for continued world peace.

> *And it shall come to pass in the last days, that the mountain of the LORD'S house shall be established in the top of the mountains and shall be exalted above the hills; and all nations shall flow unto it. And many people shall go and say, "Come, and let us go up to the mountain of the LORD, to the house of the God of Jacob; and He will teach us of his ways, and we will walk in his paths." **For out of Zion shall go forth the law, and the word of the LORD from Jerusalem**. And He shall judge among the nations and shall rebuke many people: and they shall beat their swords into plowshares, and their spears into pruninghooks: nation shall not lift up sword against nation, neither shall they learn war anymore. ~ Isaiah 2:2-4*

A common misconception about the Millennium is that only believers will populate the earth, which could not be further from the truth. When Christ comes to judge the earth, he will not wipe out every unbeliever, but will only destroy the armies of the Earth that fought against him at Armageddon. The remainder from the nations involved in that battle are given mercy to live and to repopulate the earth. While these may still be condemned to judgement for having taken the *Mark of the Beast*, Zechariah is clear that unbelievers remain after Armageddon. The rule of Christ will be required to keep the nations of the earth subdued.

> *And it shall come to pass, that **everyone who is left of all the nations which came against Jerusalem shall go up from year to year to worship the King**, the LORD of hosts, and to keep the Feast of Tabernacles. And it shall be that whichever of the*

families of the earth do not come up to Jerusalem to worship the King, the LORD of hosts, on them there will be no rain. If the family of Egypt will not come up and enter in, they shall have no rain; they shall receive the plague with which the LORD strikes the nations who do not come up to keep the Feast of Tabernacles. This shall be the punishment of Egypt and the punishment of all the nations that do not come up to keep the Feast of Tabernacles. ~ Zechariah 14:16

During this time, the religious practice of the nations will be a simple one. Just as Baptism and Communion were ordinances given by Christ to the Church to be practiced until he comes, Christ will give this Feast of Tabernacles (or Feast of Booths) to be practiced throughout *the Millennium*. By this holiday, he will note which nations fear Him and which do not. When Zechariah says, *"This shall be the punishment of Egypt...,"* he may be prophesying that Egypt will be guilty of this offense or he may simply be declaring that Egypt, whose waters had dried up, would signify the judgement of those nations who refuse this ordinance.

For the Feast of Tabernacles, every family in the earth will be made to come up to Jerusalem and dwell in tents for one week, repeating an ancient feast which the Israelites were given to practice after being delivered from Egypt. In this feast, the Israelites were made to remember their temporary dwellings in which they lived, between being delivered from bondage to Pharaoh and the time they entered their *Promised Land*. In the Millennium, the world will be made to remember their deliverance from Antichrist, who had enslaved the whole world. By this feast, they will be taught that their mortal flesh is a temporary dwelling and that they are awaiting a new body, free from the corruption of sin and death.

The Restored Earth

From the great shaking which happened at the 6th seal and the subsequent devastations, the Earth will be significantly different than it was, having different poles, seasons, and constellations. For this reason, it will be a type of *New Heavens and New Earth;* a minor fulfillment of that prophecy which will be fulfilled more completely at the end of the age.

> *For, behold, __I create new heavens and a new earth__: and the former shall not be remembered, nor come into mind. But be glad and rejoice forever in that which I create: for, behold, I create Jerusalem a rejoicing, and her people a joy. And I will rejoice in Jerusalem, and joy in my people: and the voice of weeping shall be no more heard in her, nor the voice of crying. ~ Isaiah 65:17*

During the Millennium, the earth will be restored in some limited sense to a state like the time before the flood, in which people lived to be much older than eighty years. While the cause of the change is unclear, it is evident that the human lifespan will increase, as one who dies at the age of one hundred will be considered an accursed sinner, having died in their childhood.

> There will not be an infant, nor an old man that has not filled his days. For the child will die a hundred years old; but the sinner who is a hundred years old will be considered accursed. ~ Isaiah 65:20

While the resurrected saints will not be given in marriage, the mortal Jews and Gentile who survive Armageddon will live on to repopulate the planet. Their occupation will be simple: building farms, cultivating land, planting, harvesting, and enjoying the fruits of their labor for hundreds of years in peace and security.

> And they shall build houses, and inhabit them; and they shall plant vineyards, and eat the fruit of them. They shall not build, and another inhabit; they shall not plant, and another eat. For as the days of a tree are the days of my people, and mine elect shall long enjoy the work of their hands. They shall not labor in vain, nor bring forth for trouble; for they are the seed of the blessed of the LORD, and their offspring with them.
> ~ Isaiah 65:21-23

The animal life on Earth will lose its fear of mankind. The carnivores will become herbivores, and every animal on earth will be safe to play with.

> The wolf and the lamb shall feed together, and the lion shall eat straw like the bullock: and dust shall be the serpent's meat. They shall not hurt nor destroy in all my holy mountain, says the LORD. ~ Isaiah 65:25

> The wolf also shall dwell with the lamb, the leopard shall lie down with the young goat, the calf and the young lion and the fatling together; and a little child shall lead them. The cow and the bear shall graze; Their young ones shall lie down together; and the lion shall eat straw like the ox. The nursing child shall play by the cobra's hole, and the weaned child shall put his hand in the viper's den. They shall not hurt nor destroy in all My holy mountain, For the earth shall be full of the knowledge of the LORD as the waters cover the sea. ~ Isaiah 11:6-9

This will be the general state of the Earth throughout *the Millennium* as Christ rules over the nations. Sin may still cause some people to have troubles on a personal and local basis, and some nations may need to be disciplined through a lack of rain; but in general, the world will experience peace, abundance, and a total absence of war.

The Land of Israel

To define the land and territory that will be given to the nation of Israel, one must look at the original Promised Land to Abraham, which is the inherited property of his *Seed*: Jesus Christ. The *Promised Land* was given in three prophecies, detailing the borders of Abraham's land.

> *"Lift your eyes now and look from the place where you are: northward, southward, eastward, and westward; for all the land which you see I give to you and your descendants forever." ~ Genesis 13:14-15*

> *On the same day the LORD made a covenant with Abram, saying: "To your descendants I have given this land, from **the river of Egypt** to the great river, **the River Euphrates** - the Kenites, the Kenezzites, the Kadmonites, the Hittites, the Perizzites, the Rephaim, the Amorites, the Canaanites, the Girgashites, and the Jebusites." ~ Genesis 15:18-19*

> *"Also, I give to you and your descendants after you the land in which you are a stranger, all the land of Canaan, as an everlasting possession; and I will be their God."*
> *~ Genesis 17:8*

The first thing to note are the rivers which are designated as the bounds of the *Promised Land*. It is important to know that the term "Nile River" is not found in the original texts of Scripture. This river was considered *"The River of Egypt,"* as the entire civilization was built on its shores. The other river mentioned was the *"Great River Euphrates,"* which starts in Central Turkey and extends through Syria and Iraq, emptying into the Persian Gulf. At its peak, ancient Israel only occupied a land from a small brook on the border of the Sinai Peninsula to the city of Damascus, during the reign of David and Solomon. Applying the plain understanding to the original promises, one cannot consider this a complete fulfillment.

To understand this prophecy fully, one must understand God's delivering work through Abraham during his lifetime. When Abraham was in the land, Lot was taken captive after a battle between the five kings of Sodom and Gomorrah and the four Kings of the East *(Genesis 14)*. These kings ruled the lands which today are represented in Turkey, Iraq, Iran, and Syria. Because of this battle, the strongest kings around the Euphrates River were defeated, allowing four kingdoms to arise: the Amorites, who dominated between the Jordan and the Euphrates River, the Hittites, who dominated what is now Western Turkey, the Assyrians, who came to power in Eastern Turkey and Syria, and Egypt, which dominated along the Nile. Each of these kingdoms owed their rise to Abraham defeating the *Kings of the East*, yet Abraham did not get the rewards for this victory in his day. In *the Millennium*, Christ is awarded all the territory which God had delivered through Abraham.

> *And the LORD will strike Egypt, He will strike and heal it; they will return to the LORD, and He will be entreated by them and heal them. In that day there will be a highway from Egypt to Assyria, and the Assyrian will come into Egypt and the Egyptian into Assyria, and the Egyptians will serve with the Assyrians. In that day, Israel will be one of three with Egypt and Assyria, a blessing in the midst of the land, whom the LORD of hosts shall bless, saying, "Blessed is Egypt My people, and Assyria the work of My hands, and Israel My inheritance." ~ Isaiah 19:22-25*

This entire territory is claimed by Christ, though it is not entirely given to the Children of Israel. The twelve tribes will be ruled by the Twenty Four Elders and abide in a land that extends to the south roughly as far as their current border between the "brook of Egypt" and the Red Sea port of Elat, and extend north to the extent of the territory administered by the Kingdom of David and Solomon, extending to the area of Homs, Syria to the north, running east to the Euphrates before extending back toward the Sea and down to Elat again.

This land will be divided horizontally from North to South, after a pattern measured out in *Ezekiel 46-48*, noting that the resurrected Tribe of Dan, will have an allotment of land with their brethren. The two sons of Joseph will each still have their own allotment as well, giving Joseph a double portion. The twelve tribes will have their allotment measured out equally like twelve stripes, stacked vertically; seven of the stripes above the Temple City of Jerusalem, with the other five to the south. The territory around the temple will be set aside, one part for the Levites and one part for the princes *(Ezekiel 46:16-18)*. These *"princes"* seem to be the resurrected royal line of David, who will be tasked with keeping the herds and flocks to be used in the sacrifices. The remaining land allotment will be for the Lord and will be shared by the Priests of Zadok, who serve as the official staff of his estate and the ministers in the restored Millennial Temple.

Finally, the ancient city of Tyre, once and ally and friend of David and Solomon, will again become a trade partner, being the main port city of Israel during *the Millennium*. The children of Israel will be occupied with making this former desert land bloom; with the ministry of the temple; with hospitality, and with spreading the Gospel unto the nations. They will not be engaged in common trade but will occupy their original purpose of being a nation of priests unto God. Their common needs will be supplied by Tyre, being their merchant class throughout the Millennium.

And it will be after the end of seventy years, the LORD will visit Tyre, and she shall turn to her hire and shall commit fornication with all the kingdoms of the world on the face of the earth. And her goods and her wages shall be holiness to the LORD. It shall not be treasured nor laid up, for her goods shall be for those who dwell before the LORD, to eat enough, and for a choice covering. ~ Isaiah 23:17-18

The Temple Worship

Ezekiel 40-42 gives detail as to the location and dimensions of the new temple. It will not be built on the current Temple Mount, as it is too large to fit on that ground but will be based *"south of the mountain" (Ezekiel 40: 2).* In the Millennium, the *Mercy Seat* will be the throne of Christ, from which he will carry out his judgements.

Afterward he brought me to the gate, the gate that faces toward the east. And behold, the glory of the God of Israel came from the way of the east. His voice was like the sound of many waters; and the earth shone with His glory…And the glory of the LORD came into the temple by way of the gate which faces toward the east. The Spirit lifted me up and brought me into the inner court; and behold, the glory of the LORD filled the temple.
~ Ezekiel 43:1-5

When this temple is completed, it will be defiled by *the Antichrist*, even housing his corpse, requiring it to be cleansed before Christ takes his seat there. Like the purification during the time of the Maccabees *(John 10:22)*, this cleansing will take some time before Christ enters.

*Then I heard Him speaking to me from the temple, while a man stood beside me. And He said to me, "Son of man, this is the place of My throne and the place of the soles of My feet, where I will dwell in the midst of the children of Israel forever. No more shall the house of Israel defile My holy name, they nor their kings, by **their harlotry** or with **the carcasses of their kings** on their high places. When they set their threshold by My threshold, and their doorpost by My doorpost, with **a wall between them and Me**, they defiled My holy name by the abominations which they committed; therefore, I have consumed them in My anger. Now **let them put their harlotry and the carcasses of their kings far away from Me**, and I will dwell in their midst forever."*
~ Ezekiel 43:6-9

In the passage above, Christ describes the great harlotry of Israel in the last days, putting another *way* before the people of earth by which to gain eternal life in their reinstitution of the Old Covenant, ultimately resulting in placing the carcass of the slain Antichrist in the Temple. Christ is making it clear that any other way to God is no way at all, but a wall between God and man.

And the LORD said to me, "This gate shall be shut; it shall not be opened, and no man shall enter by it, because the LORD God of Israel has entered by it; therefore, it shall be shut. As for the prince, because he is the prince, he may sit in it to eat bread before the LORD; he shall enter by way of the vestibule of the gateway and go out the same way."
~ Ezekiel 44:2

After Christ enters the Temple, the east gate will be shut. Only the resurrected King David will be allowed to enter by a special gateway to eat with the Lord. The Levites will carry out the sacrifices as a memorial of what Christ did in his atoning death and resurrection. These priests, who served in the temple until it was defiled by *the Beast*, will be able to carry out the sacrifices for the people, but not to minister before the Lord because of their sinful leadership under the Antichrist.

*"And the Levites who went far from Me, when Israel went astray, who strayed away from Me after their idols, they shall bear their iniquity. Yet they shall be ministers in My sanctuary, as gatekeepers of the house and ministers of the house; they shall slay the burnt offering and the sacrifice for the people, and they shall stand before them to minister to them. **Because they ministered to them before their idols and caused the house of Israel to fall into iniquity**, therefore I have raised My hand in an oath against them," says the Lord GOD, "that they shall bear their iniquity. And they shall not come near Me to minister to Me as priest, nor come near any of My holy things, nor into the Most Holy Place; but **they shall bear their shame and their abominations which they have committed**. Nevertheless, I will make them keep charge of the temple, for all its work, and for all that has to be done in it." ~ Ezekiel 44:10-14*

Christ will establish Zadok—the high priest in the days of David—to serve him in the temple. Zadok, after whom the Sadducees are named, inherited the ancient promise that the Lord made to his ancestor Phineas. In the wilderness, when the Israelites began to sin by fornicating with their pagan neighbors, God sent a plague to wipe out Israel until Phineas, in his zeal, ran a spear through a couple who were fornicating *(Numbers 25:7-13)*. This family alone will be able to minister to the Lord.

"But the priests, the Levites, the sons of Zadok, who kept charge of My sanctuary when the children of Israel went astray from Me, shall come near Me to minister to Me; and they shall stand before Me to offer to Me the fat and the blood," says the Lord GOD. "They shall enter My sanctuary, and they shall come near My table to minister to Me, and they shall keep My charge." ~ Ezekiel 44:15-16

The Millennium Underground

While the earth is maintained for a thousand years in perfect peace, there will be those who will have fled underground even before *Daniel's 70ᵗʰ week*. In the Book of Joshua, the kings who had been covered by the rocks in the caves were pulled out and put to death; however, there is no such indication of anything like this happening in the beginning of *the Millennium*. These people continue underground until the day when Satan is unleashed one last time to deceive the nations.

> *And they shall go into the holes of the rocks, and into the caves of the earth, for fear of the LORD, and for the glory of his majesty, when he arises to shake terribly the earth. In that day a man shall cast his idols of silver, and his idols of gold, which they made each one for himself to worship, to the moles and to the bats; To go into the clefts of the rocks, and into the tops of the ragged rocks, for fear of the LORD, and for the glory of his majesty, when he arises to shake terribly the earth. ~ Isaiah 2:18-21*

This wicked remnant from the previous world will prefer living in the darkness where they can continue with their idols. They may live and multiply underground, awaiting Satan as he arises from the *Bottomless Pit*, to make war against Christ's kingdom at the end of the Millennium.

> *... in that day that the LORD will punish the host of exalted ones on high, and kings of the earth on the earth. They will be gathered together as prisoners are gathered in the pit and will be shut up in the prison; After many days they will be punished.*
> *~ Isaiah 24:21-22*

Satan is Loosed: The Millennium Ends

While Christ will rule the world in perfect peace, this *Great Sabbath* will not last forever. God will designate a limited time during which he will endure the sinful hearts of the unbelieving. This extension of grace, like the two thousand years of Church history, like God's thousand years of patience with the nation of Israel, and like God's thousand-year extension of Adam's life, will eventually come to an end. For a thousand years, Christ will treat them with every grace, giving them righteous judgement and supplying their every material need. Still, when the opportunity arises to rebel against Him, many will leap at the opportunity.

> *When the thousand years are ended, Satan shall be loosed out of his prison, and shall go out to deceive the nations which are **in the four corners of the earth, Gog and Magog,** to gather them together to battle: the number of whom is as the sand of the sea. And they went up on the breadth of the earth, and compassed the camp of the saints about, and the beloved city, ~ Revelation 20:7-8*

Some speculate that his prison is in the belly of the Earth; called *"bottomless"* because it sits at the Earth's core. While it is uncertain from where Satan is released, it is clear that he goes immediately to the edges of the earth, to the lands furthest from the presence of Christ. As time wears on, those who love Chris will naturally move closer to Jerusalem as the faithful did in the days when Israel and Judah were divided *(2ⁿᵈ Chronicles 11:14)*. Those who hate Him will gradually move away, preferring the harsher living at the edges of the world.

These nations will gradually begin to rebel, refusing to bring their families to the Feast of Tabernacles, moving Christ to withhold rain from their lands. In their shortage of food, they will begin to blame the King of Israel, forgetting his former grace. When Satan is released, he will capitalize on this bitterness, revitalizing the lie that Christ is not the Creator of the universe but an alien creature, bent on stealing the resources of Earth. He will convince them that their only hope is to band together against Christ in a *war to end all wars*. One can only imagine the beauty and subtlety of Satan when he is released from his prison to captivate the wicked one last time.

In the end, the hordes of Earth will surround Jerusalem, fulfilling the second iteration of the Gog-Magog invasion. But in this battle, God will not plead against them with hailstones and confusion, or even with nuclear weapons. In this instance, the Earth will experience a flood of fire like the outpouring of water that destroyed the Earth in the days of Noah. Those who love the Lord will flock to *the New Jerusalem* to be saved from the coming Judgement. At the end of the Millennium, *the New Jerusalem* will serve as a second Ark, saving billions of souls as the Earth and the Heavens are consumed with the fiery consumption of the glory of God.

> ***...and fire came down from God out of heaven and devoured them***. *And the devil that deceived them was cast into the lake of fire and brimstone, where the Beast and the False Prophet are, and shall be tormented day and night for ever and ever.*
> ~ *Revelation 20:9-10*

The New Jerusalem: The Second Ark

The New Jerusalem, a moon-sized cubical city, will hover above the earth as a large satellite during the Millennium. This heavenly place, where the throne of the Father rests, is likely the place to which the Church is raptured, just as Jesus taught.

> *In My Father's house are many mansions; if it were not so, I would have told you. I go to prepare a place for you. And if I go and prepare a place for you, I will come again and receive you to Myself, so that where I am, you may be also.* ~ *John 14:2-3*

In *Revelation 21*, an angel invites John to see *"The Bride, the Lamb's Wife."* The New Jerusalem is the destination of every believer, making the city as much *The Bride* as the Church that is within. While the angel shows the city to John after describing the

Millennium, this will not be its first appearance. Like the other major characters of *The Revelation, the New Jerusalem* is introduced at its primary contribution to the narrative, detailing events before and after this point of reference.

> *And one of the seven angels who had the seven vials full of the seven last plagues came to me and talked with me, saying, "Come here, I will show you the Bride, the Lamb's wife." And he carried me away in the Spirit to a great and high mountain and showed me that great city, the holy Jerusalem, descending out of Heaven from God, having the glory of God. And its light was like a stone most precious, even like a jasper stone, clear as crystal.*
>
> *And it had a great and high wall, with twelve gates. And at the gates were twelve angels, and names inscribed, which are __the names of the twelve tribes of the sons of Israel__: From the east three gates, from the north three gates, from the south three gates, and from the west three gates. And the wall of the city had twelve foundations, and in them were __the names of the twelve apostles of the Lamb__.*
>
> *~ Revelation 21:9-14*

This city is approximately 1500 miles cubed, constructed of pure gold, with an outer wall of jasper stone, 200 feet thick. This jasper, being most commonly red in appearance due to its heavy iron content, will likely cause this city to look like a large red meteor from a distance. Compared to the Moon, which is only a bit larger at just 2159 miles in diameter, *the New Jerusalem* will likely be the object that passes by the Earth during the 6th seal, causing the Sun to turn to darkness and the Moon to turn to blood, having a gravity that would shake the entire earth.

> *And he who talked with me had a golden reed to measure the city and its gates and its wall. And the city lies four-square, and the length is as large as the breadth. And he measured the city with the reed, twelve thousand stadia. The length and the breadth and the height of it are equal. And he measured its wall, a hundred and forty-four cubits, according to the measure of a man, that is, of an angel.*
>
> *__And the wall was made of jasper; and the city was pure gold__, like clear glass. And the foundations of the wall of the city had been adorned with every precious stone. The first foundation, jasper; the second, sapphire; the third, chalcedony; the fourth, emerald; the fifth, sardonyx; the sixth, sardius; the seventh, chrysolite; the eighth, beryl; the ninth, topaz; the tenth, chrysoprase; the eleventh, hyacinth; the twelfth, amethyst. And the twelve gates were twelve pearls. Respectively, each one of the gates was one pearl. And the street of the city was pure gold, as transparent glass. ~ Revelation 21:15-21*

This city would be too large to rest on the surface of the planet, as its cubical shape would far exceed the curvature of the earth. Its base would cover half of the continental United States, while its height would reach far beyond the atmosphere of earth. The volume of the city will be so great that if each person were given a cubic mile, it would hold four billion people.

> *And I saw no temple in it, for the Lord God Almighty is its temple, even the Lamb. And the city had no need of the sun, nor of the moon, that they might shine in it, for the glory of God illuminated it, and its lamp is the Lamb. And the nations of those who are saved will walk in the light of it; and the* **_kings of the earth bring their glory and honor into it._** *And its gates may not be shut at all by day, for there shall be no night there. And they shall bring the glory and honor of the nations into it. And* **_there shall in no way enter into it anything that defiles, or any making an abomination or a lie; but only those who are written in the Lamb's Book of Life._** ~ *Revelation 21:22-27*

During the Millennium, access to this city seems to be the exclusive right of the resurrected *Bride of Christ*. The kings of the earth will bring their treasure into the city, both in materials, and perhaps even in redeemed people. At the fiery judgement at the end of the Millennium, *the New Jerusalem* will be a house for every believer who has ever lived, *the Bride* having prepared a place for them just as Christ has been doing for *the Bride* throughout the present age. It is in this city that the Church will dwell with God until He brings them to a New Earth at the end of the age.

> *And he showed me a pure river of water of life, clear as crystal, proceeding out of the throne of God and of the Lamb. In the midst of its street, and of the river, from here and from there, was the Tree of Life, which bore twelve fruits, each yielding its fruit according to one month.* **_And the leaves of the tree were for the healing of the nations._** ~ *Revelation 22:1-2*

The leaves of the *"Tree of Life"* which grow within the city are used to heal the nations throughout the Millennium, making it clear that it will appear beforehand. The *Bride of Christ* will live primarily in this city, deploying to various parts of the Earth for missions of healing, counsel, and diplomacy. This tree, by which they will heal the nations, is the very *"Tree of Life"* which was blocked from Adam and Eve after they sinned. While its fruits yield eternal life to the one who eats, even its leaves can apparently heal any ailment, supplying a universal medicine to mankind.

> *Blessed are they that do His commandments, that they may have right to the tree of life and may enter in through the gates into the city. Outside are dogs, and sorcerers, and whoremongers, and murderers, and idolaters, and whosoever loves to tell lies.*
> ~ *Revelation 22:14-15*

At the end of the Millennium, *the New Jerusalem* will serve its major purpose to save every believing soul on the Earth. *The New Jerusalem* will serve as a second Ark for all the redeemed throughout history; those who have their hope in the expectation of a

New Heavens and New Earth. Every believer, who received the grace of God throughout the Earth's 7000-year history will be collected into this great city. As Earth's history ends, *the New Jerusalem* will ascend like Noah's Ark, while fire falls from heaven to devour the earth, even as Peter prophesied:

> *...the heavens shall pass away with a great noise, **and the elements shall melt with fervent heat**, the earth also and the works that are therein shall be burned up. Seeing then that all these things shall be dissolved, what manner of persons ought ye to be in all holy conversation and godliness, looking for and hasting unto the coming of the day of God, **wherein the heavens being on fire shall be dissolved, and the elements shall melt with fervent heat**? Nevertheless we, according to his promise, look for new heavens and a new earth, wherein dwells righteousness. ~ 2nd Peter 11:13*

This fire will not fall on the earth in a limited scope, or even destroy the earth alone, but it will expand to the ends of the universe, consuming the entire corrupted creation in the holy fire of God. How long this will last is unknown, but as this transpires, every soul of man will be resurrected to face judgment at the *Great White Throne*; each given perfect justice from God.

The Great White Throne

> *Then I saw a great white throne and Him who sat on it, from whose face the earth and the heaven fled away. And there was found no place for them. And I saw the dead, small and great, standing before God, and books were opened. And another book was opened, which is the Book of Life. And the dead were judged according to their works, by the things which were written in the books. ~ Revelation 20:11-12*

In heaven there are three kinds of books: The first is the *Book of Life* in which every living soul is written. There is not one book that has been written in which names are blotted out, and a separate book in which names are later written for redemption. Rather, there is one *Book of Life*, in which Christ will receive as an inheritance, containing the names of all his people throughout all earth, through all time. Therefore, this book is called, *"The Book of Life" (Revelation 17:8)* and *"The Book of Life of the Lamb" (Revelation 13:8)*, having been purchased by his blood. Be assured, that the testimony of Scripture is clear. Those who are found written in the *Book of Life* are saved, and those who are not found are condemned, because they are blotted out for their unbelief.

> *If not, blot me, I pray, out of your book which you have written. And the LORD said... "Whoever has sinned against me, him will **I blot out of my book**." ~ Exodus 32:32-33*
> *Let them be blotted out of the book of the living, and not be written with the righteous.*

~ Psalm 69:28

No name is written down upon some decisional act to believe in Christ. Rather, those who retain the revelation which God gives to every man and believe God's testimony of salvation are *"found written"* when the books are opened.

> *… and at that time your people shall be delivered, every one that shall be **found written in the book**. ~ Daniel 12:1*

It is clear that a real threat exists to have one's name blotted out of this book. This is not the loss of salvation, negating the promise of the Holy Spirit, but the blotting out of those who were hardened in unbelief, who despised the grace of the Gospel.

> *He that overcomes, the same shall be clothed in white raiment; and **I will not blot out his name out of the book of life**, but I will confess his name before my Father, and before his angels. ~ Revelation 3:5*

The next books are the records of our lives and deeds. Every word spoken and every choice made, whether in the heart or in action, will be brought to judgement. That which reflects belief in the faithfulness of God will be rewarded while that which reflects unbelief will be judged.

> *You tell of my wanderings: you put my tears into your bottle: are they not in your book? ~ Psalms 56:8*
>
> *Oh, that my words were written! Oh, that they were inscribed in a book! That they were engraved on a rock with an iron pen and lead, forever! For I know that my Redeemer lives, and He shall stand at last on the earth; And after my skin is destroyed, this I know, that in my flesh I shall see God. ~ Job 19:23-26*
>
> *Then those who feared the LORD spoke to one another, and the LORD listened and heard them. So, a book of remembrance was written before Him for those who fear the LORD and who meditate on His name. ~ Malachi 3: 16*
>
> *"… every idle word men may speak they will give account of it in the day of judgment. For by your words you will be justified, and by your words you will be condemned." ~ Matthew 12: 36-37*

The final book is the Gospel, which is the Word of God and the person of Jesus Christ. For those who believed in Christ, their sinful deeds will have been blotted out. For those who have rejected Christ and trusted in their own works, their names are blotted out of the Book of Life.

> *For as many as have sinned without law shall also perish without law: and as many as have sinned in the law shall be judged by the law… In the day when God shall judge the secrets of men by Jesus Christ according to my gospel. ~ Romans 2:12*

[221]

After this judgement, every unbeliever will be assigned their eternal destiny, which will include both the eternal burning of *the Lake of Fire* and the lonesome torment of *the Outer Darkness*; the wrath of God poured out without mercy forever and ever. They will find themselves eternally enslaved to their nature of sin; never repenting or ceasing to gnash their teeth; never finding death or rest from their torment. In the end, Death and Hades, those agents of Satan who served the purpose of holding his captives, will also be disposed into *the Lake of Fire*.

> *The sea gave up the dead who were in it, and Death and Hades delivered up the dead who were in them. And they were judged, each one according to his works. Then Death and Hades were cast into the lake of fire. This is the second death. And anyone not found written in the Book of Life was cast into the lake of fire.* ~ Revelation 20:11-13

The Scriptures do not say how long we will spend in *the New Jerusalem*, or how long this trial will take place. Considering the eternal gravity of the judgement, we may wait and hear every single testimony of every fellow man until all the billions that have lived are judged in the open. It will be established that no man had been deprived of the knowledge of God or the revelation of His desire to save them. In the end, every soul will have established their place in the city by their testimony of grace or the justice of their rejection to *the Lake of Fire*.

Outside the city will be a void of fiery torment as God dissolves the cosmos to make an entirely new creation. Earth was corrupted by man's sin, while Heaven was defiled by Satan and his angels. God will throw it all into the fire before He allows a rebel to defile His abode. Just as David left the throne of Israel to wander the wilderness while Absalom defiled his house, God will reveal that He does not need a creation in which to dwell, as his greatness is beyond measure…*seeing the heaven and heaven of heavens cannot contain him.* (2nd Chronicles 2:6).

The Lake of Fire and the Outer Darkness

> *And it came to pass, that, when the sun went down, and it was dark, behold __a smoking furnace__, and __a burning lamp__ that passed between those pieces.* ~ Genesis 15:17

While words cannot properly express the nature of the lake of fire, the Bible does give a few terms that can help us understand the nature of this judgement. First and foremost, it must be understood that this eternal judgement is both, *"in the presence of the Lord"* (Revelation 14:10) and *"away from the presence of the Lord"* (2nd Thessalonians 1:9). While many believe the *Lake of Fire* to be a place where God is not, this destination will manifest His presence, but will be absent of His mercy and love. While this is hard to fathom, one can imagine the sun, as the radiant glory of God's presence, and then magnify that radiance beyond the bounds of the universe. If the gracious and loving presence of God were in the center of that Sun and the destructive glory of His wrath were on the outside, it would be this surface to which the wicked will be finally abandoned. For this reason, God often reveals Himself in Scripture as both a *"consuming fire"* (1st Timothy 6:16; Hebrews 12:29) and *"clothed in thick darkness"* (Psalms 18:11; Psalms 97: 2; 1st Kings 8:12).

While this judgement is fiery, it will not be light and beautiful as we imagine a fire to be. As nothing exists outside of or apart from God, there can only be a suffocating *outer darkness* remaining. This is not a vast expanse of empty space, but the compressing darkness of the void. One must imagine the inescapable gravity of a black hole, greater than the universe, compressing upon the gravity of His infinite being. For the unbelieving, what remains is only this dark, smoking, smoldering death forever and ever. However, for those who believe in Him, and accept the grace that comes through His Son, eternity will be completely absent this wrath, and only full of His mercy, love, and endless provision in the New Heavens and New Earth.

The Eternal State: The New Heavens and New Earth

God will begin again with a brand-new creation, incorruptible, unfading, and forever expanding in beauty, glory, and joy unspeakable. Unlike Noah's flood, He will not start again with a few people who are prone to sin, but with billions, redeemed in love, and alive in hope; acquainted with the folly of sin, and established in the mercy of grace; fully knowledgeable of the wisdom and mercy of God.

> *Now I saw a new heaven and a new earth, for the first heaven and the first earth had passed away. Also, there was no more sea. Then I, John, saw the holy city, the New Jerusalem, coming down out of heaven from God, prepared as a bride adorned for her husband. ~ Revelation 21:1-2*

In this new creation, the great city will come to rest on the surface of the New Earth, as the great tabernacle of God's glorious presence.

> *I heard a great voice out of heaven saying, "Behold, the tabernacle of God is with men, and He will dwell with them, and they shall be his people, and God himself shall be with them, and be their God. And God shall wipe away all tears from their eyes; and there shall be no more death, neither sorrow, nor crying, neither shall there be any more pain: for the former things are passed away." ~ Revelation 21: 1-4*

From this New Earth, we may expand throughout a new universe, colonizing planets or flying through endless heavens. While the possibilities are endless, there will always be that eternal home where His throne will rest, as our Father waits to see us face-to-face.

> And there shall be no more curse: but the throne of God and of the Lamb shall be in it; and his servants shall serve him: And they shall see his face; and his name shall be in their foreheads. And there shall be no night there; and they need no candle, neither light of the sun; for the Lord God gives them light: and they shall reign for ever and ever.
> ~ Revelation 22:3-5

This ends the history of the earth, and the furthest extent of Biblical prophecy. Beyond this point, we have only the promise that God has prepared for us things beyond anything we can hope or imagine. The sins of our past will be forgotten, and no temptation will enter in again. Our bond with Christ will remain unbroken in our complete freedom to follow our hearts' desire.

> And He that sat upon the throne said, "Behold, I make all things new." And He said unto me, "Write: for these words are true and faithful." ~ Revelation 21:5

The Benediction: The Closing Words of Christ

> And He said unto me, "It is finished. I am Alpha and Omega, the beginning and the end. I will give unto him that is thirsty of the fountain of the water of life freely. **He that overcomes shall inherit all things**; and I will be his God, and he shall be my son. But the fearful, and unbelieving, and the abominable, and murderers, and whoremongers, and sorcerers, and idolaters, and all liars, shall have their part in the lake which burns with fire and brimstone: which is the second death. ~ Revelation 21:6-8

When Christ says, *"He that overcomes,"* this is not a work to be performed, but a surrender to his mercy. Just as Jacob *"prevailed with God"* when he clung to His heel in desperation *(Genesis 32:28)*, we overcome when we admit we need His life and goodness. With that final admonition, the Angel of the Lord closes the Revelation.

> Then he said to me, "These words are faithful and true." And the Lord God of the holy prophets sent His angel to show His servants the things which must shortly take place. Behold, I am coming quickly! Blessed is he who keeps the words of the prophecy of this book." Now I, John, saw and heard these things. And when I heard and saw, I fell down to worship before the feet of the angel who showed me these things. Then he said to me, "See that you do not do that. For I am your fellow servant, and of your brethren the prophets, and of those who keep the words of this book. Worship God."
> ~ Revelation 22:6-9

And he said unto me, "Seal not the sayings of the prophecy of this book: for the time is at hand. He that is unjust, let him be unjust still: and he which is filthy, let him be filthy still: and he that is righteous, let him be righteous still: and he that is holy, let him be holy still. And behold, I come quickly; and my reward is with me, to give every man according as his work shall be. I am Alpha and Omega, the beginning and the end, the first and the last. Blessed are they that do his commandments, that they may have right to the tree of life and may enter in through the gates into the city. For without are dogs, and sorcerers, and whoremongers, and murderers, and idolaters, and whosoever loves and makes a lie. ~ Revelation 22:10-15

Jesus than gives a final call to all mankind to come to him who alone can save.

*I, Jesus, have sent mine angel to testify unto you these things in the churches. I am the root and the offspring of David, and the bright and morning star. And the Spirit and the Bride say, "Come." And let him that hears say, "Come." And let him that is thirsty "come." **And whosoever will, let him take the water of life freely.***

~ Revelation 22:16-17

Just as the book opens, in the end, Christ takes great care to testify to the authority of the Book and the importance of keeping it whole.

For I testify unto every man that hears the words of the prophecy of this book, "If any man shall add unto these things, God shall add unto him the plagues that are written in this book: And if any man shall take away from the words of the book of this prophecy, God shall take away his part out of the book of life, and out of the holy city, and from the things which are written in this book." He which testifies these things says, "Surely I come quickly." Amen. Even so, "Come, Lord Jesus." The grace of our Lord Jesus Christ be with you all. Amen. ~ Revelation 22:18-20

This is *The Revelation of Jesus Christ*, the prophecy of his coming, and our great hope. This is not some mysterious literature which man cannot possibly understand, but the capstone of the Word of God, meant to be understood and kept by the mature. It summarizes all the prophecies yet unfulfilled, drawing them into a narrative that we can understand, so that, when deception abounds, we will not be shaken with the world. Instead:

… when these things begin to happen, look up and lift up your heads, because your redemption draws near. ~ Luke 21:28

And this may be that final generation, who will live to see these things come to pass. Even so… come Lord Jesus, come.

The End

APPENDIX - A Hermeneutic of Prophetic Study

Without a hermeneutic which can be justified Scripturally, any interpretation of prophecy cannot be established as being more than a reasonable speculation. Unfortunately, with an accumulating number of theories and speculations coming forward in print publication and eBooks, as well as internet formats like YouTube and others, the vast number opinions can turn the subject matter into white noise and dull the senses of the reader to such a degree that they avoid the topic altogether. While there are many well-reasoned and well-written books on *The Revelation* and other prophetic Scripture, there seems to be a shortage of teaching literature on the hermeneutics of Bible Prophecy in general. The purpose of this appendix is to give a framework for that topic of scholarship that seems to be so lacking in the Church.

While there are many books on *The Revelation* whose commentaries and argumentation seem to reasonably establish how to interpret the book, most of these typically will only give an account of how they have interpreted various parts of the book without guiding the reader to understand the modes of interpretation they have employed *apart* from their interpretation of the book. While they may attempt to prove how their means of interpretation is superior to an alternative interpretation of a passage, they fail to establish their mode of interpretation as a valid principal on its own merit. Ultimately, they fail to establish how their means of interpretation is valid

[227]

based on the internal evidence of Scripture, demonstrating its general usage apart from their own application in the present context.

This appendix is meant to distinguish this book as being more than an interpretation *The Revelation*, but an interpretation drawn from a hermeneutic that establishes how to study prophecy in general. The intent is to allow the reader to pick up a book of prophecy, whether it be Isaiah, Jeremiah, or any other, and clearly distinguish between that which was meant for the hearer at the time it was written, that which has been fulfilled historically, and that which is meant to—either exclusively or redundantly—belong to the body of prophecy meant to support the eschatological narrative. While this methodology is far from perfect and can be improved upon, it is an attempt to establish a system of how prophecy should be interpreted, which stands apart to be tested for its Scriptural relevancy alone.

The formation of this set of hermeneutical principals was born out of years of discontent with prevailing eschatological theories, resulting in two major convictions that became the bounds of its formation: First, that the rules for interpreting prophecy should be found in Scripture alone, without requiring some exterior rules to dictate how one should interpret. Second, that the ways in which Scripture is interpreted, particularly related to unfulfilled prophecy, could be ascertained by understanding of how Jesus and his Apostles interpreted other fulfilled prophecies as recorded in the New Testament. By reverse-engineering their interpretations, these established modes of interpretation can be formed into a system of rules that can be reapplied toward other prophecies that have not been expressly interpreted by the Apostles.

If employed correctly, these modes of interpretation should help to corroborate one measure of interpretation over alternatives, reinforcing and illuminating an intended interpretation of the eschatological narrative. At a minimum, these rules should help to establish some boundaries as to the interpretation of prophecy that would serve to divide reasonable theories from the various speculations that would alienate believers from a fruitful understanding on the topic. They should help to establish the bounds by which to understand if varied interpretations could be reconciled as *both-and,* or if one interpretation should be indisputably accepted to the exclusion of the other. Holding the New Covenant truth of the Gospel in prime focus, we should be able to establish the passages which belong to the eschatological narrative, combining them into a cohesive narrative, both corroborating and elaborating upon the message of *The Revelation*.

Knowing God: The Purpose of Prophecy

Prophecy is as important a topic of study as any other element of theology or Biblical study. While many Christians diminish the study of prophecy as an informational pursuit that is less important to one's spiritual development than other facets of biblical knowledge, I believe the study of prophecy, both fulfilled and unfulfilled, is as intimate and relational as any other facet. However, understanding this requires deep meditation on why God chooses to give prophecy in the first place. Proceeding from a belief in God's faithfulness, as well as his desire to make Himself known to his servants, we should give careful attention to all He has said, learning to adopt his measure of priorities as our own.

Having a common understanding of the way God gives and keeps his promises, as well as understanding *why* He chooses his modes of delivery, is paramount in guarding against vain speculation, heresy, and fruitless division. Because we know that *"God is not the author of confusion,"* we must proceed by faith to demonstrate that point from His Word alone. Both the *way* and the *why* are not only important toward developing a common understanding between believers, but also in developing an unshakable trust toward God as these dangerous times begin to unfold before our eyes. To this end, we must first understand the way God has spoken of about these topics in Scripture, looking carefully for God's express reasoning for why He does things the way He does.

Of first import is that Prophecy is about Knowing God: Before any prophecy was given through a man in the office of a prophet, God first prophesied to man Himself. These prophecies were made by God in the manner of judgements, pronouncements, and promises which were made to demonstrate His authority, His wisdom, and His faithfulness. His purposes from the very beginning were always to respond intentionally with foreknowledge, being eternally aware of the sinful propensity of man, having foreordained His means of salvation. In His unfolding revelation, God sought painstakingly to demonstrate what the Gospel declares: that Christ was *"slain before the foundation of the world"* for the sin he knew we would commit in lieu of a temptation He knew would come; demonstrating the depths of his forbearance and the wisdom of His allowance, meant to reveal an attribute of his character which would not otherwise be manifest to his creatures: His agape love.

God declares the End from the Beginning: When seeking to interpret prophecy, one must hold the Word to the highest standard of scrutiny, believing that God, *"who cannot lie"* is not conveying information loosely with vague intent. Rather, one must believe that God is choosing His Words in the most careful manner, never to confuse or deceive us but to demonstrate Himself as being both fully capable and fully trustworthy. While God gives many promises about what He intends to do and many statements about who He is, this one passage should stand out to every student of prophecy as a baseline of His exclusive mastery of all history, having dictated the ends of creation from the dawn of time.

> *Remember the former things of old, For I am God, and there is no other; I am God, and there is none like Me. **Declaring the end from the beginning**, and, from ancient times things that are not yet done, Saying, "My counsel shall stand, And I will do all My pleasure" ~ Isaiah 46:9-10*

God boasts that He has already declared the end from the beginning. God reveals this attribute, distinguishing Himself alone from all others as having the authority to declare the end from the beginning, accomplishing every purpose according to the pleasure of His will. This statement cannot be diminished from its most literal understanding. This is not just a generic statement about God's ability to carry out a proposition despite opposition. Rather, it is a statement that every single event that transpires from the beginning to the end of time is according to an original intention which had been expressed from the start.

In fact, if one were to study the creation account of *Genesis chapter 1* with a thorough knowledge of the progressive revelation of God's unfolding plan from Genesis to Revelation, one would find in type and symbol, every unconditional promise, every objective, and every distinction in the purpose of God. If one were to study the account of the creation of man and woman in *Genesis 2*, one would find the mystery of Christ and the Church, hidden in a type. If one were to study the fall of mankind in *Genesis 3*, one could find the measure of election and rejection in God's threefold intention to save the meek, to crush the proud, and to destroy every work of the enemy of our souls. If one were to study the murder of Abel in *Genesis 4*, one could find the essence of true and false religion, of works and grace, and of unmerited protection against a deserved wrath by the death of an innocent man whose blood speaks to God on our behalf.

Every intention of God's revelation in the entire Bible is embedded in these pre-historic accounts of our first family and the God who made them. Still, it was His purpose to reveal these in a mystery, only to later point them out to us by the Holy Spirit. The reason why, when properly understood, made the soul of Paul leap with holy admiration at the manifold wisdom employed from on high.

God always give His intentions in advance: God's purpose in documenting His intentions from the beginning is to produce faith in those who would meditate on these former things. His expectation is for us to grow, not just in the general knowledge of these mysteries, but in knowledge of the intimate detail in which these intentions were dealt forth in advance, to demonstrate Himself as the God who cares intimately about our lives and steps, and the fate of every hair upon our heads. It is in this loving purpose that God intends for us to carefully ponder these former things, growing in understanding of all that He has foretold, both through the words and the lives of his ancient servants.

Through His Servants (The Prophets): Under the Old Covenant, God revealed His will through His servants, the prophets. From Abel, to Zechariah, saying: *"Surely the Lord GOD does nothing, unless He reveals His secret to His servants the prophets." ~ Amos 3:7*

Through His Son: When the Old Covenant fulfilled its purpose to reveal the sinfulness of man, God sent His Son to reveal the righteousness of God and the intended propitiation for our sins, as it is written, *"God, who at various times and in various ways spoke in time past to the fathers by the prophets, has in these last days spoken to us by His Son..." ~ Hebrews 1:1*

Through His Friends (the Apostles): And having revealed Himself to those He would later send, He called them friends, saying, *"No longer do I call you servants, for a servant does not know what his master is doing; but I have called you friends, for all things that I heard from My Father I have made known to you." ~ John 15:15*

God withholds information for our benefit: God's withholding of information, whether to test us or to provoke the response He requires for our salvation, is never arbitrary. While mankind continually went astray from Him, either hiding from Him in shame or resisting Him in self-righteousness, God was always the faithful shepherd, pursuing the lost, and revealing Himself to those who did not seek Him, goading them toward Himself *(Ecclesiastes 12:11)*. His reasoning for proclaiming His plan in a mystery was not to conceal His trustworthiness but had a twofold purpose that could only be revealed after His salvific work was accomplished for us by Jesus Christ. The two reasons were as follows:

1) **_To reveal our hearts:_** Knowing the doubtfulness of our hearts, God first determined to expose that doubt before demonstrating His faithfulness, as it is written, *...But this He said to test him, for He Himself knew what He would do.* (*John 6:6)*

2) **_To elude our enemy:_** But not only for this purpose, according to His ancient purpose, God sought to frustrate and defeat the enemy of our souls, as it is written, *... none of the princes of this world knew: for had they known it, they would not have crucified the Lord of glory.* ~ *1ˢᵗ Corinthians 2:8*

The Revelation of God's Attributes

In both Attribute and Character, He is God: God's attributes are important in establishing His ability, both to save and to punish; to help and to withhold. Still, His attributes are not worth knowing without knowing His character: that He is trustworthy, merciful, patient, and kind to even the most undeserving. God understands that if there is no means of mercy by which we can receive forgiveness, then there can be no motive but to continue in our pleasure, knowing that our judgement is certain. Therefore, God uses prophecy to painstakingly demonstrate that He is love, knowing both in advance that we would sin, and demonstrating in advance how He would make provision for us.

> *If You, LORD, should mark iniquities, O Lord, who could stand? But there is forgiveness with You, That You may be feared.* ~ *Psalm 130:3-4*

God's Sovereignty is more important than His Clarity: While God seeks for us to know that He is loving and merciful, if God were required to justify any of His choices to his creatures, He would cease to be God. He does not keep back information from us for His good, but for our good, so that we learn what is the substance of faith, patience, and trusting in Him. In this, God both reveals the end from the beginning, and reveals progressively what He meant by His earlier revelations, giving mankind only what they need to continue in faith until He has accomplished the next purpose in His redemptive plan for us.

He is not a man, as I am, that I might answer Him, that we should come to trial together. There is no arbiter between us, who might lay his hand on us both. ~ Job 9:32-33

You asked, "Who is this who hides counsel without knowledge?" Therefore, I have uttered what I did not understand; things too wonderful for me, which I did not know…Therefore, I abhor myself, and repent in dust and ashes. ~ Job 42:1-6

The Authority of the Word of God

God holds Himself accountable to His own Word: God does not give His Word carelessly or generally, but reveals His Word with the utmost precision, expecting that we hold Him to every Word He has spoken.

The secret things belong to the LORD our God, but those things which are revealed belong to us and to our children forever, that we may do all the words of this law. ~ Deuteronomy 29:29

I will worship toward Your holy temple and praise Your Name, for Your lovingkindness and Your truth; For You have magnified Your word above all Your Name. ~ Psalm 138:2

God never contradicts Himself: No matter what we fail to understand, God never contradicts Himself, intending for us to reconcile the various mysterious things in His Word, leaping in wonder and joy at the revelation if these things as He reveals His secret will unto us.

It is the glory of God to conceal a matter, But the glory of kings is to search out a matter. ~ Proverbs 25:2

In the Mystery is always Mercy: If there is some inexplicable or contradictory thing in the Word of God, the proper understanding always reveals God as being more merciful than supposed. While He keeps his Word literally, He divides language according to Himself in order to retain the right to be merciful toward those to turn from their sin and repent, showing the superiority of mercy as His original intention.

The Bible is Self-Sufficient: The Bible requires no other measure of truth to act upon it as it defines itself and explains itself according to God's will. If Israel were only given the five books of the Pentateuch, they would have every promise secured to be assured of every outcome which has come about since then. If they had only the

Book of Genesis, they would have the same security. While God reveals the details of His plan progressively, He always gives a sufficient account to demonstrate that the final outcome was always His original intent, and that the Word given is a sufficient revelation to guide us in His perfect will.

> *All Scripture is given by inspiration of God, and is profitable for doctrine, for reproof, for correction, for instruction in righteousness, that the man of God may be complete, thoroughly equipped for every good work. ~ 2nd Timothy 3:16*
>
> *The words of the wise are like goads, and the words of scholars are like well-driven nails, given by one Shepherd. ~ Ecclesiastes 12:11*

The Bible is Reconcilable: The Bible contains many statements that seem irreconcilable without additional revelation. While this truth is already within the Scripture, it must be brought to light by the Holy Spirit. God has no intention to confuse the reader but to draw them into deeper understanding of Him, provoking them through things they may not understand on the surface. This deeper understanding is the very substance of the New Testament, which the Apostles had to uncover in from the Old Testament as they were pressed to move away from all they had previously known, toward an original intent they now understood.

> *… consider that the longsuffering of our Lord is salvation--as also our beloved brother Paul, according to the wisdom given to him, has written to you, as also in all his epistles, speaking in them of these things, in which are some things hard to understand, which untaught and unstable people twist to their own destruction, as they do also the rest of the Scriptures. ~ 2nd Peter 3:14*

The things the Apostles unveiled were not the exhaustive revelation of this deeper understanding but were sufficient to establish that the death of Christ, His two comings, the New Covenant, and the ministry of the Gospel to the Gentiles were all laid out beforehand. They demonstrated that God was not changing His mind but unveiling that which He intended to do all along. The interpretation of unfulfilled prophecy is merely the continuation of this unveiling in the belief that God foreordained everything that would transpire between his two comings.

Milk before Meat: While there is much to uncover, the pressing concern is that this quest for additional knowledge does not supplant the prerogative to obey the plain speaking of the Word. Paul teaches that a teacher is made ready by growing in discernment through the obedience of the *"pure milk of the Word."*

> *For though by this time you ought to be teachers, you need someone to teach you again the first principles of the oracles of God; and you have come to need milk and not solid*

food. For everyone who partakes only of milk is unskilled in the word of righteousness, for he is a babe. But solid food belongs to those who are of full age, that is, those who by reason of use have their senses exercised to discern both good and evil.

~ Hebrews 5:12-14

Those who seek to bypass obedience and still gain deeper knowledge will find themselves going down a gnostic path, *"always learning, but never coming to the knowledge of the truth." (2nd Timothy 3:7),* becoming deceived by sin and heresy. However, those who persist in being renewed by the Word, seeking to know and understand God as they continue in obedience to what they know, will be met with clear a consistent revelation and deeper knowledge, not exceeding, but developing, reinforcing, and elaborating upon the that which is plainly written for the purpose of growing in love and usefulness to Him.

Christ is the End and Revelation of All Prophecy: The true meaning of biblical prophecy is not merely the knowledge of the future but the knowledge and clear testimony of Christ, revealed throughout the creation.

...for the testimony of Jesus is the spirit of prophecy. ~ Revelation 19:10

Prophecy is more than just a revelation of what God foretold in the past, or even the testimony of what will happen in the future. Prophecy, at its heart, is a necessity between God and mankind, without which, reconciliation would be impossible. It draws us in to understand more and more about the depths of His power over the creation, over history, and over the outcomes of the lives of every creature. It reveals to us the intimate knowledge which He possesses over our hearts and motives; our fears and inadequacies; and our inability to be otherwise. It shows how God foresaw every consequence of our free will in the introduction of sin and death into the world, under which all the creation presently groans.

Beyond this, it shows His divine choice in allowing this consequence to unfold, knowing in intimate detail, mankind's incapacity to improve their condition; knowing that every effort, whether individual of collective, would only exacerbate their problem. It reveals how God has been fully aware of a powerful enemy force within His own kingdom, allowing that enemy's intentions to manifest on a grand scale in order to reveal a nature that could in no other way be revealed to His creation. It reveals His intention to display a love that surpasses all understanding, forgiving even our greatest sins at the cost that only He could pay with the most painful, self-denying sacrifice. It reveals how God, in His wisdom, designed a creature that could die, and yet live, being *born-again* in the inner man to be saved from His holy wrath to come.

If one seeks to understand the undergirding mysteries of the unfolding plan of God, one must be prepared to have their human reasoning broken from all man-centered logic, legalism, and earthly conformity. One must be surrendered to the fact that God is undoubtedly good, yet reconcilable only to Himself, giving His every Word with the greatest care and precision in order to draw the simple toward wisdom. God is no liar, but He does test men with His Word, even as He tested Abraham with the sacrifice of Isaac; even as He tested Moses in threatening to destroy all Israel; even as Christ tested his disciple Phillip here:

> *When Jesus then lifted up his eyes, and saw a great company come unto him, he says unto Philip, "Whence shall we buy bread, that these may eat?" And this **He said to prove him: for he himself knew what he would do.** ~ John 6:5-6*

The Lord always tests those He loves, daring them to trust Him. He calls them to search Him, knowing that He cannot lie. He hearkens them to solve His riddle, unveiling the depth of His wisdom and mercy, growing steadfast against all doubt.

> *In hope of eternal life, which God, that cannot lie, promised before the world began.* ~ Titus 1:2

Types of Prophecy Given

In the Old Testament, there were several kinds of prophecy given. Listed here are several types of prophecy that can be demonstrated as being used to reveal God's prophetic plan. The first two, *Prophetic Inquiry* and *Prophetic Validation*, were only relevant for the Old Testament Prophets and Priests, to stand as an authoritative intermediary between God and man. While prophets are part of the New Covenant and are found in the Book of Acts, they do not hold this intermediary function. This authority was abolished as Christ became the sole mediator between God and the faithful believers in the Church.

Prophetic Inquiry: A prophetic answer given in response to a direct inquiry from the Lord, given through a Prophet or High Priest. When God ordained the Levitical Priesthood, He gave two stones called Urim and Thummim by which the priests were to *cast lots* in order to divine an answer. It is from this practice that the proverb is given, "*The lot is cast into the lap, but its every decision is from the LORD.*" ~ Proverbs 16:33

And you shall put in the breastplate of judgment the Urim and the Thummim, and they shall be over Aaron's heart when he goes in before the LORD. So, Aaron shall bear the judgment of the children of Israel over his heart before the LORD continually.

~ Exodus 28:30

And when Saul enquired of the LORD, the LORD answered him not, neither by dreams, nor by Urim, nor by prophets. ~ 1ˢᵗ Samuel 28:6

Prophecies of Validation: Prophetic words, upheld by God in order to establish the validity of the prophet as speaking for God Himself.

So, Samuel grew, and the LORD was with him and let none of his words fall to the ground. And all Israel from Dan to Beersheba knew that Samuel had been established as a prophet of the LORD. ~ 1ˢᵗ Samuel 3:19-20

*Then the king sent to him a captain of fifty with his fifty men. So, he went up to him; and there he was, sitting on the top of a hill. And he spoke to him: "Man of God, the king has said, 'Come down!'" So, Elijah answered and said to the captain of fifty, "**If I am a man of God**, then let fire come down from heaven and consume you and your fifty men." And fire came down from heaven and consumed him and his fifty.*

~ 2ⁿᵈ Kings 1:9-10

*So, the king of Israel said, "Take Micaiah, and return him to Amon the governor of the city and to Joash the king's son; and say, 'Thus says the king: "Put this fellow in prison and feed him with bread of affliction and water of affliction, until I come in peace." But Micaiah said, "**If you ever return in peace, the LORD has not spoken by me.**" And he said, "Take heed, all you people!" ~ 1ˢᵗ Kings 22:26-28*

Express Prophecy: Express statements, made by the Lord directly or via a prophet, promising a future outcome. These kinds of prophecies did not cease with the Old Covenant, nor were they exclusive to the twelve apostles, but documented as being given through people like Agabus, Silas, and the daughters of Phillip in Acts.

While some will contend that believing these kinds of prophecies amounts to an open cannon of Scripture, they must understand that both in the Old and the New Covenant, there were many prophets and prophecies given that were never added to Scripture. Rather, these words were tested and considered in light of their context and measured against Scriptural revelation. While some prophecies had an immediate context only, others were recognized as having a greater context by which they needed to be preserved in the cannon of Scripture.

Go, and say to Hezekiah, "Thus says the LORD, the God of David your father, 'I have heard your prayer, I have seen your tears: behold, I will add unto your days fifteen years.'" ~ Isaiah 38:5

And when he was come unto us, he took Paul's girdle, and bound his own hands and feet, and said, "Thus says the Holy Ghost, 'So shall the Jews at Jerusalem bind the man that owns this girdle and shall deliver him into the hands of the Gentiles.'" ~ Acts 21:11

While the types of prophecy above would have been the most plainly understood, several other types were inferred, both in the Old Testament cannon and in in the teachings of Jesus and his Apostles.

Narrative as Prophecy: A narrative of events, by which the events and details, foreshadow or symbolize a prophecy of some future event or revelation. Often, these things were not known to be prophetic until after their fulfillment, as the pattern or symbols involved demonstrate a future event or some spiritual truth yet to be revealed.

*Then some of the scribes and Pharisees answered, saying, "Teacher, we want to see a sign from You." But He answered and said to them, "An evil and adulterous generation seeks after a sign, and no sign will be given to it except **the sign of the prophet Jonah**. For as Jonah was three days and three nights in the belly of the whale, so will the Son of Man be three days and three nights in the heart of the earth." ~ Matthew 12:38-40*

While some narratives are meant to foreshadow the actions of Christ by the actions of some prophet, others, like this teaching by Paul, demonstrates that the Old Testament narratives and personalities often establish a deeper spiritual truth beyond just an historical record.

*For it is written that Abraham had two sons: the one by a bondwoman, the other by a freewoman. But he who was of the bondwoman was born according to the flesh, and he of the freewoman through promise, **which things are symbolic.***

For these are the two covenants: *the one from Mount Sinai which gives birth to bondage, which is Hagar – for this Hagar is Mount Sinai in Arabia, and corresponds to Jerusalem which now is, and is in bondage with her children – but the Jerusalem above is free, which is the mother of us all. For it is written: "Rejoice, O barren, you who do not bear! Break forth and shout, you who are not in labor! For the desolate has many more children than she who has a husband."*

Now we, brethren, as Isaac was, are children of promise. But, as he who was born according to the flesh then persecuted him who was born according to the Spirit, even so it is now. Nevertheless, what does the Scripture say? "Cast out the bondwoman and her son, for the son of the bondwoman shall not be heir with the son of the freewoman." So then, brethren, we are not children of the bondwoman but of the free. ~ Galatians 4:22:31

Names as Prophecy: A name may represent some destiny that the person will fulfill, or some event that will happen in their lifetime. Place names can also have a prophetic significance, as their names are often given in relation to a past person or event, while relaying a prophetic expression about some future person or event.

> And unto Eber were born two sons: the name of one was Peleg; for in his days was the earth divided; ~ Genesis 10:25

> For this Melchizedek, king of Salem, priest of the Most High God, who met Abraham returning from the slaughter of the kings and blessed him, to whom also Abraham gave a tenth part of all, first being translated "king of righteousness," and then also king of Salem, meaning "king of peace," ~ Hebrews 7:1

> And he said, "Is not he rightly named Jacob? for he has supplanted me these two times. He took away my birthright. And, behold, now he has taken away my blessing. ~ Genesis 27:36

Numerical Prophecy: Numbers that are used repeatedly can have a prophetic significance. While the practice of numerology— assuming a mystical significance in *all* numbers—is an occult practice and not appropriate for a believer, finding clear patterns of numbers in the Bible may yield some prophetic significance. In many cases, the significance of a number is contained in its first usage.

One example is with the numbers 12 and 70. The first example of these in Scripture are with the 12 sons of Israel and the 70 nations that are divided at the tower of Babel in *Genesis 10*. These numbers will continue to appear as a pair throughout Scripture. This continues as Jacob goes down into Egypt with both 12 sons and a total of 70 souls when his grandchildren and great-grandchildren are counted *(Exodus 1:5)*. Immediately after Israel is delivered from Egypt, they are led to twelve springs and seventy olive trees by which they were given rest. These symbolized the Jews and Gentiles, both held in bondage to sin, who would be delivered through Christ at the Passover. God would make this truth plain in later passage in Deuteronomy saying,

> Remember the days of old, Consider the years of many generations. Ask your father, and he will show you; Your elders, and they will tell you: When the Most High divided their inheritance to the nations, When He separated the sons of Adam, **He set the boundaries of the peoples According to the number of the children of Israel**. For the LORD'S portion is His people; Jacob is the place of His inheritance. ~ Deuteronomy 32:7-9

God chooses seventy years to represent Israel's captivity to the kingdom of Babylon, and seventy *"sevens"* (or weeks of years) to represent Israel's greater captivity to the Gentiles. Later, in Jesus's earthly ministry, he sent out twelve apostles *(Luke 9)*, followed by another seventy *(Luke 10)*. In this, Jesus was forecasting his intent to evangelize the Gospel both to the Jews and to the Gentiles after He had achieved their salvation through his death and resurrection.

In Scripture, the numbers 40, 400, and 4000 represent a time of testing or waiting. The Israelites waited 40 days for Moses on the Mountain and spent 40 years in the wilderness for doubting God. Abraham's descendants were aliens and afflicted for 400 years, while Adam's descendants were alienated from God and afflicted because of sin for 4000 years. The time between the promise to Abraham and the deliverance of the nation was 400 years, while the time between the final word of Scripture and the deliverance from sin were 400 years.

In Daniel's prophecy of 70 weeks there are 434 between the time Jerusalem is rebuilt until Messiah is killed *(Daniel 9:26)*, while if one carefully counts the years from creation to the crucifixion, there are 4034 years total from the Creation until Christ's crucifixion. Likewise, while there were 430 years between the giving of the *"seed"* promise to Abraham and receiving the Law, there were also 4030 years between the giving the *"seed"* promise to Eve, and the preaching of the Kingdom at the beginning of Jesus' ministry.

If one were to look carefully, they would find symbols of the Trinity when Abraham meets the Lord *in Genesis 18,* as he entertains three persons and intermittently refers to the one speaking as *"He"* and *"They"* referring to both *"The Lord"* and to *"Three Men."* These kinds of numerical coincidences are part of God's mysterious prophetic imprint. While these things do not add new doctrine, they are present to reinforce existing doctrine and other express prophecies in a way that demonstrates that God always proclaimed the end from the beginning.

Key Phrase Prophecies: An example of a key phrase prophecy is in *Genesis 22*. This passage tells the story of Abraham being tested to sacrifice Isaac. While Abraham has two sons at this time—Isaac and Ishmael—God keeps referring to Isaac as his *"only son."* The purpose of this is to draw a prophetic connection between Isaac and Jesus, God's only Son, who would be sacrificed for our sins in the future.

> ... *"Take now your son, **your only son** Isaac, whom you love, and go to the land of Moriah, and offer him there as a burnt offering on one of the mountains of which I shall tell you." ~ Genesis 22:2*
>
> *Then the Angel of the LORD called to Abraham a second time out of heaven, and said: "By Myself I have sworn, says the LORD, because you have done this thing, and have not withheld your son, **your only son.**" ~ Genesis 22:15-16*

Prophecy from Silence: Inconsistent sayings, demanding explanation, the understanding of which is met in the fulfillment of a prophecy. In the example below, there is a problem when God tells Adam that He will die *"in the day"* that he eats of the Tree of Knowledge. Yet, Adam lived almost a thousand years after he committed this transgression *(Genesis 5:5)*.

This discrepancy is resolved by a Psalm written by Moses, which establishes that a day to God is like thousand years, understanding that God first established a Day, *(Genesis 1:5)*, before He created the rising and setting sun by which we record a passing day *(Genesis 1:15-18)*. Peter reiterates this in *2nd Peter*, demonstrating that the *"Day of the Lord"* is both the day He appears *"like a thief,"* and also the thousand years that Christ reigns on earth in the Millennial Kingdom.

> *…but of the tree of the knowledge of good and evil you shall not eat, for **in the day that you eat of it** you shall surely die. ~ Genesis 2:17*
>
> ***For a thousand years in Your sight are like yesterday when it is past**, And like a watch in the night. ~ Psalm 90:4*

Paul taught that Adam did in fact die, in a spiritual sense, having become spiritually alienated from God on the day that he ate. It is out of this discrepancy and its resolution that we have the *already-not yet* paradigm that also reconciles the discrepancies between preterist and futurist views of eschatology, allowing for several prophecies that are presently fulfilled spiritually, while we also await their literal, material fulfillment.

> *I was alive once without the law, but when the commandment came, sin revived, and I died. And the commandment, which was to bring life, I found to bring death. **For sin, taking occasion by the commandment, deceived me, and by it killed me**.*
>
> *~ Romans 7:9*

Ritual as Prophecy: Various feasts, holy days, and rituals, of which the meaning of the practice is fulfilled in some future event. Most of these signify various aspects of Christ's sacrifice for our sin. While there are too many to list, the hyssop and the blood are an example.

> *And **you shall take a bunch of hyssop**, dip it in the blood that is in the basin, and strike the lintel and the two doorposts with the blood that is in the basin. And none of you shall go out of the door of his house until morning. For the LORD will pass through to strike the Egyptians; and when He sees the blood on the lintel and on the two doorposts, the LORD will pass over the door and not allow the destroyer to come into*

your houses to strike you. And you shall observe this thing as an ordinance for you and your sons forever. ~ Exodus 12:22

*Now there was set a vessel full of vinegar: and they filled a sponge with vinegar, and **put it upon hyssop**, and put it to his mouth. ~ John 19:29*

*For when Moses had spoken every precept to all the people according to the law, he took the blood of calves and of goats, with water, and scarlet wool, and **hyssop, and sprinkled both the book, and all the people**, ~ Hebrews 9:19*

*Then answered all the people, and said, **His blood be on us, and on our children**. ~ Matthew 27:25*

***Purge me with hyssop**, and I shall be clean: wash me, and I shall be whiter than snow. ~ Psalms 51:7*

Creation as Prophecy: Knowing the God proclaimed, *"the end from the beginning,"* we can look carefully at God's testimony of the creation and find the entirety of human history embedded within the seven days of creation. The divisions occurring in the first four days represent the separation by God of certain people unto holiness, represented in his covenant promises and toward Eve, Noah, Abraham, and David, which are all fulfilled in Christ. The creation of *"living creatures"* in the next two days represent the life-giving spread of the Gospel for two thousand years, while the final day represents the Sabbath rest as the earth is subdued by the rule of Christ in the Millennium. When we take the time to appreciate the order and precision of God's order of creation, we realize that there was a wisdom beyond any ideas of natural science or evolution, proving that supernatural material creation was the means by which God did literally *"declare the end from the beginning."*

Types of Prophetic Fulfillment

Simple fulfillment: The prophecy is given, and later fulfilled, clearly validating its divine origin. The simplest prophecies do not require explanation as to how the prophecy is connected with its fulfillment.

Now it came to pass, when Jesus had finished all these sayings, that He said to His disciples, "You know that after two days is the Passover, and the Son of Man will be delivered up to be crucified." ~ Matthew 26:1-2

Hyper-Literal Fulfillment: The fulfillment of the prophecy, is carefully dictated by the exactness of the language, painting an even more distinct picture that what might have been earlier supposed. In this example, Paul makes the word *"seed"* hyper-literal excluding the plural meaning of the word. The result is a pattern of something related to Christ, and to the Church who are both many and one, *"In Christ."*

[242]

*Now to Abraham and his Seed were the promises made. **He does not say, "and to seeds," as of many, but as of one**, "and to your Seed," who is Christ. ~ Galatians 3:16*

*And I will make you seed as the dust of the earth: so that if a man can number the dust of the earth, then shall **your seed** also be numbered. ~ Genesis 13:16*

*And I will give unto you, and to **your seed** after you, the land wherein you are a stranger, all the land of Canaan, for an everlasting possession; and I will be **their** God. ~ Genesis 17:8*

Typological Fulfillment: An historic person, image, or event, while being an historical account of something that happened, can also be a prophetic allusion to some spiritual truth, later to be revealed.

*Moreover, brethren, I do not want you to be unaware that all our fathers were under the cloud, all passed through the sea, all were baptized into Moses in the cloud and in the sea, all ate the same spiritual food, and all drank the same spiritual drink. For they drank of **that spiritual Rock that followed them, and that Rock was Christ.** ~ 1st Corinthians 10:1-6*

Multiple Fulfillment: The prophecy is fulfilled at one point in history to a degree, leaving a future, more complete fulfillment. An example is in the prophecy of a virgin bearing a child in Isaiah.

Therefore, the Lord Himself will give you a sign: Behold, the virgin shall conceive and bear a Son, and shall call His name Immanuel. ~ Isaiah 7:14

In its context, this prophecy was given as an immediate sign to King Ahaz of Judah, to signify God's promise to remove northern Israel and Damascus, who were at the time enemies that were opposing him.

*Then I went to the prophetess, and she conceived and bore a son… "Now therefore, behold, the Lord brings up over them the waters of the river, strong and mighty – the king of Assyria and all his glory; … And the stretching out of his wings will fill the breadth of Your land, **O Immanuel.** Be shattered, O you peoples, and be broken in pieces! Give ear, all you from far countries. Gird yourselves, but be broken in pieces; Gird yourselves, but be broken in pieces. Take counsel together, but it will come to nothing; Speak the word, but it will not stand, **for God is with us**." ~ Isaiah 8:3*

Yet, in the remainder of the prophecy, it was determined by the Apostles that a later fulfillment was needed, with the understanding that this child could not sufficiently fulfill the prophecy in its entirety.

"For unto us a Child is born, unto us a Son is given; And the government will be upon His shoulder. And His name will be called Wonderful, Counselor, Mighty God, Everlasting Father, Prince of Peace. Of the increase of His government and peace there

will be no end, upon the throne of David and over his kingdom, to order it and establish it with judgment and justice from that time forward, even forever. The zeal of the LORD of hosts will perform this." ~ Isaiah 9:6

For this reason, Matthew concluded that while the earlier partial fulfilment was valid, the latter fulfillment in Christ was the expectation that was always intended, giving the prophecy a *dual fulfillment*, both in the days of Isaiah and in the days of Jesus' birth.

Behold, a virgin shall be with child, and shall bring forth a son, and they shall call his name Emmanuel, which being interpreted is, God with us. ~ Matthew 1:23

Spiritual-Material or Already-Not Yet: The prophecy is fulfilled in one sense spiritually, while maintaining the expectation of another material fulfillment. Most often, these things pertain to the Church, the new birth, and the Kingdom of Heaven.

Now when He was asked by the Pharisees when the Kingdom of God would come, He ...said, "The Kingdom of God does not come with observation" nor will they say, 'See here!' or 'See there!' For indeed, the kingdom of God is within you." ~ Luke 17:20-21

*When they are already budding, you see and know for yourselves that summer is now near. So, you also, **when you see these things** happening, know **that the Kingdom of God is near**. ~ Luke 21:30-31*

Gapped fulfillment: The prophecy contains a pattern of *book ends* in which the prophecy has a part that is fulfilled, followed by an undisclosed gap of time, followed by a fulfillment of the remainder. While not exclusively, the prophetic gap is often composed of the time in which the Gentiles are gathered into the Church.

And He taught in their synagogues, being glorified by all. So, He came to Nazareth, where He had been brought up. And as His custom was, He went into the synagogue on the Sabbath day, and stood up to read. And He was handed the book of the prophet Isaiah. And when He had opened the book, He found the place where it was written:

*"The Spirit of the LORD is upon Me, Because He has anointed Me To preach the gospel to the poor; He has sent Me to heal the brokenhearted, o proclaim liberty to the captives and recovery of sight to the blind; to set at liberty those who are oppressed; **to proclaim the acceptable year of the LORD**."*

Then He closed the book and gave it back to the attendant and sat down. And the eyes of all who were in the synagogue were fixed on Him. And He began to say to them, "Today this Scripture is fulfilled in your hearing." ~ Luke 4:15-21

In this prophecy, Jesus reads a prophecy in Isaiah about to the halfway point, stopping mid-sentence without reading the statement, *"and the day of vengeance of our God."* In His omission, Jesus is hiding the *mystery* of the ingathering of the Gentiles between his two comings.

*"The Spirit of the Lord GOD is upon Me, Because the LORD has anointed Me To preach good tidings to the poor; He has sent Me to heal the brokenhearted, To proclaim liberty to the captives, And the opening of the prison to those who are bound; **To proclaim the acceptable year of the LORD, And the day of vengeance of our God**; To comfort all who mourn, To console those who mourn in Zion, To give them beauty for ashes, The oil of joy for mourning, The garment of praise for the spirit of heaviness; That they may be called trees of righteousness, The planting of the LORD, that He may be glorified."*

~ Isaiah 61:1

Understanding these kinds of prophecy and different ways in which they were fulfilled can help clarify the meaning of many prophecies in the Old Testament that have not yet been fulfilled. This meaning allows the reader to incorporate these prophecies into a cohesive narrative of that which has already been fulfilled, leaving as a remainder a number of unfulfilled prophecies that can be incorporated to form a cohesive narrative of what remains in the events surrounding the second coming. In studying these remaining prophecies, this book has been compiled toward the intent of elaborating a clear and realistic narrative, corresponding with the chronological testimony of the Book of Revelation. While the form of this hermeneutical system is presented for debate, correction, and improvement, it should help point the reader in the direction of self-study that will lend credibility to its interpretation.

I hope this work can serve to edify the reader in their study of Scripture, and to increase their hope as they expectantly trust the Lord while they wait for His return. Thank you for taking the time to read this writing.

Yours in Christ,

Aaron Matthew Fochtman

Made in the USA
Monee, IL
13 January 2022

88824456R00136